The Body Ecology Diet^{SM}

Recovering Your Health and Rebuilding Your Immunity

by DONNA GATES
with LINDA SCHATZ

Published by
B.E.D. Publications
1266 West Paces Ferry Road, Suite 505
Atlanta, Georgia 30327, U.S.A.

SIXTH EDITION

Book Cover Design, Illustrations and
Typesetting : Trent Wilson Advertising

Library of Congress Cataloging-in-Publication Data
Gates, Donna with Schatz, Linda
The Body Ecology Diet:
Recovering Your Health and Rebuilding Your Immunity
by Donna Gates with Linda Schatz–1st ed
Includes bibliographical references.

ISBN 0-9638458-9-6
$19.95 Softcover
1. Health. 2. Immune Disorders. 3. Candidiasis. 4. Nutrition.
5. Body Ecology. 6. Diet. I. Title, Gates, Donna, 1946

Please Note!

This book synthesizes information from many sources and points of view, including modern medical science, ancient Chinese medicine, naturopathy, and the authors' personal study, observation, and experience. The conclusions expressed herein are those of the authors.

The Body Ecology Diet is written and published as an information resource and educational guide for both professionals and non-professionals. It should not be used as a substitute for your physician's advice. Be sure to work with a physician who knows the importance of diet in healing and who has experience in treating Candida Related Complex and other immune disorders. While we endorse the Body Ecology Diet and related recommendations, you should make your decision based on all the information at hand, knowing that you are the primary force in directing your own life and health.

This Book Is For...

People who have symptoms of a weak immune system and want to boost their immunity.

Holistic health care practitioners whose clients have candidiasis or other immune system deficiencies. Your clients will thrive on the Body Ecology Diet and get more out of their sessions with you.

Doctors who prescribe antibiotics, birth control pills, radiation, chemotherapy, cortisone, steroids, etc. The Body Ecology Diet will help your patients avoid an overgrowth of harmful yeast during therapy and then help them restore their inner ecosystems and prevent future illness.

You Should Read This Book If:

✔ You suspect or know you have candidiasis (CRC), chronic fatigue syndrome, cancer, AIDS, or other immune system deficiencies.

✔ You have known or suspected food allergies or frequent digestive problems.

✔ You have frequent skin rashes, constipation, or PMS.

✔ You are bothered by headaches, or muscle or joint pains.

✔ You always seem to be tired, nervous, or depressed, or your memory seems to be poor.

✔ You are sensitive to tobacco, perfume, or other chemical odors.

✔ You have taken birth control pills.

✔ You have been plagued and frustrated by symptoms that persist no matter what you do to get rid of them.

✔ You have a history of drug use, including extensive use of antibiotics or illegal drugs.

✔ You want to ensure the health of your children and other loved ones.

✔ You want to prevent major disease that doesn't manifest until years after the seeds have been sown: cancer, AIDS, heart disease.

Candidiasis and Its Relation to AIDS, Cancer, Chronic Fatigue, and Other Immune Disorders

Welcome to the Body Ecology Diet (B.E.D.), a proven way to enhance your health and clear up the symptoms of candidiasis, an overgrowth of yeast. As long as a candida overgrowth exists in your body, the immune system is so overwhelmed that it cannot even begin to do its real job, which is to fight invaders such as AIDS, chronic fatigue syndrome, herpes, or rebellious groups of cells (cancer). Candidiasis reflects an immune system under siege, and until you bring the candidiasis under control through diet, rest, exercise, and a determined attitude, other immune-compromised conditions cannot be conquered. We need to focus on the candida as the first step to improving immunity. So while this book is written specifically for people with candidiasis, it is just as valuable for those with related immune-compromised conditions.

The Body Ecology Diet offers a framework for the rest of your life. It provides basic tools that will help you restore and maintain the balance and vitality your body deserves. It goes *with* the flow of nature, not against it. It strengthens your immunity. The Diet can bring a greater sense of calm to your life by providing clear guidelines and principles.

Does this mean you'll never eat pizza, hamburgers, or dessert again? Not necessarily! In its strictest, therapeutic form, the Diet is designed to heal a serious, life-threatening inner imbalance. If you have the will power to follow it for three months to a year (depending on the severity of your imbalance), you will become well...well enough to eat those foods again (although not to excess). In grappling with candida to regain your health, you will become sensitive to the needs and requirements of your body. You will learn what works and what doesn't, and you will start appreciating the value of healthy eating. You will adapt the Diet to your lifestyle, invent your own recipes and favorite food combinations. You will even enjoy the special desserts we've created.

At first, the Diet limits the foods you can have, but as your health improves, you can try a wider variety of healthy foods. Then occasional divergence even from these foods will not do the harm it does now. If some of your symptoms reappear, you'll be able to return to the basic Diet and get yourself back on an even keel.

Tips for Reading and Mastering the Body Ecology Diet

There's a lot of information packed into these pages! You'll be excited to find answers to your health concerns—but you'll probably be overwhelmed by all the things to know and do as you begin the Diet. Don't worry—everything will fall in place once you start experimenting with the foods on the Diet.

Read the book all the way through, highlighting the ideas and actions you consider important. Then, once you've *completed* the book and started on the Diet, go back and highlight in a *different* color, because you'll have a different point of view.

You may find some information is repeated in different chapters and sections. That's because we believe it's important enough to be emphasized in more than one place. Now, let us begin.

Donna's Story

"A long path of study, experimentation, prayer, and faith has brought me to the point where I am today: a healthy, optimistic woman who wants to share what I've learned. But to reach this point, I've been through many ups and downs in my campaign to overcome candidiasis, a condition that saps the very core of one's vitality and well-being.

"I was born with a sensitive constitution, including an allergy to milk. I had constant lung problems and colds. When my skin broke out during my teen years, I started taking antibiotics. My skin was very yellow, I had low energy, and sometimes I'd be very 'spacey' for no apparent reason. The antibiotics led to food allergies and digestive problems—and my skin didn't clear up unless I took the antibiotics every day. I went to a dermatologist and complained that the antibiotics made my stomach burn and gave me indigestion, but he said not to worry: people stay on antibiotics for years without problems.

"I was vain, so I did stick with the antibiotics until I was in my 30s. Yet I knew something was wrong and, with my very sensitive body, I had clues it was connected to the food I was eating. So I began my intensive search for answers.

"I tried macrobiotics, natural hygiene, raw foods, megavitamin therapy. I studied with some of the greatest teachers in these disciplines. Everything I did improved my health somewhat, but not completely. Finally, deeply frustrated, I 'let go' and prayed for help. It was then that I met Dr. William Crook.

"Dr. Crook was a pioneer in treating people with candidiasis, and his books have helped millions. I learned from him, as I had from all my other teachers to date, but still even he did not have the final answers. So, after six years of relentless searching, using the most important truths from all I have studied, I developed the Body Ecology Diet, which goes *beyond* all these disciplines to really set you up forever with a balanced, inner ecology. I've learned how we strayed from the optimum health that our Creator intended for us, and how we can return there.

"Everyone who has faithfully followed the Body Ecology Diet has improved dramatically, and I am thrilled to share it with you. I'm confident this book will change your life. If your immune system has weakened to the point where you've developed candidiasis, and you've spent a lot of money, time, and effort to find a cure, I promise you that the Body Ecology Diet will be the end of your search."

Donna Gates
Atlanta, GA

Linda's Story

"The Body Ecology Diet has helped lift me out of the worst nightmare of my life. When I met Donna, I had spent nearly four years trying to figure out why I was plagued with persistent symptoms of vaginitis, headaches, food allergies, and urinary and G.I. upsets. I had been to many doctors, tried traditional and non-traditional medicines and regimes, spent hundreds and hundreds of dollars—and I still wasn't symptom-free. I had eliminated all sugar, alcohol, and dairy from my diet, taken umpteen vitamin and mineral supplements, and tried internal cleansing cures until I was blue in the face. I was exercising regularly and had learned relaxation techniques.

"I was probably the healthiest sick person around. But until I started the Diet, my symptoms continued. Then I learned from Donna how to use the principle of Food Combining and, for me, this was the key to accelerating the rate of my improvement.

"I was so tired of doing things that didn't work, that when I found something that did, I went at it with a vengeance. I tried to do absolutely everything Donna teaches. She says make vegetable soup—I ate it even though mine consistently turned out mediocre. She advocates having soup for breakfast—I did it.

"I'm thrilled to report that most of my symptoms have disappeared, and the rest are under control. At this writing, my health remains excellent, I'm reintroducing foods into my diet and, for the first time in several years, I'm at peace with my body.

"The Diet's recipes *really* helped. At first, it was difficult to change my way of thinking about menus and meals, but after a short while it became second nature. This book represents Donna's many years of accumulated knowledge and application; everything she says is valuable and pertinent. She and I are committed to improvements in your health, so we ask you to read this book carefully and follow the suggestions and guidelines. Here's to your health!"

Linda Schatz
Alexandria, VA

About the Authors

DONNA GATES is an expert on candidiasis (CRC) and related immune disorders. She has done extensive research on how these debilitating conditions affect the body, mind, and spirit. She developed and tested the Body Ecology Diet on many different people who have all improved their health by following the basic principles of the Diet. Donna is a nutritional consultant and home economist. She has studied with the top macrobiotic teachers, and she graduated from Lima Osawa's cooking academy in Japan. She holds an M.Ed. in Counseling from Loyola University and a B.S. in Early Childhood Development from the University of Georgia.

LINDA SCHATZ is a professional writer and editor. She is co-author of *Managing By Influence* (Prentice Hall) and has been a newswriter for ABC News and "Good Morning America." She also coaches authors on how to write books and book proposals. Her specialties are self-help books in areas such as health, nutrition, and business. Linda holds an M.A. in Communication from Stanford University and a B.S. in Journalism from the University of California, Berkeley.

Acknowledgements

Since 1994 when the first edition of The Body Ecology Diet was published, many wonderful people have contributed to making it a best seller. To my friends, family, and business associates I offer my heart-felt thanks. And to those of you I haven't met, I am grateful beyond words for your help in carrying this work forward by sharing my book with others.

I will always appreciate the help of Linda Schatz and Heidi Wohl who came into my life at an extraordinarily busy time. I was struggling with how to get all the information that was stored in my mind written down in an organized manner to help the growing number of people who had heard about my work. Both women had come to my classes to learn how to heal themselves of candidiasis. While they say they are grateful for what I gave them, it is I, and you the readers, who are benefiting enormously from their selfless, consistent, determination in helping bring this book to fruition.

Wondering how I could reach greater numbers of people more quickly, I asked The Creator for help, and He answered abundantly. Bob Walberg and Robert Gaffney, the visionaries who brought America flax seed oil, came to my rescue. Today, thanks to Bob and Robert, an incredible team of very devoted Body Ecology/Omega Nutrition employees are behind the scenes providing my books and the products I recommend.

There are two other special men that I absolutely must thank, Richard Thomas and his son Jim, who made a long-held wish come true. My secret wish was for a restaurant where people could experience a Body Ecology meal, lovingly prepared and served, featuring Omega Nutrition oils, organic grains and vegetables, free-range chicken, and even ocean and cultured vegetables. Today, such a restaurant exists. In addition to serving delicious meals at the R. Thomas and Son Deluxe Grill on Peachtree Street in Atlanta, the restaurant delivers Body Ecology meals and cultured vegetables to local health food stores, making it easy for BEDers to stay on The Diet.

Finally, to the One Who created us all, Who has patiently watched us make mistakes yet has never given up on us . . . and Who is (with strict love) guiding us back into the Light, I owe my deepest and most sincere gratitude.

This book is dedicated to those who have the discernment to recognize the truth and the courage to live it.

Donna Gates

Table of Contents

PART ONE

Introduction: A Silent Spring Within

CHAPTER 1
Outer Ecology, Inner Ecology

Many years ago, Rachel Carson, author of *The Silent Spring*, warned that we are slowly destroying the ecological balance of our planet by adding chemicals to our crops. She deplored the pesticides that leach into our food and water supplies, affecting our health and the health of future generations.

In a similar manner, we are destroying the delicate balance of the ecosystem that exists within our own bodies. This intricate ecosystem is inhabited by microorganisms that play an important role in keeping us looking young and feeling healthy and strong. These friendly creatures, lactic bacteria, reside in the digestive tract, strengthen the immune system, and help the body defend against "unfriendly" bacteria and the pathogens that cause disease.

In fact, both friendly and unfriendly microorganisms are always present in our bodies, but when we are healthy, the friendly greatly outnumber the unfriendly, keeping our inner ecosystem in harmony. However, many factors weaken our immunity and upset this balance: the chemicals we add to our food and environment, fast food diets, the stress in our daily lives, and the widespread use of medicines, especially antibiotics and hormones. And when the body is in this weakened state, the unfriendly bacteria can multiply quickly, giving symptoms such as headaches, flu, skin rashes, food allergies, and other potentially more serious disorders.

This book is about restoring your inner health, strengthening your immune system, and establishing a pattern of living and eating well that will extend your vitality for years to come. The Body Ecology Diet provides basic tools you can use for the rest of your life, tools to help you achieve a new balance in your life. *Anyone*—ill or not—can benefit from the Diet.

It is time to restore the ecology of our planet and the ecology of our bodies. By rebuilding our health and our immunity, we can restore our inner ecology, and we will have a much better chance to achieve all our goals, including restoring the ecology of our outer world.

The Two Faces of Antibiotics

Some 40 years ago, antibiotics ("against life") became the "magic bullets" in curing disease. They were considered miracle drugs. Doctors prescribed antibiotics for such simple maladies as colds and skin acne. But antibiotics kill not only disease-causing bacteria, they also kill beneficial bacteria, upset the body's inner ecology, and allow unfriendly organisms to take over.

One of the most common types of unfriendly organisms is Candida albicans. It is a pathogenic yeast or fungus normally present on inner and outer body surfaces, and it co-exists in our digestive tract and in a woman's vagina alongside the friendly microorganisms. It must consume sugars to survive. It is an opportunistic organism, and it rapidly takes advantage of any weakness in our system. So if we're eating improperly, or taking antibiotics, or changing our chemistry with birth control pills, we are providing the candida with a perfect environment in which to grab control. The vagina and intestines are especially susceptible. For example, only two days on antibiotics precipitates candida overgrowth in a susceptible person.[1] When yeast multiplies, it produces toxic waste products, which circulate in the body and further weaken the immune and endocrine systems.

Symptoms of Candidiasis

The overgrowth of candida constitutes a condition we call candidiasis or Candida Related Complex (CRC). It has been linked to *many* symptoms, including food allergies, digestive disorders, PMS, skin rashes, chronic constipation, recurring headaches, chronic vaginitis, chemical and environmental sensitivities, poor memory, mental fuzziness, and loss of sex drive. CRC occurs side by side with other diseases such as chronic fatigue, cancer, AIDS, Epstein-Barr virus, bronchitis, pneumonia, and immune system deficiencies. Experts estimate that 80 million Americans have candidiasis, but the majority don't attribute their symptoms to this modern epidemic.

To reverse this overgrowth of candida, we must restore an inner environment that prevents candida from taking over. This requires two major actions: killing off the bad yeast and other opportunistic parasitic organisms, and recolonizing the friendly bacteria. Both are essential to reestablishing your inner ecology; it won't do any good to reestablish new colonies of friendly bacteria without improving the environment so they can prosper.

[1]De Schepper, 1986

A parallel exists in the outer world. Suppose we wanted to revive populations of endangered species, such as the whooping crane or North American condor. We could breed in captivity some of the few remaining birds, then release them into their former territory. But if the conditions endangering them in the first place were not changed (such as inadequate food or contaminated nesting sites), they would not be able to survive or reproduce.

Hurdles in Restoring Your Body Ecology

When antibiotics were first used, they could kill off almost any strain of infection-causing bacteria. But eventually, these bacteria altered their genetic makeup and started resisting the drugs. Now generations of these resisters have multiplied and become even stronger. They have an astounding ability to adjust to different environments. So the task of eliminating them is formidable, but the key is changing the environment so they cannot survive. The Body Ecology Diet improves your inner habitat so that unfriendly organisms cannot predominate.

A parallel with the overuse of antibiotics exists in our excessive use of pesticides. Insects have become resistant to many pesticides, forcing manufacturers to keep changing their formulae. In addition, the pesticides often kill harmless creatures—other insects, birds, animals, and plants. This compares with the die-off of friendly bacteria from antibiotics.

Emphasizing Probiotics

Friendly bacteria (also known as probiotics, "for life"), such as lactobacillus, streptococcus, and bifidus, and beneficial yeast (saccharomyces kefir and Torula kefir) are essential to a wide range of bodily functions. They help white blood cells fight disease, they control putrefactive bacteria in the intestines, they provide important nutrients for building the blood, they assist digestion, they protect the intestinal mucosa, they prevent diarrhea and constipation, and they contribute to bowel elimination. They also manufacture important B vitamins and are the most abundant source of Vitamin B-12.

Health food stores sell bottles of probiotics, which are usually kept in the refrigerator so they won't lose their potency.

Antibiotics should be taken only when absolutely necessary, and when you must take them, stay strictly on the Diet. Start a course of *probiotics* as soon as the *antibiotic* therapy is completed. We'll tell you more about friendly bacteria throughout the book. (See page 131 for the recommended therapeutic dose.)

How It All Started

Most of us begin life with a clean bill of health, a perfect body inside and out. Experts disagree on exactly where a baby's friendly bacteria comes from, but we do know that mother's milk promotes its growth. As breast feeding continues, the bacteria establish themselves in the baby's digestive tract and in the vagina of the female infant. It takes about three months for an inner ecosystem to settle in, and after this period of time, the infant's amount of lactic (friendly) bacteria closely resembles the mother's.

As the child's inner ecology develops, the beneficial bacteria thrive on natural sugars from breast milk, and then from food, particularly complex carbohydrates. These sugars transform into lactic acid, which the friendly bacteria need to survive. Once the friendly bacteria establish colonies in the intestines, they have created an ideal, self-sustaining habitat, which ideally should endure throughout adulthood, but for most people does not. When this habitat changes, we are at risk.

How Ecosystems Change

Nature gives us two forces to contend with: the process of change, called succession, and the constant attempt to return to stability, or homeostasis. These occur in our inner as well as our outer worlds.

For example, imagine that during a summer storm lightning sparks a forest fire. Rain extinguishes the fire, and most living creatures leave the site. Then, a natural succession begins. The next year, maybe some grass grows in the clearing, and you might see a few butterflies and insects return. A year later, small animals scamper through the meadow. The next summer, shrubs and tree seedlings push up through the ground. Finally, the site becomes woodland again, with its unique balance of plant and animal life. A change occurred but, in time, there was a gradual return to stability.

When humans grow into puberty and adulthood, the chemistry of the digestive tract changes as well. Our inner ecosystem goes through succession. In infants, certain strains of friendly bacteria predominate, but as we grow older, other types become more common. Yet, throughout, our bodies always attempt to return to homeostasis, to that inner equilibrium of ecological balance.

The things that destroy ecological balance, such as a bulldozer in the woods, or a long-term course of antibiotics, are the factors that give rise to the invasion of new species, which further alter the environment and establish new ecosystems. When this happens inside us, it lays the foundation for disease to occur.

Benefits of the Body Ecology Diet

The Diet helps restore your inner environment, which in turn will create the basis for a lifetime of true health.

The Diet will help you:
1. Strengthen your organs, digestive tract, and immune system.
2. Starve the yeast.
3. Cleanse your body of waste discarded by the dying yeast.
4. Balance your internal chemistry.
5. Reestablish and feed your inner ecosystem.

The Diet also will help you just plain feel better, physically and mentally. You may have experienced for a short time—or for years—some or all of the symptoms we've mentioned. The Diet and the principles it is built on offer answers you've been seeking. Now, a look at the principles of the Body Ecology Diet.

CHAPTER 2
Overview of the Key Principles of the Body Ecology Diet

The Body Ecology Diet is a synthesis of seven principles of eating and healing. They are pillars of the holistic health field. Some of them are thousands of years old, such as the Chinese concept of yin and yang (contraction/expansion). Others, such as the theory of blood types, are more recent.

The Diet weaves these principles together like pieces in a puzzle. They can create a framework for healthy eating for the rest of your life. They are clear and complementary. This book shows you how to integrate them into your daily routine. When they are properly implemented, you will see your symptoms disappear and your overall health improve.

Principle #1... Expansion/ Contraction

Certain foods, such as salt, meat, and poultry, cause the body to contract. Stress also causes a contraction or tightening. When the body is too tight, it cannot function properly: circulation slows down, elimination of waste comes to a standstill (constipation).

Other foods, like sugar, alcohol, and coffee, cause the body to expand, open up, and relax. People who eat large amounts of contracting foods, such as salt and salty animal foods, crave *expanding* foods in the body's natural attempt to achieve balance. For example, when we eat salty popcorn at the movies, we often return to the refreshment stand for a sweet drink.

A third group of foods, which is neither too contracting nor too expanding, creates a naturally balanced condition in the body. These foods are the cornerstone of the Diet. You will be delighted to learn they are delicious and readily available.

To regain optimal health and an ideal inner ecology, our goal must be to eat foods that balance and complement one another, so we feel neither too contracted nor expanded. The Body Ecology Diet will show you how to do this.

Principle #2... Acid/Alkaline

Acid rain has polluted our forests, lakes, and streams, endangering a wide range of living animals and plants. In the same manner, increased acidity due to poor diets has altered our internal chemistry, our pH balance, destroying the beneficial flora of our inner ecosystem.

Illness occurs when our bodies are too toxic and therefore too acidic. Understanding how to rebalance our internal chemistry holds a secret to success in healing; restoring the acid/alkaline pH balance is essential. The optimal pH for bodily fluids is slightly alkaline. The Body Ecology Diet recommends foods that make your body more alkaline, resulting in the proper pH for bodily functions and for beneficial bacteria to flourish.

Principle #3... Blood Types

Canadian naturopath Dr. James D'Adamo has developed and tested a theory that specifies what foods we should eat depending on our blood type. Japanese researchers also are validating the theory. We offer it as a fascinating clue to better understand your body and as part of the answer to why we have individual needs and varying rates of healing.

According to this theory, for example, people with Type A blood are more likely to be lactose intolerant and allergic to dairy products. They find them to be very mucous-forming. In contrast, once Type Os reestablish their body ecology, they may be able to eat dairy foods a few times a week without suffering any allergic reactions or excessive mucous.

Dr. D'Adamo's theory covers foods, recommended modes of exercise, and even explains who is best suited to become a vegetarian. It is a valuable clue to restoring your inner ecology.

Principle #4... Cleansing

This is nature's way of allowing our bodies to get rid of unwanted toxins and foreign substances. Aging blood cells and tissues constantly break down and are replaced by new cells and tissues. The cellular debris must be carried away, and cleansing is the process that does this. A speck of dust gets in your eye, and you start tearing—it's a way to cleanse out the dust. A virus invades your system and you get a cold or fever—it's your immune system at work to drive out the virus. The Diet encourages you to *welcome* cleansings, because they *always* result in a higher level of health and immunity.

Principle #5...
Proper Food
Combining

This proven system of eating compatible foods at each meal aids digestion and enhances overall health. When you eat foods that don't combine correctly, the digestive system gets mixed signals about which digestive juices and enzymes to release. Food remains in the digestive tract longer than it should, and it starts fermenting. This produces sugars that feed yeast and parasites, and further weakens the digestive tract and immune system.

The rotting food becomes poison, polluting the ecology of our inner world. It's a gruesome image, but it's accurate. As the stagnant food builds up on the walls of the digestive tract, it forms a landscape that only viruses, cancer cells, and parasites can tolerate, just as rats and other scavengers live off city land-fills and industrial waste sites.

Proper food combining greatly reduces gas, bloating, and excess weight. It is essential for establishing a clean, efficient internal environment. You can learn it by following three basic rules, and we'll give plenty of examples and menus.

Principle #6...
The 80/20
Principles

When you have candidiasis or other immune system diseases, it is essential that the food you eat be properly assimilated and then eliminated. A healthy digestive tract is able to do this. But many people weaken their digestive tracts by overeating or eating poorly combined foods. This puts too heavy a workload on the digestive system. The 80/20 rules guide you in eating moderately to reduce that load.

RULE NUMBER ONE: Eat until your stomach is 80% full, leaving 20% available for digesting. RULE NUMBER TWO: 80% of the food on your plate should be land and/or ocean[2] vegetables. The remaining 20% can be protein or grains and starchy vegetables.

By following the 80/20 and the food combining principles, you will never again leave the table feeling over-full or bloated.

Principle #7...
Step By Step

This principle underlies all the other facets of the Body Ecology Diet. It addresses the question, How long will it take to heal? And it reflects our observations of nature.

Everything in nature, in both our inner and outer lives, occurs in a step-by-step, orderly manner—and this process cannot be violated without damaging consequences. Plants and animals grow step by step; we heal step by step. If we interrupt the

[2]See Chapter 12 for a list of ocean vegetables.

healing process, for example with antibiotics, we interrupt the step-by-step cleansing taking place within our bodies, and disease burrows deeper into our tissues. We can choose how quickly we step through the healing process, but we cannot alter the natural progression of steps. By the time you read the Step By Step chapter, you'll have a good grasp on how to take your own steps toward better health.

As you read this book and start practicing the Diet, you will become very familiar with these principles. They are the foundation of your new way of life.

CHAPTER 3

Tips for Success in Using Body Ecology Diet and This Book

✔ The B.E.D. is a "how come" as well as a "how to" guide to healthier eating. First, read it through, so you'll begin grasping the basic principles, and this will help enhance your determination to stick to the Diet. Then, begin following the Diet *without becoming overwhelmed* by its many recommendations. The beginning may be difficult for you, because it may be a whole new way of eating and cooking, so do your best, knowing that your reward *will* be renewed health and vitality. It gets much easier as time goes on.

✔ Try the recipes we recommend. Most require just a few simple ingredients and not much preparation time. They're nutritious—and delicious.

✔ This diet works! You could see dramatic results within the first few days, especially if you have severe symptoms and start attacking them at the point where you'll get the greatest return on your investment of effort. For example, the very first action is to eliminate *all* forms of sugar from your diet.

✔ The Body Ecology Diet has helped many, many people overcome conditions that made them feel miserable. Everyone is different, so everyone heals at a different rate. You need to trust the recommendations of the Diet, and—very important—know your body and how it responds.

✔ Consider forming a support group with others on the Diet. You can trade recipes, solve problems, and hear one another's concerns. This is very valuable, especially in the beginning of your healing.

✔ Know that eventually you will be able to reintroduce foods not now on the Diet, such as fruits, beans, and other grains. Be patient.

✔ THE BOTTOM LINE:
  1. Read the book.
  2. Plan menus using foods you like; then shop for these foods.
  3. Use the foods in our recipes, always cooking extra for several meals and snacks.
  4. Reread the book until the principles are clear.

CHAPTER 4
How It All Started

The yeast organism, Candida albicans, has been around for thousands of years, but only in modern times has it overtaken our bodies and compromised our immunity.

Yeast and Fungus: The Silent Invaders

Candida albicans is one of several yeast and fungal organisms present in our bodies. Normally, "friendly bacteria" balance these organisms so they do not grow out of control, and a strong immune system oversees it all. But when we throw our body ecology out of balance by ingesting too much sugar, antibiotics, poor quality air and water, or compromise our health in other ways, the candida grows out of control and causes a variety of other symptoms.

A prominent University of California immunologist, Alan Levin, estimates that one out of three Americans is adversely affected by candida.[3] A single-cell organism, it reproduces asexually and thrives on some of the body's by-products: dead tissue and sugars from food. Unless its source of food is eliminated, it quickly monopolizes entire bodily systems, such as the digestive tract, and can cause mild to severe discomfort. Candida, when it becomes acute, is frequently the major cause of death especially in victims of cancer and AIDS.

How Do You Know You Have Candidiasis?

From time to time in your life, you've almost certainly had fevers, stomach upsets, ear problems, headaches, skin rashes, aches and pains, and other physical complaints. Normally, these clear up fairly quickly, and the symptoms do not recur frequently. If they do recur, and you go to your doctor with one or several of these complaints but there is no apparent explanation or cure, then you may have a yeast-related condition.

Although researchers are now developing lab tests on blood and feces to diagnose yeast-related conditions, the primary methods used to date have been a medical history and response to treatment. Use the questionnaire and score sheet in Figure 1 to help decide if your problems are yeast-connected. It was developed by Dr. William Crook, a pioneer in diagnosing and treating candidiasis. The questionnaire is fairly accurate for self-diagnosis of CRC. The best way to figure out whether you have candidiasis is to try the Body Ecology Diet for 10 days and observe whether your symptoms begin clearing up.

[3]Lorenzani, 1986

FIGURE 1

Candida Questionnaire and Score Sheet*

This questionnaire lists factors in your medical history that promote the growth of the common yeast, **Candida Albicans** (Section A), and symptoms commonly found in individuals with yeast-connected illness (Sections B and C).

For each yes answer in Section A, circle the Point Score in that section. Total your score, and record it in the box at the end of the section. Then move on to Sections B and C, and score as directed.

Section A: History

	Point Score
1. Have you taken tetracyclines (Sumycin®, Panmycin®, Vibramycin®, Minocin®, etc.) or other antibiotics for acne for 1 month (or longer)?	50
2. Have you, at any time in your life, taken other "broad spectrum" antibiotics for respiratory, urinary or other infections for 2 months or longer, or for shorter periods 4 or more times in a 1-year span?	50
3. Have you taken a broad spectrum antibiotic drug – even for one period?	6
4. Have you, at any time in your life, been bothered by persistent prostatitis, vaginitis, or other problems affecting your reproductive organs?	25
5. Have you been pregnant… 2 or more times?	5
1 time?	3
6. Have you taken birth control pills for…more than 2 years?	15
6 months to 2 years?	8
7. Have you taken prednisone, Decadron®, or other cortisone-type drugs by mouth or inhalation** for… more than 2 weeks?	15
2 weeks or less?	6
8. Does exposure to perfumes, insecticides, fabric shop odors, or other chemicals provoke… moderate to severe symptoms?	20
mild symptoms?	5
9. Are your symptoms worse on damp, muggy days or in moldy places?	20
10. Have you had athlete's foot, ringworm, "jock itch" or other chronic fungus infections of the skin or nails? Have such infections been… severe or persistent?	20
mild or moderate?	10
11. Do you crave sugar?	10
12. Do you crave breads?	10
13. Do you crave alcoholic beverages?	10
14. Does tobacco smoke **really** bother you?	10
Total Score, Section A	

*Filling out and scoring this questionnaire should help you and your physician evaluate how Candida Albicans may be contributing to your health problems. Yet it will not provide an automatic yes or no answer. A comprehensive history and physical examination are important. In addition, laboratory studies, x-rays, and other types of tests may also be appropriate.

**The use of nasal or bronchial sprays containing cortisone and/or other steroids promotes overgrowth in the respiratory tract.

Section B: Major Symptoms

For each symptom that is present, enter the appropriate number in the Point Score column:

If a symptom is **occasional or mild** ....score 3 points.

If a symptom is **frequent and/or moderately severe** ....score 6 points.

If a symptom is **severe and/or disabling** ....score 9 points.

Total the score for this section, and record it in the box at the end of this section.

	Point Score
1. Fatigue or lethargy	
2. Feeling of being "drained"	
3. Poor memory	
4. Feeling "spacey" or "unreal"	
5. Inability to make decisions	
6. Numbness, burning or tingling	
7. Insomnia	
8. Muscle aches	
9. Muscle weakness or paralysis	
10. Pain and/or swelling in joints	
11. Abdominal pain	
12. Constipation	
13. Diarrhea	
14. Bloating, belching or intestinal gas	
15. Troublesome vaginal burning, itching or discharge	
16. Prostatitis	
17. Impotence	
18. Loss of sexual desire or feeling	
19. Endometriosis or infertility	
20. Cramps and/or other menstrual irregularities	
21. Premenstrual tension	
22. Attacks of anxiety or crying	
23. Cold hands or feet and/or chilliness	
24. Shaking or irritable when hungry	
Total Score, Section B	

Section C: Other Symptoms*

For each symptom that is present, enter the appropriate number in the Point Score column:

If a symptom is **occasional or mild** ....score **3** points.
If a symptom is **frequent and/or moderately severe**.............................score **6** points.
If a symptom is **severe and/or persistent**...score **9** points.

Total the score for this section, and record it in the box at the end of this section.

	Point Score
1. Drowsiness	
2. Irritability or jitteryness	
3. Incoordination	
4. Inability to concentrate	
5. Frequent mood swings	
6. Headaches	
7. Dizziness/loss of balance	
8. Pressure above ears…feeling of head swelling	
9. Tendency to bruise easily	
10. Chronic rashes or itching	
11. Psoriasis or recurrent hives	
12. Indigestion or heartburn	
13. Food sensitivity or intolerance	
14. Mucus in stools	
15. Rectal itching	
16. Dry mouth or throat	
17. Rash or blisters in mouth	
18. Bad breath	
19. Foot, hair or body odor not relieved by washing	
20. Nasal congestion or post nasal drip	

(This section is continued on the next page.)

---

*While the symptoms in this section occur commonly in patients with yeast-connected illness, they also occur commonly in patients who do not have candida.

Section C: Other Symptoms (continued)

For each symptom that is present, enter the appropriate number in the Point Score column:

If a symptom is **occasional or mild** ....score **3** points.

If a symptom is **frequent and/or moderately severe** ....score **6** points.

If a symptom is **severe and/or persistent** ....score **9** points.

	Total your score from previous page	
21. Nasal itching		
22. Sore throat		
23. Laryngitis, loss of voice		
24. Cough or recurrent bronchitis		
25. Pain or tightness in chest		
26. Wheezing or shortness of breath		
27. Urinary frequency, urgency, or incontinence		
28. Burning on urination		
29. Spots in front of eyes or erratic vision		
30. Burning or tearing of eyes		
31. Recurrent infections or fluid in ears		
32. Ear pain or deafness		
	Total Score, Section C	
	Total Score, Section B	
	Total Score, Section A	
GRAND TOTAL SCORE (add totals from Sections A, B and C)		

The Grand Total Score will help you and your physician decide if your health problems are yeast-connected. Scores for women will run higher, as 7 items in this questionnaire apply exclusively to women, while only 2 apply exclusively to men.

Yeast-connected health problems are almost certainly present in women with scores **over 180**, and in men with scores **over 140**.

Yeast-connected health problems are probably present in women with scores **over 120**, and in men with scores **over 90**.

Yeast-connected health problems are possibly present in women with scores **over 60**, and in men with scores **over 40**.

With scores less than 60 for women and 40 for men, yeast are less apt to cause health problems.

This questionnaire is available in quantity from Professional Books, Inc., P.O. Box 3246, Jackson, TN 38302. Prices upon request. Copyright 1984. *The Yeast Connection* by William G. Crook, M.D. Reprinted with permission.

Candida—
A Downward
Spiral

Candida overgrowth is a vicious cycle. Our diets are full of sugars that feed the yeast. In women, pregnancy and the use of birth control pills create hormonal changes that encourage yeast overgrowth. Antibiotics, found extensively in our food supply and prescribed by doctors, kill not only bad bacteria but also the friendly bacteria that normally inhabit our tissues, so this sets up an environment where yeast can multiply uncontrollably. A normal, strong immune system can keep yeast under control. But when yeast do overgrow, they release toxins, which weaken the immune system. At this point, the weakened immune system can no longer defend against germs, bacteria, and viruses, so these organisms multiply and quickly invade tissues and organs, causing infections. If you take antibiotics to get rid of these infections, the cycle starts all over.

Some of the most important current medical research involves the immune system and diseases related to a weak immune response, such as AIDS, Epstein-Barr, cancer, and other serious conditions. Candidiasis is not a disease in itself; it is a condition indicating an internal imbalance. Its symptoms may mask, overshadow or accompany the presence of other diseases, such as AIDS and cancer. So if your immune system is occupied dealing with candidiasis, it does not have the strength to fight these other critical illnesses. The good news is that candidiasis can be corrected naturally using the Body Ecology Diet.

Diet Is
The Key

The crux of getting well is healthy eating, not medicine or vitamin pills. If you don't feed your body with essential vitamins, minerals, and other elements obtained from the right foods eaten in the right way, your body will never be strong enough to take over on its own. It will not be able to heal itself as it was created to do. By following the Body Ecology Diet, you will *naturally and easily* regain strength, health, and well-being—and judging from the comments we often receive, you may be surprised to find that you even enjoy it!

A few people still regard candidiasis as a "fad" or fake disease, but this misunderstanding is starting to clear up. Patients whose recurring symptoms and complaints cannot be resolved by traditionally-trained doctors and specialists often are referred to psychologists for treatment. Yet when these patients begin a yeast-control diet and lifestyle, they respond splendidly, and their symptoms clear up. Even if Dr. Crook's yeast questionnaire does not prove conclusively that you have candidiasis, when you start the Body Ecology Diet, we guarantee your health will improve and your symptoms will start disappearing.

Where Candida Grows

Candida easily overruns the intestinal tract and the vagina, sinuses, and surface of the tongue. It also can burrow deeper into various organs of people with severely suppressed immune systems. It can mass around the heart and affect the liver and the nervous and circulatory systems. In women, it can affect the reproductive organs.

Once candida colonizes in the liver, it precipitates a craving for alcohol and sweets. If it attacks the nervous system, it can be responsible for mood swings, memory loss, confusion, and inability to concentrate.

The goal of the Body Ecology Diet is not to eliminate candida completely—this is impossible. It can live as an innocuous organism within our bodies. Instead, the goal is to *balance our systems*, control the overgrowth, and bring ourselves back to health where a strong immune system prevails.

Our next step is to investigate the basic principles of the Body Ecology Diet.

PART TWO

Principles of the Body Ecology Diet

CHAPTER 5
The Principle of Expansion and Contraction

For more than 5000 years Oriental philosophers have been using the extraordinary principle of yin/yang to explain how the universe works. In healing, as in all aspects of life, this simple, accurate universal law provides some answers to apparently mysterious conditions such as cancer, chronic fatigue syndrome, and candidiasis. The idea of mastering yin/yang is often over-whelming and could require a lifetime of study. To simplify matters, we are extracting the aspects of yin/yang that most apply to foods and healing. We call this the expansion/contrac-tion principle. It stems from observations of natural phenomena. If mastering it at first seems a little complicated, relax—this principle is built right into the Body Ecology Diet. We present it here so you can obtain a basic understanding of how it works.

Ancient philosophers and healers observed that there are opposing forces in nature always seeking a balance. These opposing forces are not simply forces against one another, but are actually two parts of one whole. For example, male and female appear to be opposites, yet they really are extremes along the continuum of sexuality. "Maleness" is understood more clearly when compared with "femaleness." Left is better understood in relation to right. Up helps us explain what down is.

While these forces appear to be opposites or even antagonistic forces, they really are complementary. For example, left complements right, since knowledge of left and right allows us to navigate and explore. Most of us would agree that male complements female and vice versa.

When you combine any two complementary opposites, you can arrive at an ideal or a balance. For example, hot and cold create warmth.

The expansion/contraction principle is useful in understanding energy or Ki (life force within our bodies). Contracting energy or Ki is *stored* energy, while expanding energy is *released* energy. Contracting energy is *closed* and *tight*, while expanding energy is *open*, *relaxed*, and *active*. Expanding energy has a *fiery* nature, while contracting energy is like the nature of *water*...yielding, accepting, but persistent. The contracting force is soft, dark, surrendering, and intuitive in nature. Expansion indicates strength, brightness, and intense, forceful, potent energy (as in the energy of the sun).

It might be useful to point out here that extremes of contraction or expansion Ki are not ideal energy states when we are looking at the energy of our body. The ideal is the balance or mid-point of the two—when we feel calmly centered and truly strong.

Illness, therefore, is either extreme constrictive...closed and tightened energy, or extreme expansive...kinetic, nervous, uncomfortably intense energy. Candida itself is a rapidly growing, expanding fungus that thrives in the impure, dark, moist, contracted areas of the body.

To heal this condition we must stop the growth of this aggressive fungus by withholding the food it needs and simultaneously change the imbalanced, weakened state of the immune system to a positive, energetic one. Eating appropriate foods is vital, because foods, too, are classified according to the expansion/contraction principle.

How the Expansion/ Contraction Principle Affects the Foods We Eat

Some foods, such as salt, cause a contraction phenomenon within the body. Salt induces contraction of the cellular fluids. Too much salt can cause dehydration or extreme loss of bodily fluid. When we eat salt, especially too much salt, we become thirsty. You have probably experienced this at a movie theater, if you have eaten the usual overly-salted popcorn and become very thirsty.

Foods with salt inside them, such as animal foods[4] and salty cheese, also produce a contracting effect. Therefore, beef, pork, lamb, poultry, eggs, and fish are contracting foods. When we eat them, we feel more uptight or closed. A diet high in these foods can cause constipation.

Some foods, such as sugar, cause expansion to take place within the body. The blood stream quickly absorbs sugar and produces energy. If you notice that you're feeling too contracted, you also might observe that you're beginning to crave something expansive (with sugar in it) to help you relax or feel more open. All foods with sugar in them (fruits, most dairy products, sweetened pastries, candy) are expanding foods.

The Body Ecology Diet will teach you how to balance the foods you eat. Some foods are naturally balanced, and you'll want to eat them often. Please study the following expansion/ contraction chart carefully before reading on.

---

[4]The blood of animals is salty.

FIGURE 2

The Expansion/Contraction Continuum

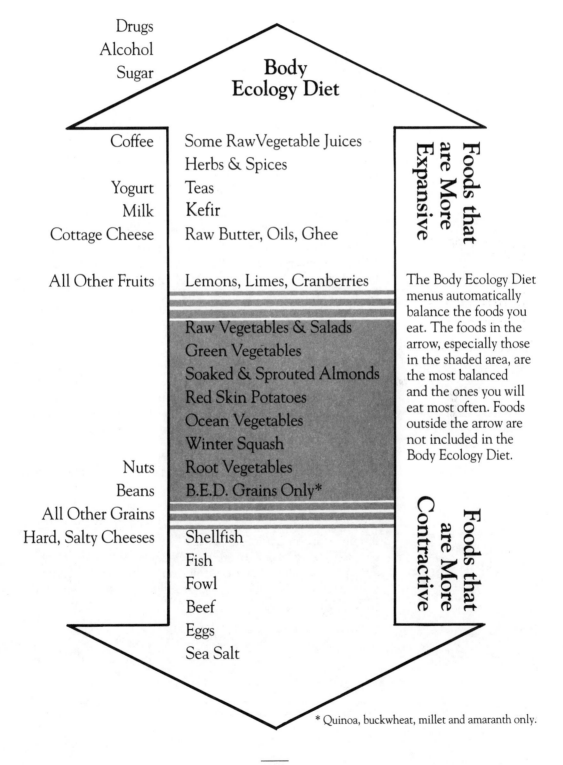

Drugs
Alcohol
Sugar

Body Ecology Diet

Coffee — Some Raw Vegetable Juices
Herbs & Spices
Yogurt — Teas
Milk — Kefir
Cottage Cheese — Raw Butter, Oils, Ghee

All Other Fruits — Lemons, Limes, Cranberries

Raw Vegetables & Salads
Green Vegetables
Soaked & Sprouted Almonds
Red Skin Potatoes
Ocean Vegetables
Winter Squash
Nuts — Root Vegetables
Beans — B.E.D. Grains Only*
All Other Grains
Hard, Salty Cheeses — Shellfish
Fish
Fowl
Beef
Eggs
Sea Salt

Foods that are More Expansive

The Body Ecology Diet menus automatically balance the foods you eat. The foods in the arrow, especially those in the shaded area, are the most balanced and the ones you will eat most often. Foods outside the arrow are not included in the Body Ecology Diet.

Foods that are More Contractive

* Quinoa, buckwheat, millet and amaranth only.

Besides sugar, note that alcohol, coffee, and drugs have an expanding effect. When consumed in excess, they cause too much expansion, and you can feel "spaced out," confused, and unfocused.

Since a healthy body always strives toward balance, too much expanding food creates a craving for contracting food and vice versa. For example, if you eat too much salt or animal food, you will crave sweets to make a balance. Eating this way puts your body on an undesirable seesaw. It's best to eat foods in the *middle* of the expansion/contraction spectrum, and when you do eat slightly toward one end or the other, choose foods that make a balance within the same meal. The Body Ecology Diet menus do this.

Remember that candidiasis is an expanding, rapidly growing condition within your body. To make a balance using the appropriate foods, you should eat those foods that are slightly more contracting at first. And to strengthen a weak immune system, you need to eat more from the balanced center of the expansion/contraction continuum. For example, at first you should eat more eggs (contracting) than you might normally. But always accompany them with vegetables (balanced). As your health improves, eat a larger percentage of your meals from the center of the chart (shaded area).

The Medicinal Value of Sea Salt

Salt is the most contracting food, but its role has been completely misunderstood. The ordinary table salt that most of us eat is too refined; it *lacks* the minerals we need and has harmful effects on the body. High-quality sea salt, however, is essential to life and has medicinal value in our diet.

For example, sea salt balances the expanding nature of butter and oils used in the Body Ecology Diet.

Why We Crave Sweets

Humans are contracted beings (we belong to the animal kingdom), so it is our nature to seek sweet, expanding tastes in an effort to balance the contraction. Newborn babies (tiny, contracted beings) thrive on breast milk, because it is sweet and watery; it is expanding.

The Body Ecology Diet satisfies this need with a natural sweet herb, stevia. The sweet vegetables such as onions, carrots, and butternut squash also satisfy our sweet taste. We use them abundantly in our recipes. You will feel well nourished by these foods and no longer crave foods containing sugar.

Stress causes the body to contract. This too explains why we often crave expanding foods such as candy, alcohol, and even tobacco, because in our fast-paced world, we are usually under great stress.

More On What To Eat

Whenever you eat contracting foods, it is vital to balance them with expanding foods that promote health. Since fruit is not on the Diet (and substances such as coffee, alcohol, and sugars inhibit healing), that leaves land and ocean vegetables, high-quality oil, butter, ghee, and simple herbs. These are excellent, healing foods, which contain all of nature's vitamins and minerals. The Body Ecology Diet recipes will teach you how to prepare many vegetables in ways you may never have known before, ways that will heal you.

Fish is the preferred animal food on the Diet. Among the contracting foods, fish ranks closest to the desirable shaded area (or balanced center area) of the expansion/contraction spectrum. Cold-water fish, such as tuna, salmon, and halibut, are the healthiest to eat; **avoid warm-water fish, such as orange roughy, because of the preservatives used when they are caught.**

In Summary

The foods listed within the shaded area of Figure 2, the Expansion/Contraction Continuum, provide the most healing energy for your body. Make them the main part of your diet, and when you eat outside the shaded area, make sure you balance your meals.

This does not mean you will never again eat foods outside the arrow. Indeed, once you have conquered your candidiasis and restored your immune system to health, you will be able to slowly reintroduce other healthy foods into your diet, foods such as beans, more grains, nuts, and fruits. But while you are ridding your body of candidiasis, stick with the recommended foods; your reward will be extraordinary health and well-being.

CHAPTER 6

The Principle of Acid and Alkaline

Just as our normal body temperature is 98.6 degrees F., there are other measures of a normal condition or homeostasis within the body. The levels of sugar, oxygen, and carbon dioxide within the blood must all be stable, and the pH (the balance between acid and alkaline) of the bodily fluids, including the blood, should be 7.4, slightly alkaline.

Knowledge of how to keep your body in a slightly alkaline condition is vital to restoring your health. Without this knowledge you cannot maintain the proper pH for your body to function and for the living ecosystem within you to survive.

An acid/alkaline imbalance toward too much acidity allows yeast, viruses, rebellious cancer cells, and various other parasites to thrive. Acidity also leads to conditions such as chronic fatigue, AIDS, arthritis, and allergies.

The typical American diet is high in foods that cause our bodies to become acidic. It is no wonder, then, that these serious conditions are becoming more prevalent. If you have an acidic condition from eating an acid-forming diet, your body constantly is trying to return to an alkaline state by calling on your stored reserves of alkaline minerals: sodium, calcium, potassium and magnesium. If you continue eating foods that are highly acid-forming, you leach even more alkaline minerals from your body, creating a mineral deficiency that becomes severe over time.

The Simple, Obvious Solution

To overcome an acidic condition, eat alkaline-forming foods. But with candidiasis, we can eat only those alkaline-forming foods that do not feed yeast or parasites but that do rebuild the immune system. Such foods provide the habitat for your newly established "ecosystem within" to flourish. There are ten categories of alkaline-forming foods that satisfy these requirements.

Alkaline-Forming Foods You *Can* Eat:

Most land vegetables
Ocean vegetables (see Chapter 12)
Millet, quinoa (pronounced "keen-wah"), and amaranth
    (available in health food stores; see Chapter 12)
Sea salt (good quality)
Herbs and herb teas (organically grown, see shopping list)
Seeds (except sesame)
Mineral water (sparkling and plain)

Lemons, limes, and unsweetened cranberries
Raw apple cider vinegar
Cultured vegetables (see Chapter 14)
Kefir (see Chapter 24)
Soaked and sprouted almonds[5]

Alkaline-Forming Foods Not On The Diet:

All other fruits

Fruits create an alkaline condition when metabolized and are usually very good for us. However, when you have immune system disorders, they are too high in sugar, and they feed yeast and other parasites.

Are Acid-Forming Foods Bad?

No. On the contrary, some acid-forming foods are necessary for nutritional value and for proper pH balance. The ideal acid-forming, to alkaline-forming ratio by volume for any given meal should be:

Approximately 20% of the foods on your plate should be acid-forming, and approximately 80% should be alkaline-forming.

For more information on how to create the 80/20 balance, see Chapter 10 and Figure 7.

Acid-Forming Foods You Can Eat:

Animal foods, such as beef, poultry, eggs, fish, and shellfish
Buckwheat
Organic, unrefined oils
The herb stevia

Acid-Forming Foods You Should Not Eat:

Highly acid-forming foods not on the Diet include: sugar, candy, soft drinks, flour products, beans, soybean products and tofu, nuts (except almonds) and nut butters, wine, beer, saccharin, Nutrasweet®, alcohol, and commercial refined vinegar. Since all processed foods with preservatives and chemicals are acid-forming, please avoid them.

---

[5]Almonds are usually difficult to digest because of an enzyme-inhibiting substance contained in their brown coating. Soaking and sprouting removes this inhibitor. Almond butter is too high in oil for those of us with congested livers. (See chapter on the liver.) All other nuts are too acid-forming until your inner ecosystem is recolonized.

Examples of Balanced Meals Using The 20%/80% Acid/Alkaline Rule:

Breakfast
(20%) Scrambled eggs (1-2)
(80%) with sauteed onion and greens
     Echinacea Plus Herbal Tea

Lunch
(20%) a B.E.D. grain
(80%) with sauteed onion, carrots, and peas
     Cultured vegetables or salad with salad dressing
      (using *unrefined* oil)
     Creamy broccoli soup with garlic and fennel
     Leafy green vegetables (kale, collards)

Dinner
(20%) Grilled salmon
(80%) Green beans with garlic
     Leeks and yellow squash sauteed with oregano
     Salad or cultured vegetables

Can I Eat an All Alkaline-Forming Meal?

Yes. Absolutely. All alkaline-forming meals heal and balance. They are especially recommended for the first three days of the Diet to quickly restore the body to a more normal condition. We also recommend an all-alkaline meal whenever you are cleansing (see Chapter 8).

An example of such a meal would be:
Potato corn chowder (see recipe), a medley of sautéed vegetables (onion, garlic, carrot, broccoli, red pepper, yellow squash) and a salad with the Body Ecology Diet Salad Dressing.

Do Any Foods Belong to a Neutral Group?

Yes, raw butter and ghee have a neutral pH balance.

What Else Causes Acidity?

Acidity in the blood/body fluids can be due to:
Constipation (body becomes toxic)
A deficiency of minerals (yeast and sugar-laden, refined
    foods leech minerals such as calcium, magnesium,
    potassium, sodium, etc. from our body)
Liver or kidney weakness
Overconsumption of protein from animal foods
    (see 80/20 principle, Chapter 10)
Improper food combining
    (You'll read more about this soon.)

Overeating
> People with body ecology imbalances almost always over-eat. They can't seem to satisfy their cravings, especially for sugar, bread, dairy, and fruits. This is partly because of the insatiable appetite of the yeast. Also, the lack of an inner ecosystem to help us properly digest food causes us to have nutritional deficiencies...some quite severe. So our body is desperately signaling us to feed it *real* food.

Drug use (both medicinal and hallucinogenic)
> This stimulates the organs, releasing hormones and increasing the blood sugar. Taking drugs has the same negative effect as eating sugar. The body needs a large amount of minerals to return to balance.

Exercise
> This makes the blood acidic, but when you breathe deeply and rapidly as you exercise, your body releases carbon dioxide, and the blood then becomes more alkaline.

Stress
> Negative emotions, such as anger, resentment, guilt and fear
> Fatigue caused by stress

Excess blood acidity weakens the respiratory system, resulting in less breathing, less oxygen inhaled, and, therefore, less oxygen available to your cells. This leads to further fatigue. No wonder that chronic exhaustion is a common symptom of candidiasis, chronic fatigue, AIDS, and cancer. That's why we strongly recommend deep breathing and aerobic exercise to get more oxygen into your system.

If you feel that you are forgetful, spacey, or constantly disorganized, it could be because an acidic blood condition causes a lack of mental clarity. An alkaline body contributes to clear thinking and precise action.

When cells live too long in an acidic condition, they adapt to it by mutating and becoming malignant. Long-term acidic conditions in our bodies provide perfect environments for cancer and auto-immune diseases like AIDS to flourish. Most people with these fatal diseases also have candidiasis, which results from destroying the body ecology.

Don't feel you have to master the science of acid/alkaline in order to get well. Yes, it takes some reading, study, and practice to feel comfortable with it, but The Body Ecology Diet has the Acid/Alkaline Principle built right into it. Once you become familiar with all the elements of the Diet and learn the wonderful variety of foods available to you, you will soon be incorporating this principle easily into your menu planning.

FIGURE 3

Acid/Alkaline Foods

| **What's On the Body Ecology Diet Menu** | **Acid-forming foods you can eat**
Limit to 20% of your meal:
　　Animal foods (i.e., beef, poultry, eggs, fish,
　　　　and shellfish)
　　Buckwheat
　　Organic, unrefined oils
　　Stevia (an herb)

Alkaline-forming foods you can eat
Should be 80% or more of your meal:
　　Land vegetables (most)
　　Ocean vegetables
　　Millet, quinoa, and amaranth
　　Sea salt
　　Herbs and herb teas
　　Seeds (except sesame)
　　Mineral water (plain or sparkling)
　　Lemons, limes and unsweetened
　　　　cranberries
　　Cultured Foods
　　　　Raw organic apple cider vinegar
　　　　Raw cultured vegetables
　　　　Kefir (see new Chapter 24)
　　Soaked and sprouted almonds

Neutrals
　　Butter
　　Ghee |
| **What's Not On the Menu** | **Acid-forming foods:**
　　Sugar, candy, soft drinks
　　Flour products
　　Beans, soybean products and tofu
　　Nuts and nut butters
　　Wine, beer, alcohol
　　Saccharin, NutraSweet®, Equal®
　　Commercial refined vinegar

Alkaline-forming foods:
　　Fruits (except those listed above) |

CHAPTER 7
The Principle of Blood Types

Extensive research by the Japanese and by Canadian naturopath Dr. James D'Adamo gives us additional insight into solving the riddle of candidiasis and candida-related conditions. While the Japanese research is interesting,[6] we have found Dr. D'Adamo's theories very useful in the quest to understand varying needs and rates of healing. Dr. D'Adamo found that people react differently to foods, water temperature, colors, and exercise, according to their blood types.[7] When we apply his theory to our own research, it provides an important clue to explain why each of us reacts differently to candida and why our healing requirements vary slightly. We present his conclusions as another step on the path to better health, another way of knowing yourself and how you can best heal your body. See if these ideas prove true for you; if they fit, use them.

Type O

According to Dr. D'Adamo, people with Type O blood have the best chance of overcoming candidiasis. They have a strong, well-developed physique, and their basic nature makes them physically very active. They need some protein **daily** to feel well; this could come from high-quality fish or free-range eggs. Dairy products are not as mucous-forming in Type Os as in other people; wheat and tomatoes are not as acid-forming. This doesn't mean you can run out and eat these foods with abandon. With the exception of kefir, dairy foods (with lactose...a milk sugar) feed yeast and are, therefore, not allowed on the Body Ecology Diet. But once you are well, you Os can rotate them into your diet with fewer consequences than others might have. Type Os usually can introduce new foods sooner than other blood types, once they restore their inner ecology.

The blood flow of Type Os is sluggish, so vigorous exercise is critical to improving health and feeling good. Type Os can exercise strenuously for an hour or two a day, and they'll feel great afterward.

The key word for Type Os is stimulate. Stimulate your body with alternating hot and cold water when you shower, wear strong colors like red, orange, purple, yellow. Drink American ginseng tea, which is very stimulating, and keep your diet high in iron, with lots of leafy greens, ocean vegetables, egg yolks, whole grains, soaked almonds and sardines.

[6]Toshitaka Nomi and Alexander Besher, in *You Are Your Blood Type*, link personality and blood type and give advice on how you can make decisions, improve relationships, and find success, based on blood type.
[7]D'Adamo, 1989

NOTE: The B.E.D Salad Dressing (see recipe) calls for the sea vegetable dulse, which is rich in iron. Sea vegetables have two to ten times more iron than spinach or egg yolks.

> *Jim T. is a Type O. He gets at least one hour of vigorous exercise daily either at the basketball court or his local gym. He feels best when he eats two meals with protein and non-starchy vegetables every day; he often starts the day with a vegetable omelette. Even while on vacation, he is active, enjoying sports and non-sedentary activities.*

Type As and A/B

These two types are very similar. They burn a lot of the calories they consume in mental activity and generally have a high creative potential. Their bodies are very sensitive, and they tend to be physically less active. When healthy, their thyroid glands are often overstimulated, which increases their metabolic rate. This leads to a nervous kind of kinetic energy and activity, rather than a calm, centered energy. Many of these people may never have experienced their true energy, because they've been eating the wrong foods all their lives. They may be tense, impatient, and unable to sleep well.

Candidiasis seems to overwhelm them, and it takes a longer time for them to spring back to health than it takes a Type O. Types A and A/B must introduce new foods more slowly. They may have to take extra special care of themselves but, in return, they can live very long, healthy lives.

Dr. D'Adamo feels As and A/Bs can become vegetarians. Transitioning into a vegetarian version of The Diet may work for you but we have found most As and ABs feel stronger with some protein...especially cold water fish (rich in Omega-3 fatty acids). (see page 67 "A Special Note To Vegetarians")

Wheat products are usually highly acid-forming for Types A and A/B. Wheat should not be eaten at all (because it feeds yeast). Types A and A/B may find buckwheat (a B.E.D. grain) to be too acid-forming, so, if it's a favorite of yours, cook it with more alkaline foods, such as onions, carrots, the three other B.E.D. (alkaline) grains, and good quality sea salt. The way you cook and combine foods can change the impact they have in your body.

Types A and A/B should eat the most alkaline fruits and vegetables to prevent an increase in body acidity. Try leafy greens, watercress, asparagus, broccoli, carrots, fennel, okra, cucumbers, celery, yellow squash, and green beans. Even if you were rebalanced and could eat them, the following foods have limitations for Types A and A/B:

Tomatoes and fruits such as oranges, tangerines, and apples are too acidic for you (but grapefruit is fine). Avocados are too rich in oil, so eat them sparingly. Red and green cabbage may cause excessive gas; however, the raw cultured cabbage you will be learning about later is an ideal food for you. Lentils have too high a concentration of iron and are difficult to digest. All Legumes are an example of improper food combining because they are part starch and part protein and are always difficult to digest.) Once you are free of your candida imbalance and choose to eat them, soy products such as tofu are well tolerated by As and A/Bs.

> *Donna is type A and eats mostly a vegetarian diet. Most of her daily protein comes from Kefir and Vitality Supergreen™ (more on these foods later). Occasionally, she finds herself craving animal protein…often fresh salmon. She has learned to listen to her body and always feels best when she does.*

Warm baths and showers—neither too hot nor too cold—are best for these blood types. A steam room, hot tub, or sauna are too exhausting. Exercise should be calming to soothe that nervous energy; yoga, T'ai Chi, golfing, walking, and gentle rebounding are all excellent examples. Soft pastel colors complement the lifestyles of Types A and A/B.

Type B

These people share characteristics of all other blood types. Balance and moderation are key to their lives. They can strike a good balance between mental and physical pursuits. They're constitutionally stronger than As but less muscular than Os.

Type Bs will find that wheat and dairy products are mildly mucous-forming and should only be eaten a few times a week if at all (see Chapter 12). They can vary their diet between vegetarian and animal meals. They can alternate between vigorous and calming exercise. Warm baths or showers are best, with occasional stimulation from a hot/cold combination. The full range of colors can be worn: red and orange to activate, blue and green to soothe, mauve and violet for meditation or reflection.

Type Bs just need to experiment until they find what works for them in terms of diet, exercise, and lifestyle. They can sample, pick, and choose.

Linda is a Type B, and she finds that an ideal day consists of at least one meal with grain or starchy vegetables and one with protein. She does hard aerobic exercise every other day and milder exercise, such as walking, on the alternate days. Once her body ecology was restored, she tried many different foods, tolerating some better than others.

Blood Type and Pregnancy

As a Type A, Donna's body is drawn naturally to a vegetarian diet. But when she became pregnant, she began craving animal foods, so she began eating high-quality protein flesh foods, such as fish and duck. When her son Taylor was born, she found he has Type O blood. She believes that's one of the reasons why her body had wanted more of a Type O diet. During pregnancy, the mother's body becomes subordinate to the baby's needs as it grows and becomes strong enough to live in the "outside world." Taylor's developing brain and body may have needed more animal foods than hers, so she managed to satisfy that need. Donna began nursing her son and continued eating high-quality animal foods. After about five months, her body signaled that it was ready to start changing back to her more-vegetarian diet.

A Final Note

Dr. D'Adamo strongly endorses food combining. His food recommendations differ in many details from those on the Body Ecology Diet, since he does not focus on candida and candida-related problems. But, overall, we have found our research to agree. While we present his theory so that you may have another approach to healing yourself, we also hope that researchers in the medical community will take up the D'Adamo banner and continue his search.

CHAPTER 8
The Principle of Cleansing

The principle of cleansing is the most important of the seven principles that make up the Body Ecology Diet. Yet, initially, it is the most misunderstood and least trusted of them all. The earth we live on undergoes a constant cleansing and renewal process. All creatures, including humans, live according to the truly wondrous precept of cleansing.

Cleansing allows our bodies to restore balance when the imbalance becomes too great and threatens our lives. Sadly, most of us have no understanding and no gratitude for this essential, life-saving process occurring within us. If you forget the other six principles on the Diet but begin to master this one, you are on your way to becoming well.

Cleansing is your body's natural way to get rid of waste or toxins, and it occurs daily in some form or another. Tears, urine, mucus, sweat—all are examples of body cleansing that we regard as very normal. But the body has other normal ways to eliminate harmful substances, by giving us such disruptions as fevers, colds, and skin eruptions, and we have been taught that these are bad and need to be suppressed.

NOTHING COULD BE FURTHER FROM THE TRUTH. The body is designed to rid itself naturally of toxins and waste, but when we take drugs, we drive these toxins *deeper* into our systems, and they further weaken vital organs. Eventually, the weakened organs have no energy to eliminate toxins and fight disease; they give up the fight, and the body succumbs.

Look at Figure 4. The top diagram shows a series of peaks and valleys. The peaks represent the positive times when our bodies are rebuilding. We feel great and look great. The valleys are the times of cleansing when we ache, feel tired, feverish, or ill. In the first rebuilding/cleansing cycle you see the ups and downs, but the overall trend is up: the chart of an increasingly healthy body that does not stop its cleansings. In the middle diagram, the overall trend or direction is down: the diagram of a body unable to fight off true disease, because it frequently takes medication and is not using the best weapons of healing— appropriate food, water, rest, and exercise.

We all have peaks and valleys in our health throughout our lives. The valleys are periods of cleansing we should be grateful for, because when the cleansing ends, our bodies will be free of damaging toxins, and this leads to a lifetime of greater strength and health. *You cannot heal without cleansing.*

FIGURE 4

Ups and Downs of Cleansing

**Following
the B.E.D.
principles:**

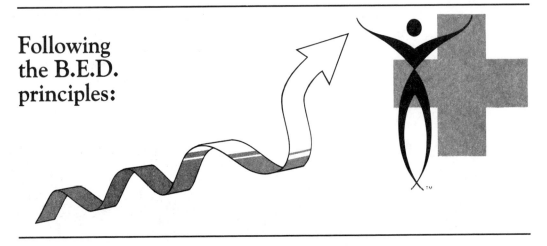

**Not following
the B.E.D.
principles:**

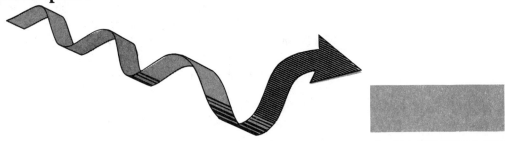

The Cycle*

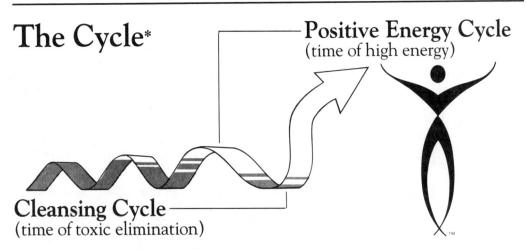

Positive Energy Cycle
(time of high energy)

Cleansing Cycle
(time of toxic elimination)

*The cycle will happen regardless of whether individual is on the B.E.D. However, following the principles of the Diet will move the individual in a positive health direction.

As you follow the Diet, ridding your body of accumulated toxins, you will have ups and downs—but you will see that, as the months pass, the overall direction will be up. Your symptoms may temporarily flare up, and sometimes you will think you are even "sicker" than before you started the Diet, but this is short-lived. It is often due to the die-off of the yeast, which creates more toxins as the body works to eliminate them. Once this group of toxins exits, you will feel much stronger. So welcome your times of cleansing, because they mean you are getting well.

Difference Between Cleansing and Disease

Cleansing is a continuing, step-by-step phenomenon. It is the natural force that drives impurities from the body: impurities resulting from the poor quality of our diets, our environment, our emotional lives. Disease, on the other hand, occurs when the body loses its ability to cleanse itself and gives up the struggle to remain pure.

The cleansing process is very simple: when the organs of elimination (lungs, liver, kidneys, colon) become overwhelmed with impurities and toxins, these toxins lodge somewhere in the cells, tissues, or muscles (usually where we have genetic weaknesses). In an attempt to maintain integrity, the body organizes a cleansing, forcing the toxins out in some disruptive form like a fever, cold, flu, rash, acne, or other "illness." If this attempt to cleanse is stopped by a drug (such as antibiotics or cold medicines) the toxins are driven deeper into the body. With each attempt at cleansing that drugs suppress, the major organs step by step give up a little of their fight until, with time, they give up altogether, becoming diseased. This is what happens in victims of cancer, chronic fatigue, candidiasis, and other immune system disorders.

Welcome the Cleansings, Which Allow You to Heal

Your most significant period of cleansing will occur during your first three months, and especially during the first few days and weeks, on the Body Ecology Diet. This is a period of great healing. You are offering your body high-quality, well-combined, healthy food that is easy to digest. It will respond by showing extensive signs of healing—only to you it may look and feel as if you're getting worse. This is just evidence that your body is throwing out those accumulated toxins. You may feel very tired. It's *extremely important* to remain strictly on the Diet during this time, to give yourself the maximum opportunity to heal. It's easy to get discouraged when you find yourself just as "sick" as before, but have faith that when this healing period ends, you definitely will feel stronger and better.

Hints to Help You Stick With the Diet During Cleansing

✔ Eat all-alkaline meals, especially during the first three days on the Diet (see Chapter 6).

✔ Eat warming foods, such as vegetable soup.

✔ Don't overeat, because this diverts your energy from cleansing to digestion.

✔ An age old remedy forgotten by our generation is to clean your colon at the first sign of a cleansing (see Chapter 17)

✔ If you crave sweets, satisfy that craving with the herb stevia. Use it in teas, or check out our recipes that use stevia.

✔ Get plenty of rest. Be kind to yourself. Let your body heal.

✔ Find someone to talk to who has already gone through this intensive initial cleansing, someone who will encourage you not to give up.

✔ Be patient. Cleansing occurs in incremental steps, just like the transition from darkness to daylight. You can't hurry it up.

When We Cleanse, Symptoms Get Worse... Temporarily

Cleansing looks like a disturbance to the entire system. Compare it to cleaning your living room. When you decide to clean your living room, you start dusting, vacuuming, cleaning the windows. The dirt and grime start to fly, you move furniture, throw things out—and if someone arrives during the middle of this, your living room looks awful. But when you're finished, it looks much better than before.

When your body starts cleansing, you may have a sore throat, skin eruptions, headaches, flu symptoms, aches and pains, depression, lethargy, increased fatigue, skin rashes, vaginal itching and discharge. This is known as the Herxheimer die-off reaction. As the yeast die off and exit through normal body channels, they release toxins that cause these symptoms. The greater the die-off, the more uncomfortable you may be. A home enema or a visit to your colon therapist at the first sign of cleansing will greatly shorten and minimize any discomfort (see Chapter 17). When the cleansing ends, you will be free of symptoms that may have plagued you for years; you will be much stronger and healthier.

How long will it take? It's different for everybody, and it depends on how long the toxins have been in your body and how deeply imbedded they are. For some, it takes three months to a year to be symptom-free; for many with severe candida imbalance, it may take longer, possibly up to three years. Most people feel a lot better after only two weeks on the Diet. You may be surprised to find yourself choosing to stay on the expanded version of the Body Ecology Diet (see Chapter 21), adding the foods you can tolerate, forever. The reward for such self-discipline will be clearly demonstrated in the quality of the way you live the rest of your life: as someone who experiences the full joy of a strong, healthy body and mind, with enough energy to do whatever you want.

The Emotional Side of Cleansing and Healing

The impact of our thoughts and feelings on the body is well documented, and the new field of psychoneuroimmunology relates this to the health of the immune system. Through techniques such as visualization, affirmations, and even prayer, we can strengthen our immune systems and enhance the cleansing/healing process. If we try to heal our bodies but remain angry, stressed, or guilty in our minds, the healing will take longer and be more difficult. But if we can cleanse our minds of negative, impure thoughts and emotions, replacing them with joy, love, and trust, the physical cleansing and healing will be easier and more fulfilling.

As your physical body cleanses (spring and fall are two natural times of potential major cleansings), you may feel inexplicably weepy, on edge, or angry. Without warning, you may feel like lashing out at someone verbally or even physically. Or you might start crying about something seemingly small. This is all part of the elimination of stored up emotional toxins connected to the physical toxins in your body—just know that these feelings are normal and it's beneficial to release them in a safe environment.

It may help you to keep in mind that nature is constantly cleansing our environment with storms, hurricanes, tidal waves, floods, ice, snow. Remember how fresh and clean spring feels after the cleansings of winter. Or, after a major spring storm, how fresh and pure the air has become.

HEALING HINTS: Take a few minutes once or several times each day to stop what you are doing, breathe deeply, and appreciate the good things about your life and surroundings. Seek the serenity and peace that are essential to good health and strength.

A Special Gift for Women

The monthly menstrual cycle offers women a special opportunity to cleanse. Not only does the uterus shed its lining during this normal process, but the entire body enters a cleansing mode. So to take advantage of this opportunity, treat yourself well. Rest a little more, plan quiet activities, eat warm, alkaline forming foods. This regular cleansing is one of the reasons women have traditionally outlived men. Men do not have this opportunity to cleanse as frequently.

The process of *pregnancy* and *childbirth* also allows women to cleanse. During birth, a tremendous amount of toxins—some built up over more than the nine months of pregnancy—leave the body with the baby and the afterbirth. Afterward, especially if she is on the Body Ecology Diet, a woman can be even healthier: her skin color may be more porcelain-like, her chronic vaginitis gone.

You Can Choose How Quickly You Want to Cleanse

The Body Ecology Diet works because it supports your body in doing what it was designed to do: cleanse. Cleansing equals healing. However, while you can't stop and never want to stop cleansings, you might like to know that you have some control over how quickly you cleanse.

When you begin conquering your immune system disorder, you simply need to follow the Diet STRICTLY, eating only the foods allowed and following the food combining rules. Yeast will begin dying off immediately, and your body will begin sending the dead yeast out through the usual channels (into the blood stream, then out in the urine, bowel movement, respiration, sweat, and, for women, through the vagina).

Remember, at first the yeast may be dying off faster than your body can handle; you may experience a variety of symptoms such as fatigue, spaciness, heaviness, depression, anger, flu, and cold symptoms. While this will clear up (usually within three to ten days), you can shorten the duration of the cleansing and "minimize your discomfort," by cleansing your colon with an enema or a colonic (see Chapter 17). It is not necessary to take candida control products or "yeast fighters" sold in health food stores, until you are ready to go to a deeper level of cleansing. Initially they may cause too much die-off. These products can be useful later when you want to go to a deeper level of healing. For now, spend your money on the best quality foods.

Don't be afraid to cleanse; expect it, even welcome it. If you find yourself cleansing so much that you cannot function, do what is recommended when you come down with a cold...cleanse the colon, rest, keep warm, and drink lots of fluids, such as hot water with lemon juice or warm teas (see shopping list).

How quickly do you want to cleanse? If you found yourself climbing a challenging mountain where everything you ever wanted was awaiting you at the top, how fast would you like to get there? Conquering this condition is like climbing a challenging mountain. You'll have to go step by step using special tools to make the job easier, but it's *you* who will decide how fast to go.

Toward A New Science

Thousands of years ago ancient Chinese healers knew the dangers of suppressing the body's natural healing process. Their work was to enhance the Ki or Chi (life force energy). Oriental medicine uses natural herbs to activate (not suppress) the energy of the cleansing organs so that they can do the job they were created to do. Medicines used by modern Western science today stop, close down or interfere with the "pushing out" process of cleansing. Medical researchers need to do a 180 degree turnabout and look for ways to *support* our cleansing organs, not *suppress* and choke the life out of them. If we would keep our bodies as pure as that of a healthy newborn babe—enzyme- and oxygen-rich—inhabited abundantly with friendly bacteria, and rich in proteins, minerals and essential fatty acids, we might be able to live for hundreds of years. We must develop a "New Medical Science" by tuning in with nature and learning from it instead of ignorantly and arrogantly fighting our natural healing process.

"Food is medicine" is an old Chinese saying. The foods we have available to each of us have special healing powers. The Body Ecology Diet incorporates exactly the foods that heal immune system disorders and weaves them into a delicious, nutritious diet plan.

But even eating the healthiest foods won't stop you from cleansing. Cleansings are nature's brilliant attempt to keep us healthy so we can enjoy a long, happy life. When we go against nature, we create unhappiness, disorder, and disease.

Our medical community must begin crossing natural healing methods with modern scientific technology, with an emphasis on wellness, prevention and wholesome nutrition—rather than continuing to support the development of drugs that damage the immune system.

CHAPTER 9

The Principle of Food Combining

Food combining means what to eat with what. It's an important feature of the B.E.D. and one reason the Diet works while other anti-candida diets do not.

Even if you no longer *eat* foods that feed your yeast, the overgrowth of yeast in your system won't disappear if you are combining these foods improperly. To conquer candidiasis, it is essential to practice the principles of proper food combining. There are two reasons for this:

1. Eating foods that are not compatible in the stomach (see below) causes fermentation. This fermentation produces alcohol and sugars, and the yeast feed off these sugars and multiply rapidly, creating more toxins in the body.

2. People with candidiasis have weak digestive tracts. Improper food combining further weakens the digestive tract by causing it to work inefficiently until it slowly breaks down.

By following the principles of proper food combining, you avoid fermentation in the digestive system, and the yeast starve to death. The healing process begins by allowing the overworked digestive tract to begin to function as it should, and a healthy digestive tract is an important first step toward the total renewal that restores your body's balanced ecology.

Benefits of Food Combining

✔ You'll feel better. You'll be less bloated and will stop having symptoms such as gas and stomach gurgling.

✔ You'll have a system to guide your choice of foods, an approach that makes it easier to decide what to eat. You'll be better able to stick with the Diet.

✔ You'll never be overweight. In fact, you'll probably lose some weight. Properly combined food is assimilated better and allows the body to metabolize it better and avoid storing fat.

✔ You'll have more energy.

The Basics

Food combining can be simplified to three basic rules.

Rule #1:

Eat fruits alone and on an empty stomach.

Fruits encourage the growth of yeast in the body, so as you begin the Body Ecology Diet, the only fruits allowed are lemons, limes, and unsweetened cranberries. These are acidic[8] or "sour" fruits. Low in sugar, they do not create yeast overgrowth. All other fruits are too sweet.

Fruits pass through the digestive system very quickly. They usually leave the stomach within 30 minutes and enter the small intestine, where they continue to digest. But if you eat them with other foods (such as a protein or starch) that take three to five hours or more to digest, the fruit is held up and starts to ferment. This means poor assimilation of nutrients but, more importantly, it sets up a perfect environment for yeast overgrowth, as they feed off the sugar produced from the fermentation.

While it's best to eat fruit alone, proper food combining allows you to eat *acidic* or sour fruits with ***protein fat*** foods such as kefir, yogurt or nuts, and seeds. For example, you could combine strawberries, blueberries, kiwi, pineapple or grapefruit with yogurt or kefir...or a handful of raw sunflower seeds. With your body ecology imbalance, however, you will not be able to tolerate these fruits at first.

As your health improves and you introduce more fruits, the first ones to try are two more "sour" fruits: grapefruit and kiwi. They are also low-sugar fruits and have enough of an acidic quality that they often don't activate yeast symptoms. The sweeter fruits have too much sugar.

The only time your digestive tract is truly empty is when you wake up in the morning. So that's the best time to eat fruit, but only if you can tolerate it without bringing on any symptoms. Please note that one of the most frequent mistakes is to introduce new foods, especially fruit, too soon, before your body ecology is restored. If you do not have a body ecology imbalance, fruit is an ideal breakfast, because it contains a lot of water, which your system needs after being asleep without fluid all night. When you wake up, we highly recommend drinking a glass of water with some lemon juice. It's an age-old way to stimulate the peristaltic action of the colon.

[8]Not to be confused with the acid/alkaline principle. For a list of acidic fruits see Chapter 21.

One exception to this rule is with lemons and animal protein. Lemon juice squeezed onto a piece of grilled salmon, for example, aids digestion and provides a nice expansion/contraction balance.

Rule #2:

Always eat protein with non-starchy and/or ocean vegetables.

When you eat protein flesh foods such as eggs, meat, poultry, and fish, your stomach produces hydrochloric acid and an enzyme called pepsin. When you eat a starch, such as a potato or rice, an enzyme called ptyalin is secreted, and an alkaline condition develops. But if you eat a protein and a starch together, the acidic and alkaline conditions neutralize each other and effectively stop all digestion. None of the enzymes can do their job, resulting in poor digestion, fermentation, and a field day for your yeast.

Non-starchy vegetables and ocean vegetables are the most compatible foods to eat with protein meals. They require neither a strong alkaline nor a strong acid condition to digest properly. So by eating protein foods with non-starchy vegetables, you can achieve optimal digestion.

RECOMMENDED NON-STARCHY VEGETABLES

Arugula	Cucumber	Onion
Asparagus	Daikon	Parsley
Bamboo shoots	Dandelion greens	Radishes (red)
Beet greens	Endive	Red bell pepper
Bok choy	Escarole	Scallions
Broccoli	Fennel	Shallots
Brussels sprouts	Garlic	Spinach (raw only)
Burdock root	Green beans	Sprouts (except
Cabbage	Jicama	mung bean)
Carrots	Kale	Swiss chard
Cauliflower	Kohlrabi	Turnips
Celeriac	Lamb's quarters	(and greens)
Celery	Leeks	Watercress
Celery root	Lettuces	Yellow squash
Chives	Mustard greens	Zucchini
Collard greens	Okra	

Non-starchy vegetables go with just about everything. You can eat them with oil, butter, ghee, animal flesh, eggs, grains, starchy vegetables (like acorn squash and potatoes), lemons, limes, and raw sunflower, caraway, flax or pumpkin seeds.

Menu Tips:

Combine:

Fish with stir-fried or steamed vegetables.

Chicken with a leafy green vegetable and an all-vegetable soup such as cream of cauliflower with dill.

A large vegetable salad with protein (chilled salmon or sliced, boiled egg) and dressing (oil-free or from organic, unrefined oils).

An onion, red pepper, and zucchini omelette or ocean vegetable omelette with steamed asparagus and garlic.

Rule #3:

Always eat grains and starchy vegetables with non-starchy and/or ocean vegetables.

Grains allowed as you begin the Body Ecology Diet are amaranth, quinoa, buckwheat, and millet. Starchy vegetables include acorn and butternut squash, lima beans, English peas, corn (fresh), water chestnuts, artichokes and jerusalem artichokes, and red skin[9] potatoes. Combine them with non-starchy vegetables or ocean vegetables for some delicious, filling meals.

Menu Tips:

Combine:

Millet casserole, a steamed leafy green vegetable, and yellow squash and leeks sautéed in butter.

Buckwheat/quinoa/millet croquettes topped with the Body Ecology Diet Gravy, steamed greens, and carrot cauliflower soup.

Dilled potato salad, watercress soup, and a leafy green salad with Body Ecology Diet Dressing.

Acorn squash stuffed with curried quinoa, broccoli with seasoned butter, and the sea vegetable hijiki with onions and carrots.

Fats and Seed Oils

At first, the only oils allowed on The Diet are freshly-pressed, organic and unrefined, sunflower seed, flax seed, borage seed, pumpkin seed, and safflower seed oils. The fats are unrefined, organic, coconut oil, butter[10], and ghee.

Never combine a large amount of fat with a protein. Large amounts of fat, especially refined fats, delay the secretion of hydrochloric acid needed to digest the protein. An example of this is mayonnaise with tuna or chicken...creating the popular "tuna salad" (usually made into an even more poorly combined sandwich). Use an oil-free dressing to make tuna, egg or chicken salads.

[9]Red skin potatoes have less gluten than other varieties and do not feed yeast.
[10]Raw butter is best if available.

Cooking Tip:

If you need a small amount of oil in your cooking to keep food from sticking to the pan, we recommend coconut oil, butter or ghee. You also might try using broth or even water to avoid the sticking.

Do not eat hydrogenated fats, such as margarine. The hydrogenation process changes the character of the oils used, making them poisonous.

Protein Fats

Avocado, olives, cheese, seeds, and nuts (except chestnuts and peanuts, which are starch) belong to a category classified as "protein fats." These foods combine best with non-starchy and green vegetables, ocean vegetables, and acid fruits.

Only a few seeds (sunflower, pumpkin, caraway, and flax) appear on the B.E.D. And only *soaked or sprouted* almonds are allowed from the nut family. Avoid all other protein fats until your body ecology is well reestablished.

Dairy

Dairy foods also belong to the category of protein fats. They should always be eaten alone and on an empty stomach. Most milk products contain milk sugar (lactose) that feeds yeast, so they are prohibited on The Diet. Lactose-free cultured dairy foods (see Kefir Chapter 24) may be safe for many of you even in the early stages of The Diet. You can combine cultured dairy foods with acidic fruits and non-starchy vegetables (especially raw, leafy greens). For example, try a kefir dressing using lemon juice and herbs for your salad.

Dried Beans, Peas, and Soybeans

These foods are not on the Diet, so you won't be eating them initially. They are both protein and starch, so you can see why they are difficult to digest and cause gas. When you get better, you may be able to introduce them and combine them safely with non-starchy green vegetables and ocean vegetables. For example, try anasazi beans cooked with onion and garlic, served with sauteed carrots, daikon, and steamed greens or a raw salad.

---

[11]Type A and A/B usually cannot tolerate uncultured dairy foods.

Sugar, Honey, Molasses, Etc.

The Diet forbids all types of sweeteners except the sweet-tasting herb stevia, because sugars feed the yeast. Once you no longer have a yeast overgrowth and your digestive tract is well-populated with friendly bacteria, you may be able to tolerate a natural sweetener such as honey, barley malt, rice or maple syrup, or molasses. Crude, unsulphured blackstrap molasses is preferred over the others because it is rich in iron, calcium and magnesium. The abundance of minerals make crude molasses the *only* sugar that is alkaline-forming. All other forms of sugar are acid-forming. Sugars should be eaten *alone;* they don't combine with any-thing! That's why you can get gas from cookies, since they combine starches, fruits, and sugars. Eventually, you may be able to have crude molasses sweetened tea first thing in the morning. If you get used to the herb stevia, you may never want to go back to sugar again.

Your Weight

Proper food combining automatically results in some weight loss, because you'll no longer be bloated with the toxins that comes from poor digestion. Some people can easily lose up to 10 pounds during the first two weeks after they start the Diet. This is all very normal—don't worry if you lose some weight. You can reach your ideal weight once your body is back in balance and building healthy tissue. If you're already thin, you may still lose some bloating; the scales may stay the same, but you'll look different.

You also may feel hungrier than usual, again because you'll have no "bloated" or full feeling after meals. So just eat more! As long as your food is properly combined, you can eat as much as you want, and not worry about gaining weight. It's fine to have four to five smaller meals throughout the day. Just allow time for a grain meal to digest (about three hours) before switching to a protein meal. Protein meals take longer than grain meals to digest—sometimes four hours.

Water

Drink at least eight glasses per day, but *not with meals*, since it dilutes your digestive enzymes. Drink water especially when you get up in the morning, to restore liquid to your system. At other times, drink no closer than 10-15 minutes before a meal, and then wait again an hour or longer after you eat. Drink water at room or body temperature—ice cold water shocks the system too much. Try to have at least half your daily water intake by mid-morning; it really revitalizes your system.

Additional Suggestions

Most people can apply these food combining rules to each meal separately—that is, eat a grain meal with vegetables for breakfast, a protein meal with vegetables for lunch, and grain and vegetables again for dinner. However, if you have an especially slow or weak digestive system, you may feel better by using food combining rules #2 and #3 for a day at a time: grains and vegetables one day, protein and vegetables the next.

If you're a vegetarian and don't eat animal protein, you'll have fewer rules to remember. If you do not eat eggs or dairy, be sure to consume large quantities of the mineral-rich ocean vegetables. At first, you may need to consider eating some protein to increase your strength and starve out the yeast.

Additional Resources

Many books are available on food combining, including one of the most popular, *Fit For Life*, by Harvey and Marilyn Diamond. We especially recommend *Food Combining* by Lee Dubelle. See the Bibliography for more resource materials. Also, you can buy a wallet-size card from your local health food store that lists different food groups and tells you which foods combine well.

Don't let all this confuse you. It takes a bit of practice, but soon it becomes second nature, and you'll automatically know what foods to eat together. Proper food combining is a key part of the Body Ecology Diet, and mastering it will reward you with better health.

FIGURE 5

B.E.D. Food Combining Chart

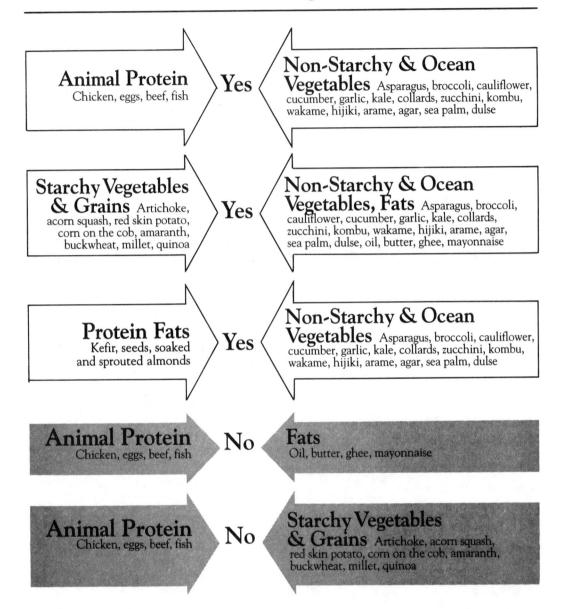

NOTES: All fruits should be eaten alone (30 minutes before or 3 hours after eating) with the exception of the acid fruits, which may be eaten with protein fats. The **only** acid fruits eaten on the B.E.D. are lemons, limes, cranberries and, later grapefruits.

SUGAR - Not on B.E.D. but should be eaten alone (30 minutes before, or 3 hours after eating). Does not combine well with any other foods.

DAIRY - Not on B.E.D. If introduced later, eat alone (3 hours before or 3 hours after eating) or with raw salads, acid fruits or seeds and nuts.

PROTEIN STARCHES - Dried peas, soybeans, and beans are not initially on B.E.D. and will be introduced later. They should then be eaten with non-starchy vegetables.

CHAPTER 10
The Principles of 80/20

When you have candidiasis or other immune system diseases, it is essential that the food you eat be properly assimilated and then eliminated. A healthy digestive tract can do this. But many people weaken their digestive tracts by overeating, which puts too heavy a workload on the digestive system. So moderation is a key factor in regaining health and maintaining it. We have two important rules, the 80/20 quantity rules, for you to keep in mind.

Rule #1:

Eat until your stomach is 80% full, leaving 20% available for digesting.

If you eat until you're 100% full (or even more), this overeating furthers yeast overgrowth. It also slows digestion tremendously. Digestion should occur promptly. If it does not, fermentation occurs, and the yeast happily feed off the sugars produced in the fermentation process. Leaving a little room in the stomach (about 20%) for the digestive juices to do their job is essential for efficient digestion and quickly turning around your body's ecology imbalance.

This is especially true if you find yourself overeating on grains, bread, and pasta. Fermentation of the natural complex sugars in grain encourages candida overgrowth. So NEVER, NEVER OVEREAT ON GRAINS OR STARCHY VEGETABLES. Limit yourself to one helping of grain. If you're still hungry, have more alkaline-forming land or ocean vegetables.

A typical American meal contains mostly acid-forming foods (such as a big serving of steak or chicken) and not enough alkaline-forming foods, such as non-starchy vegetables. Since candidiasis is an acidic condition, your body needs more alkaline land and ocean vegetables to bring it back into balance.

Rule #2:

80% of the food on your plate should be land and/or ocean vegetables. The remaining 20% can be:

Animal protein, such as poultry or fish.
A grain or combination of grains, such as quinoa or millet.
A starchy vegetable or combination of starchy vegetables, such as potatoes or corn.

Again, this helps your digestive tract. By following the 80/20 and the food combining rules, you will never again leave the table feeling over-full and bloated. You won't want to take a nap after a meal, you won't have gas, and you will feel calm and satisfied.

Applying the 80/20 Rules to Menu Planning

In the design of the Body Ecology Diet, all the principles and rules work in harmony. Thus, as we have seen, when you plan meals with the proper acid/alkaline balance, you automatically are following the 80/20 rules. At first, *breakfast* may seem the most difficult meal to fit with rule #2, but here are some suggestions:

Vegetable soup	80%
Quinoa	20%
Leftover dinner vegetables	80%
Cream of buckwheat with dulse	20%
Sautéed greens and onions	80%
Poached eggs	20%

Linda learned to eat vegetable soup for breakfast with millet, quinoa, or buckwheat stirred into it; it's just the right thing for warming up on a cold morning, it's filling, and it satisfies the body's morning need for liquid. She sometimes cooks dulse or nori into these grains; it virtually "dissolves," and yet it adds valuable minerals and vitamins to the grain.

Another Breakfast Tip:

Having an *all alkaline* breakfast is also highly recommended. During the night while we are sleeping, our body becomes more acidic. When we awaken, our first meal of the day should be high water content, expansive food. Fruits and their juices would be ideal if they did not feed the yeast. Recently a perfect solution has appeared on the health food scene…a variety of super-nutrient "green drink" mixtures. These now quite popular green drinks are a blend of energizing, powerful whole foods and herbs. Their base is a combination of cereal grasses and micro-algae. Very easy to digest and convenient if you're in a hurry, we believe so much in the value of the green drink that we created our own formula called **VITALITY *SuperGreen*™**.

Note: You'll be learning about another alkaline-forming breakfast food in our new section Part VI, The Magic of Kefir.

FIGURE 6
80%/20% Rule #1

Stop Eating When You Are 80% Full

20%

80%

Leave 20% Empty for Digestion

Don't "Top-off" Your Tummy

FIGURE 7
80%/20% Rule #2

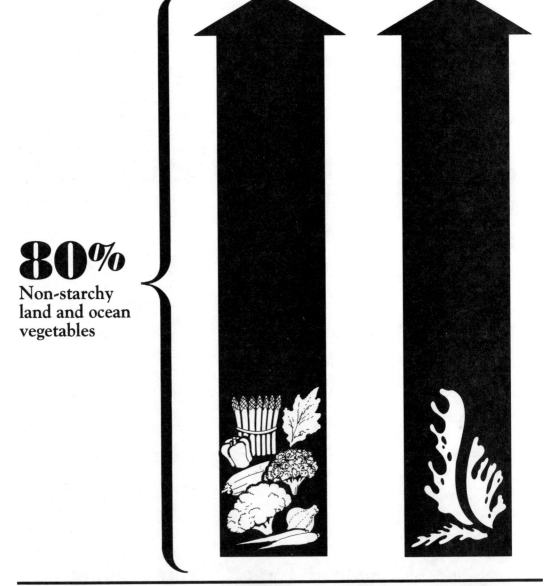

80%
Non-starchy
land and ocean
vegetables

20%
Protein flesh
foods, *or* **B.E.D.**
grains, *or* **starchy**
vegetables

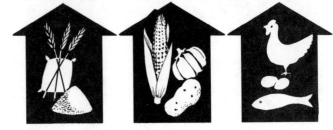

CHAPTER 11
The Principle of Step By Step

The step-by-step concept intersects with all the other principles, rules, and tips of the Body Ecology Diet; it is one of the most important healing concepts to embrace. Yet we often overlook it due to its simplicity. It answers the question: how long will it take to heal? In fact, the step-by-step principle is about time—taking the time to heal.

Nature acts in a step-by-step, orderly manner, and we cannot violate this order. The life process of birth, maturation, aging, and death illustrates this. A tree must start from a seedling and grow. The seasons of the year have an order that cannot be changed—we cannot go from winter directly to summer without having spring. In spiritual traditions, this is the principle of dawning—dawn occurs little by little in the transition from night to day, and so it goes for all things in nature.

Unfortunately, we often spurn the step-by-step principle, and our health suffers as a result. To illustrate: unwilling to take the time to get over a cold or the flu (cleansings), we take medicine and antibiotics as a "quick cure." In doing this, we halt the body's attempt to eliminate its toxins step by step. Drugs stop the cleansing process, which the body uses to get rid of illness; drugs drive disease deeper into the body, giving the potential for an even more serious illness later. But if we allow nature to take its course, cleansing and healing *will* take place, step by step.

Our unwillingness to take time got us into trouble when we replaced many home-cooked meals with fast foods. Many of us now no longer take the time to learn which foods are best for us, to plan menus, shop, and prepare them. Fast foods skip over these steps, resulting in diets that satisfy our taste and hunger needs, but not our nutritional needs.

The breakdown of our inner body ecology also occurs step by step—in fact, the increments often are so small that we don't even notice them. That's why you can become aware of a yeast overgrowth or a kidney problem, for example, and wonder how it happened all of a sudden. It didn't—it's the result of many assaults to your body ecology over a long period of time. The good news is that healing also takes place in a step-by-step sequence, and all you have to do is start.

How to Heal, Step By Step

We cannot expect instant healing—this too would violate the step-by-step principle. The impurities and toxins you've built up in your system over the years cannot be eliminated all at once—

they must be eliminated in an orderly cleansing process. But this doesn't mean it has to be slow. You can choose how quickly you go through the steps of healing. For example, when you first start the Body Ecology Diet, you may have very uncomfortable symptoms of yeast die-off, since you are no longer feeding the yeast. If you absolutely can't stand it, or if you need to feel better for work, you can slow down the cleansing by transitioning into The Diet little by little. Here are some ways you can step more quickly to health:

- ✔ Eliminate stress as much as possible.
- ✔ Eat according to the Diet—don't cheat!
- ✔ Eat foods that especially aid cleansing, such as lemons, limes, raw apple cider vinegar, and UNSALTED raw cultured vegetables (see Chapter 14).
- ✔ Eliminate medicines that suppress the cleansing process.
- ✔ Pay attention to cleansing the colon.
- ✔ Rest during periods of cleansing.
- ✔ Use probiotics to increase colonies of friendly bacteria.

Even when you take these actions, you will be following the principle of step by step. And in your inner world the colonies of friendly bacteria will be increasing in a step-by-step manner.

Success with the Diet comes step by step. That's why you must be very determined to stick with the Diet until you master it. Develop your will power, step by step. Advance with the Diet according to your personal pace, the pace that supports you the best. Persevere. When you have a setback, an old symptom or reaction, take only the next step that allows you to get back on track. The beauty of the Diet is that if you do stay with it, you *will* have success, you *will heal.*

Beginning the Diet is similar to climbing a mountain. When you're at the bottom, at the first step, you can't see the health, happiness, and prosperity that may await you at the top. But as you progress up the mountain, the top reveals itself more and more. As you start the Diet, some things may not be clear, but as you become stronger each day, step by step, your understanding and clarity increase. When you master the principles of the Diet, you'll be at the top of the mountain–vital, knowledgeable, and healthy.

That's why it is important to use your inherent ability to envision yourself in perfect, glowing health, radiating positive energy, feeling strong. By holding this vision, and using the Diet as your guide, you can achieve your goal. If you persist step by step, you will have success.

Just remember how beautiful the world looks from the top of a mountain.

PART THREE

Description
of the
Body Ecology Diet

CHAPTER 12
What *Is* the Body Ecology Diet?

Now that you're aware of the basic principles of the Diet, it's time to learn more about what foods are on it and how to combine them properly. You may think it's impossible to incorporate all the principles simultaneously, but as you will see, they all weave automatically and easily into our suggested recipes and menus.

You will be pleasantly surprised by the variety of foods you can eat on the Diet. Some of them may be new to you, so you will have the joy of discovering new tastes and textures. Some (like the ocean vegetables) are different enough that it may take some time to acquire a taste for them. But it will be worth it. Many of the foods have healing qualities, so you will especially want to concentrate on them. And by staying on the Diet, you will feel so much better in such a short time that you will soon be eagerly trying new recipes using the Diet foods.

Because of individual sensitivities, you may find that one or two of the foods on the B.E.D. do not work for you until your immune system is stronger. Don't despair. There are plenty of other foods that you can enjoy.

It's very important that you eat at least three to four meals a day, keeping in mind the 80/20 quantity rules and the principles of the Diet. You may not always feel hungry, but it's necessary to provide your body with these healing foods. This is especially important during periods of cleansing.

The cleansing effect of the Diet often causes weight loss, as stored toxins exit the body's cells. If you are naturally slim, you may even go below your average weight. In time, when your body starts rebuilding, you will naturally regain to your ideal weight, the weight at which your body functions best.

Animal Protein Foods You Can Eat

Meats, poultry, and fish are on the Diet because they do not feed the candida fungus. These foods are acid-forming and cause contraction. Keep in mind the 80/20 rule when serving yourself. (Only 20% of your meal should be an animal protein and 80% should be vegetables.) If you can, buy meat and poultry that are free from antibiotics and hormones.

At first you need to eat more animal foods than you might like or be accustomed to. A diet too high in animal protein is not healthy, but when you make your initial assault on the yeast, the extra protein will help balance the expansive nature of CRC. Gradually, as the yeast starve and die off, you can increase your grain/vegetable meals and cut down on animal protein meals. Your blood type offers a clue to how much protein you need. Types A and A/B can transition into a totally vegetarian diet. Type Os will always do best with some animal protein each day, and Bs will find themselves thriving on moderation—some animal protein meals and many meals of grain-based entrees.

Remember, fish is the preferred animal protein food on the B.E.D.; try to have some at least three times a week. Salmon and sardines are especially healthy because of their high content of Omega 3 oils, which keep the circulatory system healthy. A well-functioning circulatory system is essential to improving your immunity; the circulatory system carries vital nutrients to all parts of the body and removes waste products.

Eggs

Eggs help strengthen the thyroid, which is often weak in people with candidiasis. Since they are such a concentrated, contracting food, many of us find it best to eat them midday, when the body has plenty of time and energy to digest them. At breakfast, when you're trying to make your body more open or expanded, they may be too contracting. Still, their strongly contracting nature creates energy useful for those with very active mornings. If you sit at a desk during the day, eat them for lunch or dinner. For some, eggs are too contracting and energizing for the dinner meal. They also take longer to digest than a grain-based meal, and you may still be working to digest them at bedtime. Most people sleep better on an empty stomach, so try to eat your last meal several hours before going to sleep.

One therapeutic way to prepare eggs is to fry them "over easy" (a soft, runny yolk) in a little organic, unrefined coconut oil, butter or ghee. Then, eat only the yolk. Some people have trouble digesting the egg white.

Eggs are sorely misunderstood these days. Yes, they do have cholesterol, but they are comparatively low in fat.[12] The yolk contains lecithin, which aids in fat assimilation. Eggs actively raise the level of HDL, which is the good cholesterol, and they have the most perfect protein components of any food. Today, even though we Americans have drastically cut our egg consumption in half, there has not been a decline in heart

[12]Jennings-Sauer, 1988

disease. If you have been an egg lover and have given them up, you can now enjoy them by eating them appropriately. Remember to combine them with lots of alkaline vegetables to balance their acidic nature. Raw cultured vegetables (an excellent expansive food) make an ideal balance with the contracting power of eggs. These enzyme-rich vegetables greatly enhance digestion of protein. Blood Types A and A/B may find eggs too acid-forming and might want to eat them less frequently than Types O and B.

Menu Tip:

Try a vegetable or ocean vegetable omelette. Or serve your eggs poached or over easy on a bed of steamed greens. They are delicious scrambled with chopped and sauteed vegetables, such as red onions, shitake mushrooms, scallions, and red bell peppers.

SPECIAL NOTE: With a body ecology imbalance, animal protein foods are usually difficult to digest, since hydrochloric acid is often lacking. Here are a few tips to help:

Drinking warm water and lemon juice after the meal is an age-old remedy that really works.

Digestive plant enzymes that include protease can be very helpful.

Throughout the meal slowly drink a mixture of two tsp. raw, organic apple cider vinegar and six ounces water.

Cayenne pepper stimulates the secretion of hydrochloric acid. Sprinkle it on your protein foods or cook with it.

A Special Note to Vegetarians:

You can be a vegetarian and still conquer your candidiasis with the Body Ecology Diet. Just eat the grains, vegetables, cultured vegetables, and sea vegetables, and practice all seven principles of the B.E.D. You must be especially careful to eat well, not skip meals, and eat a wide variety of foods. Use sea salt to help make your meals a little more contracting initially and pay special attention to the popular green drink formulas with their high-protein micro-algae (spirulina, blue green algae, red marine algae, chlorella and cereal grasses. See new section on kefir too).

Other Protein Foods (Protein Fats)

Nuts are protein fats and are acid-forming. They are not on the Diet until the inner-ecosystem is restored, because they are initially too difficult to digest. Nevertheless, if you can digest them, you can enjoy raw soaked and sprouted almonds, which are alkaline and slightly expansive in nature.

To soak: Cover them with purified water in a glass or stainless steel container overnight or for 12 hours. Drain and refrigerate.

To sprout: Soak almonds in a sprouting jar 8-12 hours, then drain. Turn upside down in your dish drainer for 8 more hours, then refrigerate the almonds in an airtight container. Sprouting more than one day produces a bitter taste.

This sprouting process makes them easier to digest. Soaked almonds provide an excellent source of vegetable protein, especially for blood types A and A/B. Since nuts are protein fats, they should be eaten only with non-starchy, alkaline land and ocean vegetables. Soaked and sprouted almonds, however, combine well with any foods. Toss a handful into a leafy green salad with an oil and lemon/herb dressing. Chew them well.

Seeds allowed on the Diet are flax, sunflower, pumpkin, and caraway. Do not eat sesame seeds; for reasons we do not fully understand, they simply do not work. Seeds (alkaline) are easier to digest if eaten raw, not roasted. Flax seeds help digestion; try boiling them to make a flaxseed tea. Most people tolerate sunflower and pumpkin seeds well. Seeds fall in the middle, balanced area of the expansion/contraction continuum. As protein fats, they combine ideally with non-starchy, steamed vegetables. Or you can eat them alone on an empty stomach. Like the raw soaked almonds, they are delicious tossed into a leafy green salad with an oil and lemon/herb dressing. Also like almonds, they can be sprouted. Because they are a very concentrated food, eat them in small quantities.

Grains

The Diet allows four grains that are very low in gluten and do not feed the yeast: millet, quinoa (pronounced "keen-wah"), amaranth, and buckwheat. They may not be familiar to you, but they are readily available in health food stores and some supermarkets. The first three are alkaline-forming. Buckwheat is acid-forming, so cook it with a little bit of good quality sea salt (which is alkaline) to balance its acidity. All the grains are high in protein.

Combine these grains with vegetables (80/20 rule). Eating a grain entree for your last meal of the day is ideal, because grains digest more quickly than animal foods and you will sleep more comfortably. Never overeat on grains; overeating slows down digestion. If they stay in the stomach too long, grains begin fermenting, and this encourages yeast overgrowth.

If your condition is not severe, or once you've become more balanced, you may find that you can tolerate corn, especially blue cornmeal products. Buy *baked* (no-oil) blue cornmeal chips. They make a nice crunchy accompaniment to an all-vegetable soup or to vegetable salads.

We are proud of the grain recipes we've developed for the Body Ecology Diet. You will notice they usually have vegetables and sea vegetables cooked into the recipe, making them even easier to digest. Health food stores also sell flours made from these grains, which allow you even more options as a creative cook. However, the whole grain is much more desirable than the flour. (All flour products are mucous-forming and lack fiber.) Anti-fungal herbs, such as turmeric and some curries, make the grains even more delicious and more healing.

> When Mary J. began the Diet, her body ecology was so out of balance she could not tolerate any cooked grain at all, even the four on the Body Ecology Diet. But by sticking with the Diet, she gradually regained her strength and added the four grains, rotating them into her meals one at a time.

Mary's condition is not uncommon in those with severe cases of candidiasis, especially if the digestive tract is very weak. If you fall in this category, experiment with the Diet's four grains, eliminating the ones that don't work for you. Eat mostly land and ocean vegetables, some animal protein foods, and lots of raw cultured vegetables (more on these below). Focus on cleansing your colon and on introducing digestive enzymes that are high in Amylase. Then slowly introduce the grains, one at a time, to find your tolerance. Eat them in small quantities, soaked well before cooking and properly combined with vegetables, and you will do just fine.

An Absolute Must:

It is always recommended that you soak your grains in water for 8 to 24 hours. When the digestive tract is weak and lacking an inner ecosystem, it will not be able to break down the phytic acid found in all grains, beans, nuts and seeds. Soaking removes this enzyme inhibitor (see page 197).

Cooking Tip:

If you have Type A or A/B blood, buckwheat may be too acid-forming for you. Try cooking it with other grains, such as quinoa and millet; otherwise, you may have to forego it for now.

Vegetables

Vegetables are the most perfect foods nature has given us; they are also the most abundant foods on earth. They are rich with the vitamins and minerals needed to heal your body, and their colors, textures, and shapes add excitement to any meal.

The non-starchy vegetables (see list) form excellent combinations with just about every other food. They provide perfect balance to protein or grain meals, they are filling, and they give you a sense of well-being and health.

RECOMMENDED NON-STARCHY VEGETABLES

Arugula	Cucumbers	Parsley
Asparagus	Dandelion greens	Radishes
Bamboo shoots	Endive	(daikon & red)
Beet greens	Escarole	Red bell peppers
Bok choy	Fennel	Scallions
Broccoli	Garlic	Shallots
Brussels sprouts	Green beans	Spinach
Burdock root	Jicama	Sprouts
Cabbage	Kale	(except mung
Carrots	Kohlrabi	bean)
Cauliflower	Lamb's quarters	Swiss chard
Celeriac	Leeks	Turnips
Celery	Lettuces	Watercress
Celery root	Mustard greens	Yellow squash
Chives	Okra	Zucchini
Collard greens	Onions	

You can eat non-starchy vegetables with organic, unrefined oil, butter, ghee, animal protein, eggs, grains, starchy vegetables (like acorn squash and potatoes), lemons, limes, and protein fats, including raw sunflower, caraway, flax, or pumpkin seeds.

Leafy green vegetables, which grow above ground (turnip greens, kale, collards, beet greens), are rich in chlorophyll and help cleanse the blood. They also provide excellent sources of calcium and iron and should be included in every meal. Root vegetables, which grow underground (carrots, onions, daikon, turnips), are more contracting in nature and provide strength and winter warmth.

The starchy vegetables, such as red skin new potatoes, sweet corn, water chestnuts, winter squash, artichokes, Jerusalem artichokes, lima beans, and English peas, can be eaten as entrees and combined only with the four B.E.D. grains and the non-starchy vegetables above. Red skin potatoes are the only potatoes on the Diet; always eat the skins.

Menu Tip:

A delicious light meal could be baked red skin potatoes topped with ghee, lecithin, and herbs, plus a green salad. Potatoes also can be topped with the Body Ecology Diet Gravy (see recipe) or raw, unsalted cultured vegetables.

Ocean Vegetables

Ocean (or sea) vegetables greatly enhance the functioning of the immune system. They are rich in minerals and strengthen the thyroid. The most common ocean vegetables are:

Agar (AG-GAR)
Arame (ER-A-MAY)
Dulse (DULS)
Hijiki (HE-GEE-KEE)
Kelp
Kombu (KOM-BOO)
Nori (NOR-EE)
Sea Palm
Wakame (WA-KA-MAY)

You may be most familiar with nori, since sushi bars use nori to wrap and garnish sushi and sushi rolls. Dulse is a chewy snack for many people in the Canadian maritime provinces, where it has been harvested for centuries. Arame is good either cooked or raw. You can add raw arame, dulse, or wakame to your salads. Agar is a mild-tasting gelatin used to thicken aspics or puddings; it also aids elimination. Be sure to cook ocean vegetables with plenty of sweet vegetables, such as onions and carrots, to get a good balance between the sweet and salty tastes.

Besides the recipes we give you, macrobiotic cookbooks have recipes using sea vegetables. Simply adjust the recipes by eliminating the miso and tamari, and replace them with a little good quality sea salt—not too much, since ocean vegetables are naturally salty.

Menu Tip:

You can buy "Sea Seasonings" brand flavorings, such as Dulse with Garlic or Nori with Ginger, to sprinkle on just about everything you cook—soups, main dishes, grains, salads.

Vegetables Not on the Initial, Therapeutic Version of the Diet

Please don't eat the following vegetables. Here's why:
Beets (unless cultured), parsnips, sweet potatoes, yams—too high in natural sugars.
Mushrooms—too expansive (shitake are usually O.K.).
Avocado—actually a fruit, and oil content too high.
Tomatoes—also a fruit, but you may tolerate them occasionally, in season, with a green salad if your blood type is O or B. They will always be too acidic for As and A/Bs. When cooked, tomatoes are even more acid-forming and therefore not good for you.

Eggplant and peppers—members of the nightshade family of vegetables, they often irritate the nervous system; people who are highly sensitive or hyperactive should not eat them. Others can eat them in moderation.

Green bell peppers are red peppers picked at an early stage. They are very difficult to digest and should not be eaten. Our recipes use only red peppers, in small quantities, for flavor and color.

Brown skin potatoes—too high in gluten, and feed the yeast.

Indoor, tray-grown "wheat grass"—really a long sprout—too sweet, too expansive.

Mung bean sprouts typically have mold on them; sunflower and buckwheat sprouts are great.

Raw vs. Cooked Vegetables

People with weak digestive tracts often find it difficult to digest raw foods. (Note: raw cultured vegetables are an exception.) So as you begin the Diet, lightly steamed vegetables may be best for you. Cooked vegetables are slightly more contracting than raw ones, so they are better for people whose bodies are in expanding/ill conditions. Raw, cold foods also irritate the spleen, a key immune system organ, which must heal to bring the body back to balance. (Note: Cultured vegetables do not.)

Raw vegetables, however, are an essential source of enzymes, which aid digestion. Unsalted raw cultured vegetables and raw apple cider vinegar (see below) provide these important plant enzymes. Remember, foods properly used balance our bodies. It's important to eat both raw and cooked foods as a way of improving the body ecology.

Try to eat a salad every day using the Body Ecology Diet Dressing, and include at least 1/2 cup of unsalted cultured vegetables with your meals each day. The raw apple cider vinegar in the Body Ecology Diet Dressing helps "pre-digest" lettuce, making it easier to assimilate. And both apple cider vinegar and cultured vegetables encourage the growth of friendly bacteria. You'll see a marked improvement in your health in two to three months once you begin including these products frequently with your meals.

Here again, you can use the 80/20 rule: during the colder winter months, or if your digestive tract is weak, eat 80% cooked foods, 20% raw. During the hot summer, and as you become healthier, graduate toward eating more raw, enzyme-rich vegetables (80% raw and 20% cooked).

A Helpful Hint:

Plant enzymes with protease, amylase, cellulase and lipase are an excellent digestive aid and enzymes with hydrochloric acid, bromelain, ox bile, and pancreatin are useful for digesting a protein meal. High quality enzymes are available from your health food store. They are a must for everyone with a body ecology imbalance.

Cooking Tip:

When vegetables are steamed, some of their vitamins and minerals go into the water, so use this water in soups or even drink it to recapture these nutrients.

Fruits

The only fruits allowed at first on the Diet are lemons, limes, and cranberries, because they are not sweet enough to feed the yeast. All other fruits are too sweet. After your candida is under control and you start to introduce new foods into your diet, the first fruits to try are the so-called sour or acidic fruits—grapefruit and kiwi. These fruits are improperly named, since they are not acid-forming in your body; like all fruits, they are alkaline-forming. Grapefruit and then kiwi are the first two "sour" fruits that most people can reintroduce into their diet, but only if the body ecology is well restored.

A VERY IMPORTANT WARNING: Eating fruit too soon often brings back candida symptoms. It may take a year or longer for you to be able to eat fruits again (except lemons, limes, or cranberries).

Remember the food combining rule for fruits: eat them alone and on an empty stomach. Lemons and limes, however, are an exception to this rule. You'll find you can use them in salads or squeezed into drinks or on fish and other animal protein with no problem. Watch out for grains and starchy vegetables, though. If you are very sensitive, you may have a problem digesting lemon and lime with grains.

Once you begin to introduce other fruits back into your diet, you'll find that summer is the best season to eat them; fruits are cooling foods and help us tolerate the heat. Start slowly and look for any sign of your symptoms returning.

Raw Vegetable Juices

Although fruit juices are not on the Diet, raw vegetable juices (from certain vegetables) most certainly are. They can bring outstanding nutritional qualities to your body in an easily-assimilated form. They are digested immediately and begin cleansing and healing long before the nutrients from whole foods begin to work. Also, they require less energy to digest than whole foods. Juicing is not the same as putting something in the blender and liquefying it. A juicer machine extracts only the liquid from vegetables, leaving behind a pulp of cellulose and fiber. It is this juice that has the valuable live enzymes, vitamins, and minerals to help heal your body. Vegetable juices are extremely alkaline and expansive—so they are good for balancing acidic, contracting conditions, such as consumption of too much meat.

With body ecology imbalances, juicing properly is extremely important. Timing is everything. If you introduce juices into your diet too early or if you combine them improperly with certain foods, you will feed the yeast and parasites. Please refer to the chapter on juicing to learn more.

Dairy Products

The milk sugar (lactose) in dairy foods feed the yeast. Therefore, dairy products are not allowed when you start the B.E.D. Unfermented and pasteurized dairy products are mucous forming. Once some of your symptoms disappear, you may be able to tolerate a small amount of cultured dairy foods (kefir and yogurt). Many people do best if they are made from goat's milk. Yogurt and kefir have very little milk sugar and are usually safe if you are lactose intolerant. Because their protein is pre-digested, they stay in your stomach for a shorter time. If you eat them, enrich your kefir or yogurt with other probiotics such as acidophilus (Bio-K+) and bifidus (various strains). Combine them with raw and lightly steamed vegetables or cultured vegetables. A digestive enzyme for milk products is also recommended (see page 253). To learn why we prefer kefir to yogurt see page 164.

Herbs

Most herbs are welcome on the Diet. If you can get organically grown herbs, so much the better. You can season your dishes with basil, bay leaves, cayenne, chives, coriander, cumin, curry, dill, garlic powder, ginger, Italian and Mexican seasonings, mustard powder, marjoram, oregano, black pepper, poppy seeds, rosemary, sage, tarragon, thyme.

Herbs that are particularly healing include cayenne, curry, ginger, and garlic.

Here are some brand-name herb products we recommend:
- ✔ "Frontier Herbs" curry powder
- ✔ "Sea Seasonings" Dulse, Dulse with Garlic, Nori with Ginger, Kelp with Cayenne
- ✔ "Herbamare" (blend of herbs and sea salt)
- ✔ "Dr. Bronner's" Balanced Mineral Seasoning (green label only) – used in the Body Ecology Diet Salad Dressing
- ✔ "Trocomare" (sea salt, blend of herbs, and cayenne pepper)

Experiment with your favorite herbs and tastes as you try the recipes on the Diet. You can have a new taste experience just about every day as you vary what you cook and how you cook it.

Sea Salt

Refined table salt has gotten a justly received bad reputation during these times of concern about hypertension and heart disease. But if a mineral rich sea salt is used and used correctly, it enhances the healing value of foods besides enhancing their flavor.

The Diet uses mineral-rich sea salt medicinally at first, to restore the body's balance. Since candidiasis is a condition of too much expansion and acidity, small amounts of mineral-rich sea salt help contract and alkalize our body, bringing it into balance. That's why some of the more contracting foods, such as poultry, eggs, and even meat are desirable when you first start the Diet.

Later, you can use a moderate amount of sea salt in cooking. It's important to use just the right amount—not too much—or the body will become too contracted and start craving expanding foods, such as sugar, again. Have you ever gone to a bar and eaten a bowl of salty peanuts...or gone to a movie and had a bag of popcorn? That made you thirsty, and probably the drinks you most wanted to quench that thirst were beer or soft drinks – they both contain sugar, an expanding food.

Use sea salt when cooking buckwheat to make it less acid-forming. Other grains on the Diet are alkaline-forming, so using sea salt with them is optional. You can use a small amount of salt (just enough to heighten the natural flavors) in the final 10 to 15 minutes of cooking a soup or vegetables. When cooked for 10 minutes or more, salt chelates, blending with other foods, and does not cause such a "salty" reaction in our bodies.

We recommend a high-quality sea salt for cooking. You also can buy (in most cookware stores) a special salt grinder for table use, one with non-metallic parts that won't interact with the salt. (see shopping list for the name of our favorite sea salt)

Men and women have different needs for salt; men need a little more of sea salt's contracting quality. Women should cut way back on salt and continue to do so from the time of ovulation until they complete their period (monthly cleansing) so their bodies will easily "open up," relax, and expand ever so slightly to release the uterine lining. When a woman's body becomes too contracted from too much sea salt, she will have extreme cravings for sugary, sweet foods as her body attempts to balance itself so the lining of the uterus can be shed. If she eats too much salt during her period, she may not have a complete cleansing. After the lining is shed, a woman can increase her use of sea salt and contracting foods a bit (which will help bring on a smooth ovulation). She should still balance the contracting foods with expanding foods, of course. The more contracting foods are best to eat close to the time of ovulation. Doing so helps the ovary contract, and the tiny egg "pops out" (more on women's special needs later).

Non-Alcoholic Flavorings

At least three companies make non-alcoholic liquid flavorings you can use in Body Ecology Diet dessert recipes. St. John's Herb Garden, Inc., Frontier Herbs, and The Spicery Shoppe sell natural extracts such as almond, vanilla, banana, pineapple, and even coffee. Some have a vegetable oil (soybean) base, and some have a vegetable/glycerine oil base. *The glycerine-based flavorings are fine*. You might find that you are sensitive to one flavoring and not another, but usually these should work for you. The Spicery Shoppe makes extracts by squeezing the essential oils from foods and putting them with these bases. These oils have no sugar; therefore, they don't feed the yeast. That's why you can safely use fruit flavors such as pineapple or banana (unless you are somehow sensitive to the essential oil).

Most health food stores stock these flavorings or can order them for you.

Fermented Foods

With a few exceptions, fermented foods are not on the B.E.D. Avoid all fermented foods, such as salted and pasteurized sauerkraut, amasake, miso, soy sauce, tamari, tempeh, and rejuvelac. Kefir, a fermented or cultured food is discussed in a later chapter.

You *can have* two types of (unheated) fermented foods: raw, unfiltered apple cider vinegar and raw, unsalted cultured vegetables, made with a variety of vegetables, such as cabbage, carrots, daikon, garlic, celery, kelp, beets,[13] and herbs (see Chapter 14).

Apple cider vinegar and cultured vegetables allow the lacto-bacilli that fight yeast and other unhealthy flora to proliferate. Besides probiotics, which provide your body with beneficial flora (bifidus, acidophilus, streptococcus faecium, rhamnosus), these cultured foods will be an important factor in recolonizing your inner ecological world.

Apple cider vinegar is manufactured by several different companies. Some bottles are labeled "filtered," some "unfiltered." The unfiltered are best. Look for vinegar packaged in light-proof or dark opaque containers. This prevents photo oxidation and keeps the integrity of the product. Look for products that tell you on the label that they are raw, unpasteurized, and contain the "mother" of the vinegar, and the more of it, the better.

Rich in potassium and alkaline-forming, apple cider vinegar is an "antidote" when you've had too much salt or sugar. It's delicious in the Body Ecology Diet Salad Dressing, and you can use it to substitute for other vinegars in various recipes (even homemade mayonnaise). You can have mustard if it is made with raw apple cider vinegar (see Shopping List for brand names).

Cultured vegetables are vegetables that have been cut or shredded and left in a sanitary environment for a few days at the right temperature. This lets the lactobacilli and enzymes that are naturally present on the vegetables proliferate and help overcome the yeast. Enzymes are essential to digestion and elimination of toxins from the body. Unsalted cultured vegetables also help control sugar cravings.

You can make your own cultured vegetables or buy them in health food stores. We recommend you have at least $1/2$ cup a day as you begin the Diet. Later, you can vary the amount according to your body's needs and the extent to which you have restored your inner balance.

Making these vegetables may seem time consuming, but they are well worth it in regaining your inner ecology. They are also a very economical way to reestablish your inner ecosystem, since they cost far less than expensive probiotics.[14]

If you have a few friends or family members on The Diet, spend a Sunday afternoon making cultured vegetables together. Breaking up the work and talking makes the time pass quickly.

---

[13]Although beets are not normally on the B.E.D., they are okay in this instance, because the friendly bacteria in the cultured vegetables devour the sugar in the beets and, therefore, the sugar is no longer available to feed your yeast.

[14]The money spent on probiotics, however, is well worth it, especially in your first year of healing. Before they start the Diet, many people spend a lot of money on various avenues of healing. Instead, spend your money on high-quality foods recommended by the Diet, and on cultured vegetables and high-quality probiotics. (see also new chapter on kefir, Chapter 24)

A SPECIAL WORD OF CAUTION: Occasionally, very sensitive individuals find they have a reaction to eating these foods. This is because the cider vinegar and cultured vegetables cause a cleansing reaction that may be uncomfortable. Since few of us understand and trust the cleansing principle at first, it's possible to become frightened or intolerant of too much cleansing. If you fall in this category, hold off eating these foods for a few weeks until you no longer have a flare-up of your usual symptoms. Just follow the rest of the Diet guidelines. Don't give up on these valuable foods, though…try them later.

Water

Pure, high-quality drinking water is critical to recovering your health. Your system needs at least six to eight 8-ounce glasses each day. Try to drink half of these by mid-morning, to make up for the fluids your body missed during the night. If drinking water is not easy for you because you don't like it, flavor it by drinking herbal teas such as Echinacea Plus, Raspberry Leaf, or one of the others listed on the Shopping List at the end of this book. Adding stevia and a slice of lemon to your drinking water also works well.

If you don't drink fluids during the day because you're too busy and forget, wear a timer that signals you to take a few sips from a nearby container.

It's especially important to consume the full amount of water if you are using any colon cleansers, because they can be binding and cause constipation without adequate water. Most people underestimate the amount of water they drink in a day, so count your glasses.

Do you often find yourself full of energy just around bedtime, so you stay up too late and then feel exhausted the next morning? This condition can be a sign of simply not drinking enough water during the day.

> *One of Linda's most painful conditions associated with her candidiasis was a history of urinary tract infections. This is very common among women with yeast conditions. She developed the habit of drinking a lot of water to keep her urinary system as clear as possible. She keeps a carafe of water on her desk and sips throughout the day, and she often takes a plastic "biker's bottle" on car trips, so it will always be available when she's on the road.*

It's essential to drink pure, good quality water. Chlorine and fluoride destroy friendly bacteria in your digestive tract, so try to drink filtered water. Sparkling water is acceptable on the Diet.

The Herb Stevia

Stevia is a small shrub found primarily in China and South America. Its sweet properties have been known for centuries in Paraguay and Brazil, where it grows along their mutual border in very rich top soil. Stevia is up to 300 times sweeter than sugar, yet it is an entirely natural product that also has excellent medicinal properties. The South American Indians chew the leaves or pour water over them to make tea.

Stevia has a long history of safe and therapeutic use as an herbal sweetener and as an antifungal, anti-inflammatory, and antibiotic agent. It lacks calories, is heat stable (and therefore ideal for cooking and baking), and enhances the flavor of whatever it's used in.

It helps balance the pancreas (a healthy pancreas is essential for healthy digestion). This important gland regulates blood sugar and is often off-kilter in people with candidiasis. In Brazil, China, and other countries, stevia is recommended for diabetics and people with hypoglycemia. It helps regulate the digestive tract to produce a healthy stool, and it greatly increases energy.

In animal studies both in the U.S. and Brazil, stevia produced a significant reduction in cavities. When used with fluoride, it is even more effective.[15]

Equally important, stevia inhibits those sugar cravings, which can lure you off the Diet. Its extraordinary sweetness means you only have to use the smallest amount—just a pinch has the same impact as a cup of sugar.

Japan consumes more stevia than any other country. The Japanese grow what they can and then import tons more each year from Brazil and China. Since the 1970s, the Japanese have used stevia as a food additive in soft drinks, juices, chewing gum, pickles, frozen desserts, bean and fish paste products, and low-calorie foods.

Stevia is also popular in Holland, Nigeria, Indonesia, Costa Rica, Hong Kong, and other countries. The U.S. Food and Drug Administration (FDA) has finally approved stevia for use in the United States, but only as a dietary supplement. This means you can use it yourself, but it cannot be labeled as a sweetener in any commercially manufactured food.

Stevia has been tested extensively in human and animal studies around the world with no negative side effects. Ironically, of over 6,000 complaints on file with the FDA since 1985, about 80%

[15]Dr. Kleber, Dental Science Research Group, Purdue University

are related to the artificial sweetener NutraSweet® (16), yet it is still on the market. Stevia exists in nature; we merely *extract its essence* to satisfy our natural craving for sweets.

This book includes several recipes sweetened with a bit of white stevia powder. It is not an essential food on the B.E.D., but it can add taste and pleasure to your cooking. If it could be added to foods in the U.S., it would open up a whole new world of taste, even for people not on the Body Ecology Diet.

The FDA claims it does not have enough scientific evidence that stevia is safe, and has not approved it fully for use as a sweetener. But we suspect special interests are working to keep stevia off the American Market. In our book, **The Stevia Story: A Tale of Incredible Sweetness and Intrigue**, we go into more detail about this. Currently, the FDA allows stevia to be sold as a dietary supplement only. This means you can purchase it and use it as you like, but natural food companies who want to use stevia in drinks, dairy products, baking mixes and toothpaste are prohibited.

You can voice your support for stevia by asking the FDA to approve it in a category known as GRAS, Generally Regarded as Safe. And you can lobby your Congressional representative and the President. See Appendix B for sample letters, and be sure to check out our stevia recipes in the recipe section.

Donna has recently written a new book with Ray Sahelian, MD called **The Stevia Cookbook: Cooking with Nature's Calorie-Free Sweetener.** You can find both stevia books at your local health food store or order them from us at 1-800-511-2660.

**NOTE: Donna has created over 100 stevia recipes in this new book, but many are not recommended for someone on the first (or healing) stage of The Body Ecology Diet. (French Chocolate Ice Cream or Cheesecake would be an example.)

VISIT OUR STEVIA WEBSITE AT STEVIA.NET.

Teas

Several teas are especially healing and antifungal: mathake, echinacea, and pau d'arco (also known as Brazilian bark or Taheebo). You can have as much of these as you want! Also healing: Burdock root and Dandelion root teas, Yogi Digest-Ease tea. Avoid fruit teas and teas with citric acid, since fruit is not on the Diet.

Both Green Tea and Ginger Tea enhance digestion. You can buy Ginger Aid Tea (made with stevia from Traditional Medicinals) or even make your own.

To Make Ginger Tea

Boil several slices of ginger root in one quart of water for about 15-20 minutes. Add stevia to taste, then let the tea sit for a half hour or more. You will have ginger root tea, which you can learn to make stronger or weaker depending on your taste.

[16]Roberts, 1990

Butter, Unrefined Oils, and Fats/ Cholesterol

Rich fatty foods are definitely *not* on the Diet. High-quality *organic, unrefined* vegetable oils, butter, and ghee certainly are. Quality oils are critical for the healing process. The *unrefined* vegetable oils allowed on the Diet—safflower, sunflower, pumpkin seed, and flax seed—have the highest quality of essential fatty acids (EFAs) of any oils. These EFA oils can be used in salad dressings; coconut oil, butter and ghee are best for sautéing. **Always buy organic, unrefined oils in light-proof bottles.**

There is a critical need for the Omega-6 and Omega-3 essential fatty acids to be obtained from our diet since they are not made by our bodies. Besides being good sources of energy, Omega-6s and 3s play a key role in how oxygen is carried throughout our bodies. Found in high concentrations in the brain, they are important for normal brain function, the transmission of nerve impulses, and the regulation of our hormones. All the organic, unrefined oils on the B.E.D. are rich in Omega-6, and most of us obtain ample amounts of it. It is in the Omega-3s that we are seriously deficient. Flax seed oil is our richest source of Omega-3.

Organic, unrefined flax seed, pumpkin seed, sunflower and safflower oils are great **culinary oils** and add wonderful flavors to salad dressings. B.E.D. Essential Balance (a blend of these organic oils plus borage seed) is our favorite oil and the best oil to consume daily, since it has a perfect balance of the essential fats.[17]

To protect the heat sensitive Omega-3s, do not cook with flax seed or Essential Balance. Both of these oils can be used in salad dressings or dribbled over a baked red skin potato or grains. Therapeutically, one to two tablespoons of unrefined essential fatty acid oils should be taken once a day. Research now shows that by adding *unrefined* EFA oils to a healthy diet such as the Body Ecology Diet, normal weight can be restored in obese people. In order for this to work, though, **all refined oils** and **margarine must be removed from the diet.**

Other benefits showing up in the latest research using flax seed oil and a diet like ours are: a stronger immune system, an increase in energy, normal blood cholesterol levels, and relief of pain from arthritis. Unrefined flax seed oil is being used in clinics around the world to fight cancer, depression, emotional disorders, and even schizophrenia.

---

[17]We've included a recipe for a B.E.D. mayonnaise, but please remember that mayonnaise is not a *healing food* and should be eaten sparingly—reserved only for special occasions. Made with Essential Balance, however, our B.E.D. mayonnaise is the healthiest you can eat.

Unrefined pumpkin seed oil is delicious, very nutritious, and has medicinal properties. It is used to nourish and heal the digestive tract, fight parasites, improve circulation, help heal prostate disorders, nourish the ovaries, and help prevent dental caries.

We recommend you cook with organic, unrefined coconut oil. Contrary to the misinformation put out by the hydrogenated soy oil industries, coconut oil is actually a beneficial fat. It contains lauric acid, an important fatty acid (found abundantly in mother's milk), that has an antiviral effect in the body. Coconut oil is excellent for the thyroid and does not raise cholesterol when consumed in a diet that contains essential fatty acids (flax oil, etc.). Coconut oil is naturally stable and therefore excellent for sautéing. Also important to note, for anyone suffering from candida, coconut oil is a rich source of caprylic acid...a potent anti-fungal.

You can also sauté with butter or ghee. Ghee can be made at home or purchased from your health food store. Ghee is clarified butter, the *oil* of butter with the milk solids removed. (It's the milk solids in regular butter that contain those harmful hormones and antibiotics.) Ghee is less mucous-forming than butter and contains no lactose (milk sugar), so it is ideal for an anti-candida diet. Cooking with a mixture of half unrefined coconut oil and half ghee produces a delicious flavor. Ghee keeps longer than butter and does not require refrigeration.

You can make your own ghee. Here's how: Melt two to four 1/4-pound sticks of butter in a saucepan over medium/low heat. It will start bubbling, and you will see the white milk solids gather on the surface. Then these solids start to clear away from the surface. Allow this clearing to continue for a couple of minutes (too long and the ghee will burn). Remove pan from heat, and let it cool. The solids will sink to the bottom, and you can strain the clear yellow liquid into a jar. It keeps fine at room temperature or in the refrigerator.

If you do use butter, the best type to get is **raw butter**. Unfortunately, its sale is prohibited in most states, since it lacks preservatives, spoils easily, melts quickly, and is definitely too much trouble for the big food chains to handle. Raw butter is better because it contains the enzyme lipase, which helps digest the fat in the butter. It is lighter in color and has a delicious flavor. Ideally, butter should be made locally and delivered door to door as it was in the olden days. Today, if you really want the best butter possible, you almost need to have your own cow. If raw butter is not allowed in your state, at least buy *organic* butter from you health food store.

Avoid margarine. The hydrogenation process used in manufacturing margarine creates trans fatty acids that are harmful to your health.

Fat Intolerance

Until your inner ecosystem is restored and your digestive tract is teeming with fat digesting friendly bacteria, you may not be able to tolerate oils, butter, or fats at all and will have to avoid them completely. This is very common with a body ecology imbalance because of the toxic, congested condition of the liver and gallbladder. Symptoms of fat intolerance are: pains in the neck and shoulders, spasms in the large and small intestines, feeling tired just after eating, bloating, indigestion, belching, flatulence and/or nausea, right upper abdominal discomfort, and hard stools. Fat intolerance can be confirmed by a simple urine test or by simply eliminating fats from your diet for a week and noting any improvement in your digestion and your energy. **Digestive enzymes high in lipase should be taken with each meal.**

A small amount of *organic, unrefined* coconut oil used for sautéing (as for onions when making a pot of soup) shouldn't cause you any discomfort; salad dressings or butter on your potato may. Fortunately, we have solved this problem for you. While we often hear that our Body Ecology Diet Salad Dressing™ made with unrefined oil is the most delicious dressing folks have ever tasted, we are now getting rave reviews over our no-oil dressings. The oil has been replaced with water and xanthan gum, a natural, flavorless thickener tolerated by everyone and available at health food stores. Our B.E.D. no-oil dressings are unbelievably good (see recipes).

Note: Good news: In chapter 24 you'll learn about kefir, a cultured food rich in the B-vitamins. B-3, B-6, and B-12 play a critical role in the assimilation of fats. Once your inner eco-system is established with lots of Vitamin B producing friendly bacteria, you'll find it easier to digest fats.

Heart Healthy

While the Body Ecology Diet is gaining widespread popularity as the premier diet for candidiasis and immune disorders, it is certainly an excellent eating program for people with heart conditions and cholesterol problems. If you or someone you love has high cholesterol, eat plenty of the following:

> daikon (a large white Chinese radish)
> raw vegetables (especially carrots, red peppers, broccoli, cauliflower)
> lemons (and later grapefruit)
> garlic and ginger
> fish oils (salmon, trout, tuna)
> the B.E.D. organic, unrefined vegetable oils (coconut, flax seed, pumpkin seed, sunflower and safflower)
> lecithin
> probiotics

Reminder: Excessive amounts of fats–even the oils, butter, and ghee on the Diet– delay the secretion of gastric juices that digest protein flesh. This means those all-American tuna, egg, and chicken salads with a lot of mayo are out. (See recipe section for salad dressings you can use with protein foods.) Enjoy your butter, unrefined oil, and ghee with starches, grains, non-starchy vegetables, and ocean vegetables. You will notice that your digestion of fats is enhanced when eaten with raw, grated daikon, cultured vegetables, leafy green salads, apple cider vinegar, and lemon juice. (**Please see more on unrefined oils in the Introduction to Salads and Salad Dressings section.**)

Foods To Avoid

✓ Alcohol—its sugars feed the yeast.
✓ Breads and flour products, grains, pastas (except as discussed above)—they create too much gluten in the body, and their natural sugars feed the yeast.
✔ Citric acid–found in many foods and teas–read labels
✔ Legumes, beans, peanuts—too difficult to digest, and they cause fermentation and sugars; peanuts attract fungus during processing.
✔Mushrooms—encourage allergic reactions; they are a fungus.
✔ Nuts and nut butters—they are too acid-forming and difficult to digest.
✔ Oils (other than above)—i.e., olive, soybean, peanut, sesame —olive is a fruit; other oils come from foods not allowed. Olive oil can be introduced again later.
✔ Sugars—including honey, molasses, corn syrup, dextrose, brown rice syrup, barley malt, etc.—feed the yeast.
✔Yeast—baking and brewer's...cause allergic reactions.

Words of Encouragement

You may think there are more do's and don'ts on this Diet than you can possibly handle—but don't worry! After a little practice, eating according to the Diet will become second nature to you. You won't have to think about what goes with what; you'll learn to shop for and even crave all the foods that make you feel so much better. Just remember that the Diet absolutely works, and it takes different amounts of time for different people to feel better.

Talk about your experiences to your friends and family. You might even write a journal to chronicle your healing. If you read it a year from now, you'll marvel at your progress.

CHAPTER 13
Juicing

Machines that grind fresh raw fruits and vegetables into juices seem to be everywhere these days: in the stores, on television, pictured in books. It's a sign that people want to include healthier foods in their diets and reap the benefits of the vitamins, minerals, and enzymes in fresh produce. But juicing is not the panacea it's often portrayed to be, and for people with body ecology imbalances, it may even magnify their symptoms if they start too soon.

Is Juicing Good for You?

Yes and no. If you have a body ecology imbalance, you need to wait until you've been on the Diet at least three months and have fulfilled some other conditions before you start juicing. Once you do, however, juices can play a significant role in healing (especially of the liver—see Chapter 21) if they are understood and used appropriately. The key is learning how and when to incorporate them into your diet.

Benefits of Juicing

✔ Juices can balance an overly contracted condition.
Because of their natural sweetness and high water content, they are the most expansive form of fruits and vegetables. You can use them medicinally to correct contracted conditions. These include constipation, headaches brought on by too much salt, or the irritability and moodiness some women experience before their periods. A stressful lifestyle causes contraction, so does airplane travel. Freshly squeezed juices can bring your body right back into balance.

✔ The alkaline-forming nature of juices can balance an acidic condition and aid in cleansing.
Regular consumption of juices strengthens all bodily functions by keeping the organs, glands, and cells clean and free of the toxins that create an acidic condition. Again, juices, with their high water content, catalyze cleansing.

✔ Juices are easily digested and nutrient-rich.
Raw juices are as rich in the same nutrients, oxygen, water, and enzymes as the whole fruits and vegetables from which they're made. But juicing machines separate out the fiber, and without it, juices digest in a few minutes. Thus, these important nutrients become much more readily available, an enormous benefit for people with immune system disorders, including cancer, chronic fatigue, and AIDS. (New research shows AIDS patients have poor assimilation of nutrients even when they eat correctly and take supplements.)

✔ Juices give the digestive tract a much needed rest.

Within minutes of being consumed, juices send a quick source of fuel into the blood stream, allowing the digestive organs to take a break. The tremendous amount of energy that would be spent on digestion can then be used for cleansing and rebuilding the body.

Then Why Not Juice?

It can be costly. To do it right, you need to purchase an expensive piece of equipment ($100-300 or more). You'll also be buying enormous quantities of fresh vegetables (fruit juices, with a few exceptions, are not on the Diet). Preparing the vegetables—washing and feeding them into the juicer—takes time. And cleaning the machine can be a nuisance.

Most important, however, is the fact that most juices have a high concentration of natural sugars and therefore feed yeast and opportunistic organisms. They do not combine well with any other food. If they are eaten with protein or starches, they will cause digestive problems including fermentation and gas. How can we overcome these negatives and make juicing work for you?

Timing Is Everything

There are two important rules to remember:

Rule #1:

Don't juice until your yeast problem is completely under control.

Wait until you have detoxified your colon and have implanted significant colonies of friendly bacteria into your digestive tract. You should also see other signs that your body ecology is back into balance—for example, your symptoms of yeast overgrowth should be gone. For most people, this is at least three months or more. Remember, you don't want to feed the yeast any form of sugar. When you're ready to try juices, introduce them cautiously, as you would any other new food, and watch for signs that your body might not be ready yet.

Rule #2:

Drink juice only on an empty stomach.

Take juice as your first meal of the day. Wait at least one half hour before eating anything else.

Why are these rules necessary? Read on.

Vegetable Juices

To make most vegetable juices palatable, carrots or another sweet vegetable are used as the base. And concentrated carrot juice yields a very strong sugar. So juice blends that have a sweet base of carrot, beet, and/or fennel must follow the food combining rule for sugar, which is to eat it alone on an empty stomach at least one half hour before any other solid food. And if your yeast overgrowth is not under control, the sugar will feed it, causing a flare-up of symptoms, and you could lose the ground you've gained.

Juices made only with greens (kale, broccoli, cabbage) and non-starchy, low sugar, high water content vegetables such as cucumbers do not have to follow this special food combining rule. However, juices assimilate so rapidly, it is still always best to "chew them" alone, wait the half hour, and then eat your other foods.

"Chewing" your juice means to hold it in your mouth, allowing the digestion process to begin by mixing it with saliva. Savoring your vegetable juices in this way makes a huge difference.

Fruit Juices

Like fresh fruit, fruit juices are rich in natural sugars and are not on the Body Ecology Diet, with the exception of lemons, limes, cranberries, and (this one will surprise you) Granny Smith apples. These green, sour apples have much less sweetness than juiced carrots and make a better base for the raw juiced vegetables. And although it is a fruit, this sour apple is compatible with all vegetable juices. To ensure it does not cause a problem with the yeast, we also combine it with freshly squeezed lemon juice. The recipe at the end of this chapter is an excellent example of a juice blend that is not only surprisingly tasty, but healing as well.

You can have these juices on an empty stomach at least one half hour before eating other foods.

A glass of unsweetened cranberry juice concentrate diluted with water and sweetened with the herb stevia is excellent for strengthening the bladder and alleviating urinary tract infections. Recent research shows that compounds in cranberry juice prevent pathogenic (unfriendly) bacteria from adhering to the bladder walls.

Lemon juice and lime juice, or a combination of the two, are natural antiseptics and cleanse the digestive tract. The sourness of all three of these fruit juices helps stimulate the peristaltic action of the colon and promotes morning bowel movements. Once you begin introducing new foods and are trying grapefruit, you can also try grapefruit juice from the sourer varieties of the fruit.

More Tips on How to Make Juicing Work for You

Adapt recipes to use as little of the sweet vegetables (carrots, beets, fennel) as possible, or substitute them for green apple and lemon juice. Add a high concentration of celery, cucumber, or a combination of green vegetables that are not sweet.

When necessary, dilute some of the sweetness in your juice by adding water, either spring or filtered, and/or lemon juice.

Try to juice only what you will drink right away; do not make extra. If it sits around, even in the refrigerator, it becomes more sugary. If you must juice for several meals at one time, keep the green apple or carrot juice in a separate container from the other juices. Mix together just before drinking.

Add greens, such as parsley, kale, and watercress. You don't need a lot of these, but their high concentration of chlorophyll will help cleanse your blood and cells.

Undiluted green grass juices, like wheat grass juice, may be too expansive initially and cause nausea or dizziness. You can add just a small amount of freshly squeezed grass juice into a blend of other juices. Wheat grass juice also makes a great colon implant.

Add 1 tsp. to 1 Tbsp. raw apple cider vinegar to your juice. Its sourness balances the sweetness of the juice. You can also add Dr. Bronner's Balanced Mineral Seasoning and Sea Seasonings with Dulse, Garlic and Kelp, or Kelp with Cayenne to enhance the taste.

Add friendly bacteria to the juice; they love the sugar. If the bacteria have been cultured on dairy, there's no problem with food combining, since dairy combines well with acidic fruits and raw vegetables.

The Bottom Line

Juice fasting can be very beneficial. Try it on a day when you can stay at home and rest. Drink a lot of juice often so you don't get weak. Colon cleansing—colonics or enemas—is important during this time. Because of the cleansing effect of the juices, the colon wants to release more stagnant material than normal peristaltic movement will allow. If you want to fast longer, consult with a health care professional who's an expert on fasting.

Juicing can be very beneficial as long as you follow the rules. The investment of your time and money now will pay off in years of better health for you and savings in health care costs later in life.

The following juice recipe is an ideal mixture of good health and good taste. Most juices with this much chlorophyll are difficult to stomach, but ours, when mixed with a little Granny Smith juice, is delicious. This recipe makes one half gallon of green juice and one cup of green apple juice...enough to last for a day of juicing or for three mornings. Drinking your juices immediately after juicing is ideal, but because of the time and effort it takes to clean and juice vegetables most of us find this very inconvenient. We have found that as long as you keep the green mixture separate from the apple juice, this amount will last for 2 to 3 days.

> 6 oz. spinach juice
> 2 oz. parsley juice
> 8 oz. lettuce juice
> 10 oz. broccoli juice
> 18 oz. cucumber juice
> 20 oz. celery juice
> ginger to taste
>
> Juice separately:
> 8 oz. Granny Smith apple juice

Mix together 8 oz. of green mixture with one ounce of green apple and the juice of half a lemon. Enjoy![18]

Reminder:

Juicing at the beginning of the diet and juicing improperly can set you back seriously. *Once your body ecology is restored*, you may try introducing fresh vegetable juices very cautiously—always on an empty stomach first thing in the morning. Wait half an hour before eating other food.

VITALITY *SuperGreen*™, our micro-algae formula mentioned earlier, is an excellent drink for you even as you begin The Diet. It is delicious when added to a juice of all green vegetables. Taken alone, it contains all the nutrients your body needs to cleanse and rebuild. In the morning for breakfast, it is a super convenient way to start the day; taken in the late afternoon, it's a quick pick-me-up and revitalizer.

---

[18]A very special thanks to Arden Zinn, the juice lady of Atlanta, for her wonderful guidance and for developing a green drink that will cleanse the liver and still taste great.

CHAPTER 14
Raw Cultured Vegetables

Raw cultured vegetables have been around for thousands of years, but we have never needed them more than we do today. Rich in lactobacilli and enzymes, alkaline-forming, and loaded with vitamins, they are an ideal food that can and should be consumed with every meal.

Since they are an excellent source of Vitamin C, Dutch seamen used to carry them to prevent scurvy. For centuries, the Chinese have cultured cabbage each fall to ensure a source of greens through the winter (if they have no refrigeration). Cultured vegetables are a favorite food of the long-lived Hunzas. Yogurt ads lead us to believe that eating yogurt ensures a long life, but it's really the active cultures of friendly bacteria (lactobacilli) in the yogurt that are responsible for the health of these people. Similarly, the friendly bacteria, the enzymes, and the high lactic acid in raw cultured vegetables add to health and longevity.

They taste tangy. It may be a new taste for you, but you will soon feel that no meal is complete without them. Even better, since they are all-vegetable, they combine with either a protein or a starch meal. They are slightly to the expansive end of the expansion/contraction continuum, so they help balance the contractive nature of animal foods and sea salt. So what exactly are raw cultured vegetables?

They're sauerkraut. The Austrians coined this word, from sauer (sour) and kraut (greens or plants). But we call them raw cultured vegetables, because we don't want you to mistake them for the salted and pasteurized sauerkraut sold in supermarkets and even some health food stores. That kind of sauerkraut is definitely not on the Diet, because it is pasteurized. The pasteurization (heating) process destroys precious enzymes, and the added salt eliminates any health benefits. We'll teach you how to make these delicious raw cultured vegetables without heat or preservatives.

Benefits

✔ Raw cultured vegetables help reestablish your inner ecosystem.

The friendly bacteria in raw cultured vegetables are a less expensive alternative to probiotics (although we recommend both as you begin the Diet).

✔ They improve digestion.

Knowing the benefits of raw foods, you may have decided to include raw vegetables with each meal. Yet when you begin the Diet, your digestive tract and spleen may be too weak to tolerate them. Cultured vegetables eliminate this concern, since they are already pre-digested. This means that even before they enter your mouth, the friendly bacteria have already converted the natural sugars and starches in the vegetables into lactic acid, a job your own saliva and digestive enzymes would do anyway. The enzymes in the cultured vegetables also help digest other foods eaten with them.

✔ They increase longevity.

You could think of the friendly bacteria in raw cultured vegetables as little enzyme powerhouses. By eating the vegetables, you will maintain your own enzyme reserve and use it to eliminate toxins, rejuvenate your cells, and strengthen your immune system—which all adds up to a longer, healthier life.

✔ They control cravings.

Homemade cultured vegetables are ideal for appetite control and thus weight control. The veggies help take away cravings for the sweet taste in pastries, colas, bread, pasta, dairy, fruit, and other expansive foods not on the Diet.

✔ They are ideal for pregnant and nursing women.

Pregnant women should eat cultured vegetables to ensure their ecosystems will be rich in friendly bacteria. The vegetables also help alleviate morning sickness during the early part of the pregnancy. Once the baby is born, the mother should continue eating the vegetables and drinking the juice. And the liquid from the cultured vegetables can be fed to the baby in tiny spoonfuls to relieve colic.

✔ Raw cultured vegetables are alkaline and very cleansing.

They help restore balance if your body is in a toxic, acidic condition. Because they do trigger cleansing, you may have an increase in intestinal gas initially as the vegetables stir up waste and toxins in the intestinal tract. Soon, however, you will notice an improvement in your stools. To ease the discomfort of the gas, colonics and enemas are very useful during this period.

How Raw Cultured Vegetables Work

The vegetables are cultured by grinding up cabbage (or a combination of cabbage and other vegetables) and leaving it in a sanitary environment at room temperature for a few days. Friendly bacteria that are naturally present in the vegetables quickly lower the pH, making a more acidic environment so the bacteria can colonize.

By sanitary environment, we mean a large stainless steel stockpot or ceramic crock covered with cabbage leaves, a plate, and a heavy object to weight down the vegetables, and then covered with a dishtowel. Room temperature means 60-70 degrees Fahrenheit, for about six days, depending on how you like the taste. Some connoisseurs say six days are ideal, others feel only three are necessary. You can experiment and decide for yourself.

During this fermentation period, the friendly bacteria are having a heyday, reproducing and converting sugars and starches to lactic acid. Once the initial process is over, it is time to slow down the bacterial activity by putting the cultured veggies in a glass jar with a tight-fitting lid and refrigerating it. The cold will not kill the activity, just slow it down to an appropriate rate.

Ideal Times to Make the Veggies

The cooler months of fall and winter are the best times to prepare the veggies, because your room temperature is usually ideal. And since we eat more contracting foods such as salt, animal foods, and cooked vegetables in soups and stews at these times, the raw cultured veggies provide a perfect balance. During the summer, fermentation tends to occur too quickly, so it's not an ideal time to make the sauerkraut. We are drawn to eating rawer, fresh, enzyme-rich foods during the summer anyway, so nature again has provided a flawless plan.

Try to make your sauerkraut in a quantity that you and your family will consume in about two to four weeks, so you'll always be able to eat it fresh. If you do need to make it in bigger quantities and store it, that's okay too—just keep it cold and tightly covered. Properly made, it can have an eight-month shelf life. If you have a friend on the Diet, try sharing the responsibility of making the sauerkraut and sharing the yield.

Once you master the basic technique, be creative. Try different vegetable combinations, and include soaked, drained ocean vegetables like hijiki and arame. Use lemon juice, herbs (fresh or dried), seeds (dill or caraway), and juniper berries. Try leaving out the cabbage entirely and making a batch of cultured daikon.

Tips for Eating Raw Cultured Vegetables

Include at least $1/2$ cup of the veggies in any meal where you are eating a protein or starch. Use the juice in salad dressing as a replacement for the apple cider vinegar or lemon juice. You can also toss the veggies into salads, wrap them up in blue cornmeal tortillas, or serve them with crunchy blue corn chips.

Never heat the veggies, or the valuable enzymes and bacteria will be killed. If you leave them out at room temperature for awhile, they come alive and start to multiply quickly. So sometimes when you open a jar, the veggies overflow and start bubbling out the top. This is good! It just means your batch is rich with viable bacteria ready to go to work in your digestive tract and establish a new inner ecology.

Recipes

There is no one perfect way to make raw sauerkraut, but the following recipe is one we learned from one of the great cultured vegetable masters, Evan Richards, president of Rejuvenative Foods in Santa Cruz, California 831-462-6715. We are deeply grateful for his efforts and guidance. Over the last ten years he has patiently produced and sold raw cultured vegetables when very few recognized the importance of these vital foods.

The secret to making great raw cultured vegetables is in using fresh, well-cleaned vegetables that taste good and are not too mature. They should be harvested when they are sweet, juicy, tender and delicious. Good cabbage, beets, and carrots are sweet and full of many exciting flavors.

Vegetables ferment as a result of beneficial bacteria that are naturally present. Normally, the beneficial bacteria dominate and give you great tasting raw cultured vegetables. The cleaner the equipment and vegetables, the better. You do want to shake your vegetables after cleaning so as to have the least amount of water in the raw culturing vegetables.

Step 1–Use mostly cabbage (organic, green and/or red), either by itself or with beets, carrots, garlic, celery, red peppers, kelp, herbs (thyme, dill), or any other vegetable you want. Use a minimum of 10 heads of cabbage.

Grind them up with a food processor. Then place them into a large stainless steel bowl and pound them with a bat or a similar heavy, blunt object until they become a little juicy. While beating, **add freshly squeezed lemon juice** (see recipe on next page).

A Champion juicer works well for grinding vegetables, but be sure to grind them with the blank plastic piece and not the screen. This blank piece lets you grind without juicing. If you use the Champion juicer you will not need to pound the cabbage with a bat.

Step 2–Put the vegetables into a stainless steel, ceramic, or glass crock. Don't fill the crock to the brim, because the fermenting vegetables are likely to expand and overflow.

Step 3–Put lots of fresh cabbage leaves on top of the ground-up vegetables (completely covering the ground-up vegetables).

Step 4–With your hands and a little body weight, gently, yet firmly and evenly, compress the leaves.

Step 5–Put a plate that is as wide as possible in the crock.

Step 6–Put some weight on the plate. You can use a jar or something else that has some weight to it. We like to use a jar that won't leak, filled with about two-thirds of a pint of water. A little weight is good, but don't put on so much that vegetable juice is forced up above the fermenting vegetables. You want to check the fermenting vegetables a few times in the next 24-36 hours to confirm you have the right amount of weight and to make sure that the plate is sitting on the vegetables evenly.

Step 7–Cover the crock with a clean dishtowel. Let the fermenting vegetables sit in a well-ventilated room at room temperature (between 60-70 degrees) for five to seven days. The longer they sit, the stronger they become. After five to seven days (6-7 days at 60 degrees and 5-6 days at 70 degrees), throw away the old cabbage leaves and any moldy and discolored vegetables on the top. Put the remaining fermented vegetables in glass jars and refrigerate. This raw sauerkraut will last from four to eight months when kept at 34 degrees and opened minimally. Do not freeze.

Our Favorite Beginner's Recipe

We like to add freshly squeezed lemon juice to our cabbage, because it tastes delicious and retains the beautiful color in the vegetables. Here is our favorite beginner's recipe.

> For every three heads of cabbage:
> (we use 2 green cabbages and 1 red cabbage)
>
> Combine $^3/4$ to 1 cup
> freshly squeezed lemon juice and
> 3 Tbsp. dried dill weed

Put this mixture into a stainless steel bowl and beat it thoroughly with a blunt object. Put this into your crock or stainless steel stockpot and cover with at least two layers of cabbage leaves, the plate, and the heavy object. Find a cool spot in your house and let it sit for six days before unveiling it. Scrape off any foam or mildew from the top or edges, and refrigerate as above. Your batch, if you've made it correctly, should be brightly colored, juicy and sweet.

If you want to add other vegetables, use a layering method:

Grate vegetables in a food processor. Add more lemon juice and more dill (or other herbs), and then pound them as explained above. Layer cabbage in the bottom of a large pot or crock about six inches deep, then add layers of carrots, peppers, beets, celery, daikon, onions, then a layer of cabbage, etc.

Press down each layer so the vegetables will be saturated in their own juice. When the container is full, cover it with the cabbage leaves, a plate, a heavy stone or weight, and a dishcloth, and continue as above.

If you want to make another batch right away, some connoisseurs recommend starting your next batch of raw cultured vegetables in the same empty pot or crock without washing it out each time.

You will improve your technique with each batch you make.

CHAPTER 15
Cravings: How to Stay on the Diet

Like most people, you're accustomed to eating mostly what you want, when you want. Deciding to start the Body Ecology Diet requires many changes in your eating habits and even your lifestyle (you have to shop for new foods, probably at different stores, and cook them in new ways). It's very natural to start craving foods you have eliminated, and it's likely that the main craving you will have will be for a sweet taste: ANYTHING that has sugar or tastes sweet.

Sweet Dreams

Our desire for a sweet taste starts when we're born and relates to the expansion/contraction principle. Breast milk tastes sweet and helps babies—who are contracted little beings—grow and expand. The first foods babies eat are often sweet vegetables, such as winter squash, carrots, and sweet potatoes. Sweet foods are expanding. As other foods are introduced, especially the many processed foods we eat today, sugar in one form or another becomes part of most meals. By the time we're adults, we view our "need" for sweets as normal.

We grow to like and expect that sweet taste, and when we eliminate it, we start craving it. Breads, dairy, and fruit all have natural sugars that attract our sweet tastes. When the Body Ecology Diet eliminates these all at once, no wonder we crave something sweet.

Women have a particularly difficult time with sugar cravings just before their monthly period. The hormone progesterone increases, causing an increase of sugar in the blood. The yeast feed off this increased sugar, multiply and demand more food... sugar. PMS symptoms (irritability, depression, puffiness) and vaginal itching flare up. Furthermore, since most women unknowingly allow their bodies to become too contracted just before this monthly cleansing, they desperately crave sugars and other expansive foods as their bodies attempt to "open" or relax enough to shed the lining of the uterus.

How to Satisfy That Sweet Tooth

The first three days on the Diet are the most difficult. There are several good solutions to help you squelch that sweet craving.

First, try the herb stevia in a cup of tea. Stevia does taste sweet, but it does not feed your yeast overgrowth. Research shows that it balances the body's blood sugar. You can adjust the amount of stevia according to your taste. See our recipes for more ways to use this valuable herb. Artificial sweeteners are not on the diet. They suppress the immune system.

Other ways to combat your sweet tooth are sprinkling apple cider vinegar on your vegetables, drinking it in water, and eating lots of cultured vegetables. Besides providing an abundance of friendly bacteria, these enzyme-rich foods are a high-quality, alkaline, expansive food, which balances out the more contracting animal proteins and salty foods that make us crave acid-forming sugars.

The Diet uses the sweet-tasting vegetables liberally: onions, carrots, butternut and acorn squash.

Fruits are ideal foods to help open and relax a woman's body just before her monthly cleansing, but are limited until she restores her body ecology. Do drink more water with freshly squeezed lemon or lime juice (with stevia if you want).

The nutrient-rich, high protein, green algae formulas seem to have a remarkable ability to reduce and then eliminate sugar cravings. We blended **VITALITY** *SuperGreen*™ to meet this need. It is available from your health food store or call 1-800-511-2660.

In your meal planning, remember to balance expanding with contracting foods, sweet with salt. For example, when you eat contracting, salty foods, such as meat or eggs, balance them with expanding foods, such as raw vegetables and salad, using the 80/20 rule. This balance is critical. If your body becomes too contracted, you will start craving sugar and be tempted to abandon the Diet so you can have that sweet taste. DON'T DO IT! Bring your body back into balance, and then eat along the middle of the expansion/contraction continuum.

Kefir added to the Diet as a morning breakfast food curbs cravings. Cleansing the colon does too.

Binges

It takes courage and will power to stay on the Diet. One of the best ways to do this is to hold a vision of yourself without any symptoms of candidiasis, a healed body and soul. Imagine what your life will be like, free from pain, free from all the symptoms that have stopped you from doing what you want to do in life. It's a feeling that you may not have had for a long time, but it can be recaptured; you can create it for yourself. Take encouragement from this book and from the many people who have used the Diet and healed themselves.

Sometimes, however, the urge to have some "forbidden" food is just overwhelming, and people eat a little—or a lot. If that happens to you, just go back on the Diet as soon as possible. Try not to wallow in self-criticism. Just resolve not to do that again, and know that the Diet ultimately will make you feel better and more balanced, so you will not have those cravings.

Our Antidote to a Sugar Binge

We often find that when B.E.D.ers do slip off the Diet, drinking a six-ounce glass of water to which one tablespoon of apple cider vinegar has been added and/or eating one-half cup or more of the raw cultured vegetables as soon as possible reduces some of the usual negative symptoms. These alkaline-rich, cultured foods aid in digestion and convert sugars to useful lactic and acetic acid. They also supply living microorganisms that help keep the yeast under control.

Alcoholism and Bulimia

The Body Ecology Diet is especially healing for alcoholics. Their desire for sugar has led to craving the strong sugar in alcohol. Most alcoholics have some degree of candidiasis, and it has often spread to the liver. If they try to give up the alcohol without understanding how to cope with the enormously powerful cravings of billions of yeast organisms, they won't succeed. By following the Body Ecology Diet with its elimination of sugars, use of the herb stevia, raw cultured vegetables, apple cider vinegar, probiotics, and eating in a balanced way (using the expansion/contraction principle), they have a much better chance. Of course, an alcoholic still needs support on spiritual and emotional levels, too. An excellent book about this and alcoholism is general is Joan Mathews Larson's *Seven Weeks to Sobriety*, Fawcett Columbine, New York, 1993.

People with bulimia also have imbalances in their body ecology. They overeat because they are constantly feeding hordes of living organisms within their bodies, such as opportunistic bacteria, parasites and fungi. These organisms send out signals that they're famished, so bulimics keep trying to feed them—all this on top of the natural desire for sweets. If you think you are bulimic, stop feeding the fungi and parasites. On the Body Ecology Diet you can stop the cravings and gain control of your eating.

If you find yourself craving sweets, try the following before giving in to the demands of your yeast:

✔ Drink a glass of water with fresh lemon juice.

✔ Eat a leafy, green salad with B.E.D. dressing.

✔ Sprinkle apple cider vinegar on lightly steamed vegetables.

✔ Eat one-half cup raw cultured vegetables.

✔ Drink a cup of tea with the herb stevia.

Decide if the cause of your craving for sugar is:

- ✔ Your body attempting a contraction/expansion balance. (Are you eating too salty?)
- ✔ Yeast demanding to be fed.

*Lynn E. lives in North Carolina and heard about the Body Ecology Diet from her sister in Atlanta. We sent her a copy of the book. She tried the Diet for two weeks and called back to say that she couldn't resist eating something every day that fed her yeast. She wanted to get well but felt frustrated. To eliminate her cravings for sugars and bread, we encouraged her to continue the diet and put 1 Tbsp. of apple cider vinegar into a 6 oz. glass of water and drink this twice a day. We also coached her on how to make a delicious batch of raw cultured vegetables and suggested she eat a half cup with every meal. She also drank a glass of **VITALITY Super-Green**™ for breakfast and around 4:00 in the afternoon. After a month, she called back to say it had worked and that she was loving the new recipes, especially the soups.*

Trusting Your Intuition

Can you trust your intuition about what your body needs to eat? If we drank breast milk as our first food; then graduated to vegetables, fruits, and grains; properly combined our foods; and ate lots of salt-free cultured vegetables, the answer would be yes. But with a body ecology imbalance, you can never trust your intuition to tell you what your body needs. Billions of yeast and other unwelcome visitors living inside you are sending messages about what they want to eat (always a form of sugar). They do not care in the least about the needs of the body they live in.[19]

If you find yourself craving the healthy foods on the B.E.D., yes, listen to your body. For example, if you crave chicken, fish, or eggs, your body wants protein and/or has a need for more contracting and strengthening foods. The yeast are not asking, your body is.

Even if you are a natural vegetarian, at least eat some eggs. Food can be used as medicine to restore balance as needed. Once the balance is achieved, you will loose your taste for them again.

Once you've restored your body ecology, you can ask yourself before each meal, "What do I need?"

[19]To better understand the spiritual cause behind our current physical condition, we should reflect on how very much like the yeast we are. We, in a similar fashion, have been living upon the earth, not caring or realizing that it has its needs, too. Like the yeast, we have been demanding what we want...and taking it. We've become a world of weak, sensitive, vulnerable bodies, duplicating the vulnerability of our planet.

CHAPTER 16
Traveling, Eating Out, and Snacking on the Body Ecology Diet

Travel

Travel, especially on airplanes, has a contracting, acid-forming impact on the body. Many people find that when their routines are changed by being in different time zones or just being away from home, their bodies react with symptoms of contraction and acidity, such as constipation, fatigue, headaches, or stomach upsets. That's why people crave expansive foods like alcohol and sweets when they travel; their bodies are trying to get back into balance. Here's how to do it.

Eat expansive, alkaline-forming foods. Fruits would be ideal, but since they are not on the B.E.D., the next best foods are raw vegetable juices, raw vegetables, then cooked vegetables, then grains. Avoid contracting foods such as animal protein and salt.

It's important to eat lightly, too. The digestive tract slows down when we travel, so lighter foods are easier to digest. Drink lots of fluids—even more than usual. Put lemon or lime slices and a bit of stevia (if you have it) into water, preferably purified or mineral water. Drink fresh vegetable juices if you can find them (or bring some along on your trip).

For the most part, it's difficult to eat airline meals and stay on the Diet. Even the "vegetarian" meals that some airlines offer are poorly combined, poorly cooked, and made from frozen food, which has lost its "chi" or life force. You might want to bring your own food.

Better yet, encourage the airlines to start offering fresh fruit and vegetable platters and light grain dishes. They could save a lot of money and contribute to their passengers' health. Or open an airport concession where you sell freshly squeezed vegetable and fruit juices for people to take on the plane!

Restaurants

No, it's not impossible to enjoy a restaurant meal while you are on the Diet. It just takes a little planning and a lot of will power (or "won't" power, as in "I won't eat that"). Restaurants are used to requests that deviate from the menu. Many people have medical conditions or allergies that require special food, so you won't be alone in asking for what you want and what will support your health.

You can always get a delicious piece of fresh fish or grilled chicken breast with steamed veggies and a salad in any good restaurant. Order a plain salad with some lemon wedges to squeeze on top. Many people on the Body Ecology Diet carry with them a "salad dressing kit." They tuck a small travel pouch containing leak-proof plastic bottles filled with organic, unrefined oils (Essential Balance and flaxseed), apple cider vinegar and Herbamare or sea salt into their purse or briefcase. A pillbox filled with enzymes is great too. Donna also adds a bottle of Sweet N' Better liquid concentrate to her kit.

Many restaurants list vegetables as side dishes. You might order two such dishes, like steamed broccoli and green beans. A tiny vial of Herbamare seasoning in your salad kit adds flavor to any steamed vegetable. Sometimes you will find an appetizer of a platter of raw veggies and a dip; just order it without the dip and ask for lemon wedges instead.

Restaurants sometimes serve small red skin potatoes with their entrees; try ordering them separately. You could combine them with a salad and/or a vegetable side dish for a perfect Body Ecology Diet meal. Because ghee does not require refrigeration, a small jar of ghee in that kit comes in very handy if the potatoes need seasoning. Instead of the potatoes, you could have a piece of broiled fish with a salad and vegetable.

Just make up your mind before you leave your house that you won't have bread, dessert, or a poorly-combined meal when you dine out. Concentrate on enjoying the surroundings and the people you're with. If everyone at your table orders a cocktail before dinner, you order sparkling water with lemon or lime slices. Slip out that little dropper bottle of stevia concentrate (see stevia recipes to make liquid concentrate) from your salad kit, and you won't feel like you're missing a thing.

We're lucky here in Atlanta thanks to **R. Thomas Deluxe Grill** on Peachtree Road. They offer wonderful Body Ecology approved meals along with a regular menu of burgers.

Parties

Parties may be even a bit more difficult because the range of food choices is narrower. A good trick is to eat either a full or partial meal at home before the party, so you won't be tempted to eat "forbidden" foods once you're there. If you feel comfortable enough bringing your own food to eat while everyone else is eating theirs, do that. Most hosts and hostesses are very understanding and eager to make sure you have a good time; it is we who needlessly feel silly if we act differently from the rest of the people.

Snacks

Because your digestion is becoming more and more efficient and you have less of that bloated or full feeling after meals, you may feel hungry more often yet not want to eat a full meal. Here are some good, quick snacks:

- ✔ Keep a bowl of celery and carrot sticks in the refrigerator.
- ✔ Use the Body Ecology Diet Salad Dressing as a "dip" for these and other cut-up fresh veggies.
- ✔ Eat baked blue corn chips with cultured vegetables.
- ✔ Munch on popcorn and carrot sticks.
- ✔ Try raw pumpkin seeds with celery sticks.
- ✔ Keep a pot of soup in the refrigerator so you can heat up a little bit of it at a time.
- ✔ Chew on some nori, Dulse is good too, the ocean vegetable used for wrapping sushi rolls.

As time passes, you'll figure out your own best ways to stay on the Diet. You'll invent ways to eat and recipes and ideas you can pass on to others. Feel free to send them to us as well; we'd love to hear from you. (see end of book for our address)

PART FOUR

Rebuilding the Immune System

CHAPTER 17

How to Care for Your Colon

For many people, talking about the colon (large intestine), or even *reading* this chapter, may be embarrassing, and your first inclination might be to avoid the topic altogether. But colon care and cleansing are critical to healing and knowing your body and how to keep it healthy.

When we say that it's essential to have a clean colon, we mean one free of toxins, waste material, and unhealthy microorganisms that accumulate on the walls, preventing the food you eat from being properly absorbed by your body. Most people have seven to ten pounds of old fecal matter in their colons, even if they have a bowel movement every day. When this accumulation is removed by various colon cleansing procedures, the body is free to absorb the essential vitamins and minerals of the Body Ecology Diet, and healing begins.

Disease originates in the colon. When waste cannot be properly eliminated, it accumulates in the colon and then backs up into the rest of the digestive tract, then the liver and kidneys. This causes unpleasant symptoms elsewhere in the body. This can mean constipation, headaches, weight gain, skin problems, muscle and joint pain, and other more serious illnesses. Even chronic diarrhea is a symptom of improper waste elimination.

The digestive system (which includes the colon) is similar to the root system of a tree. A tree takes its nourishment and water through its root system, feeding it along the branches and out to the leaves. We take ours through the digestive tract, where the nutrients from food are carried into the blood stream, then passed along to the various organs and absorbed into the cells of our body. In either system, if there is a blockage, or if poor-quality nutrients are taken in and distributed, the entire tree—or body—is thrown out of balance, and its very life is in danger.

What the Colon Does

The diagram above compares the length of the digestive tract to the average height of a human being. With such a long distance for food to travel, you can see the potential for blockages.

The colon is not merely a long tube used for waste elimination. Its most important function is to send essential vitamins and minerals from food into the body through the colon walls. But if the walls are blocked, those nutrients never reach their destination, and toxins are absorbed into the body. Gray hair comes from improper mineral absorption. If adults had colons as pure and clean as an infant's, their hair would have rich, beautiful color!

The accumulation of waste on the walls of the colon provides the perfect breeding ground for parasites, yeast, and viruses. Many of us harbor viruses that only emerge when our immunity is low, and then we get flu or cold symptoms. The accumulation of toxins physically impairs elimination of feces and also can prevent friendly bacteria from colonizing and doing their work. It can become just like an oil spill: the environment is so polluted that even healthy animals and birds cannot survive.

Why Cleanse?

The way most of us eat these days, toxins do accumulate in our bodies, and they start in the digestive tract and colon. They build up over the years, stretching the colon out of its proper shape and position within the body. Even if you think you're in reasonably good health, if you're an adult, your digestive tract and colon undoubtedly have been abused and will profit from cleansing. If you do have a health problem, your digestive tract unquestionably is in poor condition. An initial, deliberate cleansing program, then maintenance of a clean system, are essential to healing and restoring your body ecology. If you start eating properly but don't cleanse the colon, you will slow down the healing process significantly. The two must go hand in hand.

We recognize the importance of cleaning our houses or taking our cars in for regular maintenance to prolong their effectiveness—why not take care of our bodies just as well or better? The results will be even more rewarding: a long, vital life and excellent health. The colon is the most important place to start. If you begin by cleansing the colon, the other organs then automatically begin to eliminate their waste into the colon, as our bodies were designed to do. In this manner, the toxins and waste the body has stored—sometimes for years and years—can exit naturally.

Benefits of a Healthy Colon

Reestablishing the vitality of your colon is a key part of the Body Ecology Diet. It's just as important as eating the right foods. And once you've done it, it becomes easier to stay on the Diet. As you accomplish this important goal, here are the results you can expect.

You will have much greater energy and vigor and, at the same time, an inner calm and improved mental clarity. You will enhance your ability to sleep well. You won't crave sugar anymore, because the body will be better able to absorb the sweetness in foods such as onions, carrots, and fruits.

A healthy colon greatly slows the aging process. When the body absorbs vitamins and minerals properly, the signs of age, such as gray hair and wrinkles, are slower to appear.

Finally, a properly functioning colon reduces the need for strong cleansings; you will have gentler cleansings that you don't even notice.

What Others Say About Colon Cleansing

"The road to health is the one that begins with an understanding and commitment to cleanse and detoxify the body, to restore balance, peace and harmony...."

—*Dr. Bernard Jensen, D.C., Ph.D.*

"Colon health emphasizes prevention rather than cure. It is the most important step in maintaining or regaining vital health. If the sewer system in your home is backed up, your entire home is affected. Should it be any different with your body?"

—*Norman Walker, D. Sc., health expert who died at the age of 109*

The Secret to Longevity

Cleansing is not only a basic principle of the Body Ecology Diet, it is an essential life goal. It is the secret to a long life, to looking fabulous and staying disease-free. Faithful attention to cleansing will prevent diseases that we often assume come naturally with old age. These diseases represent the accumulation of a lifetime of toxins and impurities that the body has never cleaned out.

Remember, babies are born with super-clean digestive tracts. They build a strong immune system with friendly bacteria promoted by mother's milk. When they eat properly (food combining, lots of vegetables), they do not store toxins in their digestive tracts and quickly eliminate waste matter. If we could maintain our digestive tracts and colons in the condition of a healthy year-old child, our life expectancy would be much higher than it is now, and we would be disease-free in our old age.

How Foods We Eat Move Through the Colon

Putrefaction is the process by which foods decay within the colon and generate toxins and a foul odor. Ideally, the colon should be clean enough that foods spend minimum time passing through it and do not putrefy. Much of this depends on what foods are eaten.

Foods that putrefy quickly are the same foods that spoil easily outside the body: meat, fish, eggs, dairy products. These are also the foods that form the most mucus, which in turn slows transit time. Fruits and vegetables putrefy more slowly (in your kitchen they can remain outside the refrigerator longer); they form the least amount of mucus and are the easiest to digest, passing through the body in less transit time.

Transit time is the time it takes from eating food until its residues are expelled from the body. The average transit time in Western civilization is 65 to 100 hours![20] Once the colon has been cleansed and a healthy diet is maintained, that time can be reduced to 18 to 24 hours.

The ideal, healthy stool is neither runny nor mushy; it drops from the body within seconds after sitting on the toilet; it is fully formed, but crumbles into little pieces when the toilet is flushed; and it is free from the clay-like appearance that comes from mucous-forming foods.

What Damages the Colon?

Sugar, flour products, and dairy products are among the most damaging foods to the colon. They are very mucous-forming; the mucus slowly accumulates on the walls of the colon, and even if you are eating the healthiest, most mineral or vitamin-rich foods available, the mucous barrier will prevent those nutrients from being absorbed through the colon walls and back into the body. Animal foods (meat, poultry, fish) and salt are very contracting and greatly slow transit time. That is one reason you should limit the animal flesh foods to approximately 20 percent of your plate and learn the art of using salt appropriately.

Grains, depending on your blood type, also can be mucous-forming. Blood types A and A/B have the greatest difficulty with grains. Grains are less troublesome in their whole (berry) form than when they are broken down, that is, cracked or ground into flour. Wheat is one of the most mucous-forming grains, but three of the B.E.D. grains do not form mucus— amaranth, quinoa, and millet. The fourth B.E.D. grain, buckwheat, can be mucous-forming, especially for blood types A and A/B. If buckwheat bothers you, try cooking it in combination with the other grains on the Diet and with plenty of vegetables.

Overeating also damages the colon and creates mucus. It's imperative to eat only until you're about 80 percent full to give your digestive tract a chance to function properly. Once that food is absorbed and on its way through the system, if you're hungry again, go ahead and eat more. Some people eat several small meals throughout the day and never gain weight (as long as they food combine properly[21]), because their bodies are absorbing and eliminating correctly. Overweight results from an

[20]Gray, 1986

[21]If you eat frequently throughout the day, you can assist your food combining by devoting one day only to grains and/or starchy vegetables with land and ocean vegetables; another day, combine only protein with vegetables.

accumulation of toxins the body cannot absorb for one reason or another; eliminate the toxins, and you'll lose weight naturally.

Stress and Anger—the high-impact forces in our daily lives—cause the body to become contracted and uptight; this delays or stops elimination, and constipation results.

Fatigue—not enough sleep or rest—means we don't have the energy to eliminate. The bowel movement is a cleansing, and cleansing requires energy. Some people find they can relieve constipation just by getting more sleep.

Ways To Cleanse Your Colon

Many excellent books go into more detail than we can here about methods of cleansing the colon (see the Bibliography). However, here are various therapies you might try:

Enemas

People have used enemas since ancient times to help ease elimination from the colon and aid in healing. In fact, until about 50 years ago, medical doctors frequently prescribed them as part of a normal cure for disease. Doctors would sometimes come to a patient's house to administer the enema. Now, medical professionals have little or no training in the value of enemas for helping the body eliminate toxic waste. There are two types of enemas, cleansing and retention. The cleansing enemas are not retained or held in the body; they are used to flush out the colon. Use filtered water and an enema bag...or better yet, an enema **bucket**...found at most hospital supply stores. (See page 323 of **Prescription for Nutritional Healing** by James and Phyllis Balch for more information on different types of enemas and how to do them).

Colonics

Colonic irrigation offers a pleasant and convenient way to cleanse. In addition, it bathes the entire length of the colon (over five feet), whereas an enema bathes only the lower part. When administered properly, colonics are safe, painless, and clean. They should be administered by a trained therapist with whom you establish a partnership. Find one you are comfortable with, who works at a pace that suits you, and who uses filtered water and disposable tubing and attachments.

The therapist can help you determine the condition of your colon and how often to have a colonic. In the beginning, it's a good idea to have two within a week's time to facilitate the elimination of old waste and toxins. Then, the therapist can set up however many more you might need, but you don't need to go every week forever! Once the body's inner ecology is reestablished, colonics can be used to maintain health and muscle tone periodically.

The goal of colonics is to cleanse and open the colon so it works properly and naturally. It's essential to use purified water, water without chlorine or other matter, since chlorine kills friendly bacteria. Even with the use of pure water, colonics do wash out friendly bacteria with the toxins. But a toxic colon doesn't have friendly bacteria anyway. In the early stage of cleansing, eliminating yeast, parasites, and blocks of fecal material is more important than preserving your friendly bacteria. After the colon is cleansed, you'll want to colonize your colon with friendly bacteria by taking probiotics orally, by colonic implants, and by eating raw cultured vegetables. (see new chapter on kefir, Chapter 24)

TIP: After a colonic, you may feel tired. Go home and rest, putting on warm, comfortable clothing. Pamper yourself. Take a warm bath and go to bed early. Eat light, easy-to-digest foods such as vitality broth,* steamed vegetables, and/or one of the B.E.D. pureed soups. Sip water with raw, organic apple cider vinegar or have it on a salad to restore potassium lost during the colonic. Take minerals and drink water with VITALITY SuperGreen™. Sip hot tea with stevia to help restore your blood sugar.

*Into 4 cups of water, add: 2 cups red potato peelings cut $^1/2$" thick; 2 cups celery stalks (chopped); 2 cups celery tops; 1 carrot (chopped); 1 small onion (chopped). Simmer, covered, for 30 minutes, strain liquid and drink 8 oz. every 2 to 3 hours.

Herbs

Some herbs, such as senna and cascara sagrada, act as laxatives. They are okay to use occasionally, but please don't become dependent on laxatives for elimination.

Psyllium, Soil Based Organisms and Flax Fiber

Colon cleansing products often contain psyllium or bentonite, substances that virtually pull impacted waste material off the colon walls. When using psyllium, IT'S CRUCIAL TO DRINK A LOT OF WATER. Psyllium is a bulking agent and will actually cause constipation unless you wash it through with enough liquid—certainly eight glasses a day. We prefer using Soil Based Organisms (SBO's) combined with ground flax seed meal. SBO's are a powerful way to clean putrefaction from the digestive tract helping to regulate bowel function. SBO's replenish beneficial bacteria, eliminate parasites and create a "standing army" of T-cells that significantly strengthen the immune system. Ground flax meal is anti-viral, anti-bacterial and anti-fungal. It protects your colon against cancer.

Foods That Assist Colon Cleansing

✔ Garlic is well known for its medicinal and cleansing value. It has antifungal, antimicrobial properties and can relieve gas, bloating, and water retention; it also helps digestion. You can swallow small cloves of garlic whole. Cook with it as much as possible; many of our recipes include garlic. It also comes in various supplements in which the odor has been removed.

✔ Foods high in fiber, such as grains and vegetables, also enhance cleansing. Fruits are high in fiber and water content—excellent for cleansing—but unfortunately they are not on the Diet, at least at first. If you can tolerate grapefruit, add it when your symptoms disappear. Better yet, focus on raw vegetable juices and chlorophyll-rich foods, such as leafy greens, that provide the oxygen friendly bacteria love.

✔ Eating a salad with the Body Ecology Diet Dressing each day will give you good fiber. The apple cider vinegar in the dressing is especially healing; it will help reestablish those colonies of friendly bacteria once the colon has been cleaned.

Foods on the Diet that accelerate cleansing include raw vegetable juices taken on an empty stomach, daikon, green onions, leeks, chives, turnips, spaghetti squash, and the herbs fenugreek and curry powder.

✔ Salt-free cultured vegetables (see Chapter 14) help keep the colon clean and allow friendly bacteria to grow. Remember, they must be salt-free.

✔ Flax seed tea is excellent for healing.the colon. It's especially valuable if you suffer from leaky gut or irritable bowel syndrome, a spastic colon, colitis or bloody stools. To make: Pour 12 ounces of boiling water over 1 Tbsp. flax seeds and steep for 30 minutes or longer. (Overnight is even better.) Drain and drink the liquid.

Understanding Intestinal Bacteria

In general, there are three types of bacteria in the digestive tract: pathogenic (hostile), beneficial (friendly), and neutral. Microbiologists don't have the final answers on what all the bacteria do; some colonize and some are transient, but even the transient ones can be helpful. The beneficial bacteria are easily disturbed, and especially affected by stress. The pathogens attach themselves to tissues and develop sites of infection.

It is estimated that more than 400 species of bacteria inhabit our digestive tracts, weighing up to three and one-half pounds! It could take a year or more to accomplish a complete bacteriological analysis of one tiny sample of human faeces.[22] This indicates the complexity of our inner ecosystems, and

[22]Chaitow and Trenev, *Probiotics*, 1990

shows why it is important to be aware of different factors—such as antibiotics or birth control pills—that can upset the inner balance.

The type of food we eat directly influences the type of friendly bacteria that proliferate within our systems. A diet rich in meat and fat produces different bacteria than a high complex carbohydrate/lacto-vegetarian diet. All friendly bacteria, however, produce enzymes that aid digestion. A high concentration of friendly bacteria greatly improves transit time and also may play a vital role in breaking up waste that has accumulated on the colon walls.

Given the key role of friendly bacteria in our ecosystems, it is important to continually replenish them with probiotics, cultured vegetables, and raw apple cider vinegar. You can take a minimum of 1-3 Tbsp. of probiotic powders daily until your symptoms clear up, and your inner ecosystem is well established. (Important new information is given in Part VI for reestablishing a healthy inner ecosystem.)

How Do You Know When Your Colon Is Better?

First, you'll feel better—maybe better than you have in years. You will have regular, healthy bowel movements; you won't have gas or bloating. Your breath will be fresh. If you can wake up in the morning without bad breath, without having to brush your teeth, that's a good barometer that your digestive tract is in good shape.

Parasites

Many people believe that parasites exist only in those who are exposed to unsanitary living conditions. This is not so. Parasites can attack anyone who is in a weakened state. For instance, parasites are frequently present in people who have nutritional and/or immune deficiencies. The symptoms caused by parasites can mock those of other diseases, such as flu or CRC, and parasites can even exist without causing any symptoms at all. Millions of Americans may have them in one form or another.[23]

Parasites are difficult to diagnose. If you think your candida is under control, but you still have symptoms such as gas, bloating, and allergic reactions to foods that do not feed yeast, there's a good possibility that parasites may be the culprit. A colon therapist or doctor may be able to make the diagnosis; there are also various stool tests, although many are not reliable.

[23]Luc De Schepper's *Peak Immunity* has a good discussion of possible symptoms and cures for parasites.

However, since so many people do have undetected parasites, it can't hurt to go through a program of parasite control periodically. Swallowing a whole clove of garlic is effective against parasites. Health food stores have various preparations you might want to try. ParaGONE by Renew Life Formulas is very effective and economical (800-830-4778).

Other Aspects of Colon Care

✔ Massage helps eliminate stress and relax the body, making bowel movements easier.

✔ Acupuncture can help stimulate the large intestine and balance it in its relation to other organs.

✔ Drinking enough water—eight glasses a day—is essential to proper functioning of the digestive tract and relief of constipation.

✔ Breathing deeply has a very beneficial effect on the large intestine. In Oriental medicine, the lungs and large intestine have a very strong relationship. So anything you do to strengthen the lungs also strengthens the large intestine. When you take deep breaths, you can actually feel your abdomen relax. People who smoke have weak large intestines.

✔ Exercise, of course, helps all areas of the body and especially the large intestine and lungs. The thigh muscles are on the same meridian, or energy path, as the colon, so stimulating these muscles will help tone and relax the colon.

✔ A healthy colon ensures a healthy liver. The liver eliminates its impurities into the colon, but it cannot do this unless the colon is clean and functioning properly. A diet high in refined fats and oils, overeating, and drugs all damage the liver and can cause it to "backup" with toxins; this in turn can result in problems with skin, eyes, and joints, especially the knees. So this is why many people with CRC also have skin problems: the colon is clogged, the liver is clogged, and waste tries to exit the body via the skin (see Chapter 20).

How to Maintain and Nourish a Clean Colon

There are several more actions you can take to make sure your colon is functioning at its optimal level.

Right after you wake up in the morning, begin drinking water with lemon, which in effect rehydrates your body from its overnight rest and cleansing. Your body continues to cleanse at least until mid-morning, so it's important to aid this process by drinking several glasses of water. Try to get in at least four of your daily eight glasses by midday. Adding lemon to the water gives it an antiseptic quality and helps stimulate the peristaltic action of the bowels. Morning is a good time for a bowel movement, part of the completion of the overnight cleansing process.

A daily bowel movement is desirable for adults, and there's nothing wrong with one after each meal. (Remember, babies, with their pristine digestive tracts, often move their bowels after each meal.) We've been conditioned to suppress the reflex that prompts the bowels to move each time the stomach fills up. We often wait until just the right time or place. But as part of a colon improvement program, it would be helpful to retrain your bowels. Some colon therapists recommend excusing yourself about 10 minutes after a meal and sitting on the toilet, exercising the abdominal muscles and encouraging even the slightest urge to move the bowels.

Adding chlorophyll to your water helps maintain a good acid/alkaline balance and supports the recolonizing of friendly bacteria in your body ecology; it adds oxygen. You also encourage growth of friendly bacteria by eating unsalted raw cultured vegetables, raw apple cider vinegar, and, of course, adding probiotics to your diet.

Help From Probiotics

Into a blender add one cup of water, 1 Tbsp. of probiotic powder, 1 tsp. of alcohol-free vanilla flavoring, 1 heaping tsp. of lecithin granules (opt.), and a pinch of powdered stevia herb (if available). Blend for a few seconds, and you have the Body Ecology Diet "milkshake" or "Acidophilus Milk." You can drink it first thing in the morning on an empty stomach, waiting at least one half hour before eating food. It's great for your colon. If you use a dairy-free brand, you also can use it as "milk" on top of Arrowhead Mills puffed millet cereal.

You might consider colonic implants to give you added energy and enhance the color and texture of your skin. You can implant probiotics and chlorophyll, separately or together. The best time is right after a colonic or home enema and right before bedtime.

Put at least 2 Tbsp. of probiotics and/or 2 Tbsp. of liquid chlorophyll into an enema bag or bucket, with about 4 oz. of purified water. Insert it into your colon, and when you lie down to go to sleep, the colon will be able to retain this amount of liquid.

Fasting

In Chinese medicine, food is used to heal. Eating high-quality foods is the best path to cleansing and healing; people with immune-compromised conditions are usually too weak to fast. But as you get stronger and healthier and want to cleanse very deliberately, you might try a modified fast, maybe one day a week or twice a month. Fasting gives the digestive tract a chance to rest.

Later in your healing, you can modify your pattern again, such as by drinking water and lemon juice throughout the day, and eating only a light vegetable meal in the afternoon. Once you are able to tolerate grapefruit, you can use it like lemons and lemon juice. A day when you drink only warm vegetable broth (called "pot liquor" in the South) makes an ideal modified fast.

In chapter 24 you will learn about kefir. You can fast on kefir diluted with water. The Russians and Turks do this all the time and it is a famous cure in Russian health sanitariums. Even in ancient ayurvedic texts you will find this kefir/water mixture mentioned. They call it "curd water".

TIP: Fast only on days when you also can rest, such as the weekend, to give your body the full advantage of the cleansing process.

Pacing Your Cleansing

Toxins sometimes leave the body faster than the body can eliminate them through its usual systems, and this is when a cleansing reaction occurs. We've already mentioned this Herxheimer reaction, when you may have symptoms such as a flu-like soreness, skin eruptions, dizziness, itching, emotional upheaval, sleep disorders, or intensification of a pre-existing symptom. You do have some control over how smoothly and comfortably you cleanse. If you begin the Diet and combine it with a series of colonics or home enemas, you will avoid a build-up of too many toxins...more than your body can handle at one time.

Final reminders for maintaining a healthy colon: stay on the Body Ecology Diet, adding suitable foods as you can tolerate them; remember to food combine; and exercise as appropriate for your blood type. Remember to take the cleansing process step by step so you won't become discouraged.

The Deer Exercise

The deer exercise comes from the physical, mental, and spiritual teachings of Taoism, an ancient religion and way of life. It is so named because the deer continually stimulates its sexual glands by constantly contracting and relaxing its anal muscles and moving its tail from side to side. The inner energy this creates travels to the antlers, which are valued in Chinese medicine for their great healing powers.

In people, the exercise builds sexual desire, which is often weak in those with candidiasis. It has more important physical benefits, however.

Main Benefits

It tones the anal muscles and colon, aiding peristaltic action and reducing transit time. It prevents colitis. As we age, the muscles of the colon and the bladder tend to become loose and flaccid, and that is why many older people have a difficult time controlling these functions. Deterioration of the rectal and anal muscles also can hasten the onset of hemorrhoids and cancer; exercising them reverses this process.

In men, the deer exercise also strengthens the prostate and helps prevent disease, weakness, enlargement or dysfunction of the prostate. In women, it stimulates the vaginal muscles, helping prevent and cure such problems as menstrual disorders, infections, and vaginitis.

How to Do It

The following description of the deer exercise comes from *The Book of Internal Exercises* by Stephen T. Chang with Richard C. Miller (Strawberry Hill Press, San Francisco, CA, 1978).

Do the exercise in the morning and evening. Sit in a comfortable position. Tighten the muscles around your anal opening as hard as you can, and hold this as long as you are comfortably able. (Women should tighten the vaginal muscles as well.) When done properly, this feels as if air is being drawn up into the rectum.

Don't force the process, but perform the exercise until you are tired. Stop, then repeat it when you are rested. At first, you may be able to hold the sphincter muscles tight only for several seconds. After a few weeks, if you persist, you will be able to hold them much longer without feeling tired or strained. If you do the exercise properly, you'll be aware of a pleasant feeling traveling from the base of the anus, through the spinal column, to the top of the head.

CHAPTER 18
Special Information: Women, Men, Children

Each of us is unique; each of us has different needs and diverse paths to healing. However, we can generalize about different groups of people, based on our observations, and learn what will keep them healthy.

The Nature of Woman

According to the ancient principle of yin/yang (contraction/expansion), the essential nature of woman is yin and contractive. Water is often used as a symbol describing the true essence of woman. Water is fluid, flexible, yielding to resistance; yet it is persistent in getting to where it must go. It seeks a downward path representing humbleness (not submissiveness). When it is calm, it can be gentle and still, but it also has the power to become fierce, angry, and destructive. Indispensable to all, water's positive, accepting energy nurtures and brings forth life.

In contrast, man's nature is more like the energy of fire. Traditionally, man's role in society and the family has been more outward, expanding, forceful...arousing and inspiring...more fervent...conquering and intense.

It is well recognized that man has some female nature and woman has some male energy, but the essential natures of man and woman remain quite different. Both energies are necessary for creation, and a positive balance of the two allows many harmonious arrangements to take place.

Philosophers can have a wonderful time reflecting upon this yin/yang phenomenon, but for our purposes we want to understand how woman's nature influences her needs for certain foods. What foods will give her the energy she needs to carry out her important role in her family and in society?

What Foods Are Best?

Foods that maintain the soft, fluid, accepting, yet powerful nature of a woman are *grains*, *vegetables*, and *fruit*. Salt and foods containing salt (including animal foods) cause contraction. Too much contraction hardens a woman's body, creating too much fire energy. Dairy products often have hormones that interfere with the delicate balance of a woman's own hormonal system. Sugar depletes a woman's body of essential minerals, those same minerals that determine her beauty and strength throughout her life and that during pregnancy create new life.

Because of her receptive, intuitive qualities and her mission to bear new life, a woman's body tends to gather and store energy. As a protection for her and for her baby, nature gave her a body that processes food more efficiently and stores it away for future use. A woman, then, needs less food than a man, and when she eats too much, it is stored as fat. Even if a woman has Type O blood and thrives on some animal protein, she will not need as much as a Type O man.

Sexual Organs Affected by Foods

A woman's sexual organ system is very delicate and can be damaged by excessive sugar, salt, and dairy foods. Dairy products not only contain hormones that interfere with the female hormones, but are so mucous-forming (especially in the body of a woman with Type A blood) that they are linked to serious disorders such as infertility from blocked Fallopian tubes, endometriosis, menstrual cramps, heavy menstrual flow, tender breasts, ovarian tumors and cysts, and vaginal infections.

Sugar weakens and upsets a woman's delicate endocrine balance much more than it does a man's. Especially around the time of her monthly period, too much salt can cause her body to become too contracted, which inhibits the shedding of the uterine lining.

Women and Candida

Dr. William Crook lists several reasons women develop yeast-connected health problems more than men or children:

- ✔ Hormonal changes connected with the normal menstrual cycle, as well as hormonal changes during pregnancy and adolescence, encourage yeast overgrowth.
- ✔ Birth control pills can lead to candidiasis.
- ✔ Teenage girls, very concerned about their complexions, often start long-term acne treatment with antibiotics—and this promotes yeast overgrowth.
- ✔ The anatomy of the vagina provides an ideal place for candida colonization.
- ✔ The anatomy of the urethra leads women to experience more urinary tract problems than men; antibiotics are often prescribed for this.

Caring for the Birth Canal (Vagina)

The birth canal is much more than an occasional passageway for birth; it continually functions as an avenue for cleansing. A channel to the outside, it permits unnecessary waste and damaging toxins to leave a woman's body. Constantly sloughing off toxins, it allows her body to stay cleaner and healthier...a protection or the children she might bear and a reason women outlive men. Women have more opportunities to cleanse.

A woman's emotional state is very much linked to the health of her sexual organ system and to the condition of her birth canal: if the birth canal is irritated, diseased, or the pH out of balance, the woman will feel out of sorts. Once these conditions are corrected, she'll feel better.

Yeast infections can be localized in the birth canal, but today many women have developed *systemic* candidiasis: it occurs throughout the entire body. Since the body is designed to constantly rid itself of dangerous parasites, it will eliminate those yeast organisms (especially those colonized around the sexual organs) through the vagina. This creates much confusion for a woman. When she eats foods that feed the yeast, they will reproduce and cause damage to her system. Once she is on the Body Ecology Diet, they begin dying, millions of them leaving her body through her birth canal. Therefore, even though she is conquering her yeast problem, she could see signs of vaginal discharge for a very long time. It is important, then, for a woman to know how to care for this area until her body finishes cleansing itself of the yeast.

The environment of the vagina should be acidic, and friendly bacteria only grow well in an acidic world. An alkaline condition encourages unfriendly bacteria to take hold, so it's important to maintain a clean, acidic vagina. (Male sperm is alkaline.)

DOUCHE WITH APPLE CIDER VINEGAR to achieve an acidic condition. Traditional doctors might advise douching only once a month, after menstruation; this is fine once you are completely well. For now, it's perfectly safe to douche with apple cider vinegar once, twice, or more a week, depending on your condition and especially after making love. Make sure it's raw, organic apple cider vinegar.

DOUCHE RECIPE: 1/4 cup raw, organic apple cider vinegar in 1 quart of distilled or purified water.

Following this cleansing, you can implant friendly bacteria into the birth canal by dissolving a probiotic powder (Lactobacillus bifidus) in a small amount of distilled water (2-4 oz.), then inserting it using the equivalent of a turkey baster—a small bulb or sack you can put the liquid in, with a way to squirt it into the vagina. (A travel douche bag works well, too.) This method works better than suppositories, because the liquid penetrates into the folds and crevices of the vaginal cavity, where the actual colonization takes place. The optimal time to do this is before bed, when you have the best chance of retaining that liquid. Remember, the goal is to have the friendly bacteria colonize in the vagina and grow on their own.

You also can add chlorophyll to the probiotic solution; chlorophyll provides oxygen for the friendly bacteria.

Tea tree oil is another excellent, gentle douche that is anti-fungal and antibacterial and leaves a fresh, clean feeling in the vagina. This essential oil comes from a tree that grows in Australia. It is available in health food stores. Tea tree oil also comes in suppositories, but these are more expensive. You can obtain similar results by saturating a tampon with the oil and inserting it at bedtime.

> The symptom that finally led Linda to realize she had a condition of candidiasis was an almost constant vaginal itching, irritation, and discharge. No matter what medicine she used, the itching would return; it was unbearable.
>
> Besides changing her diet, she started douching and found tea tree oil especially helpful during the week before her menstrual period, using it sometimes three to four nights in a row. The oil totally relieved the itching.

DOUCHE RECIPE: One teaspoon tea tree oil in 500 ml. (2 cups) distilled or purified water.

Making Love

A man's semen is alkaline, so after intercourse it is important to restore the acidic condition of the vagina. In addition, candida can be passed back and forth during sex, so the woman can protect herself by douching, then implanting with friendly bacteria. If you do this regularly, besides taking other steps to heal yourself, it will work—you will have success.

Candida and Sex Drive

A woman's sex drive can easily wane if she has an overgrowth of candida. In a sort of vicious cycle, she doesn't feel well, she becomes hard to live with, she has physical symptoms that are not conducive to love-making—and then her relationship can be affected. But it's very important to use the physical connection of intercourse as a way of keeping a relationship healthy.

In ancient times, Oriental healers viewed love-making as an art form and believed it had the power to restore well-being. Since woman's nature is to receive and accumulate energy, making love and releasing this stored energy through orgasm rebalances a woman and helps her feel much happier: more relaxed, accepting, intuitive, giving, and nurturing. The energy of intercourse used in a pure and honorable way can be a spiritual, emotional, and physical aid to healing.

It's a wonder that Wendy K.'s marriage held together at all. It started out like a fairy tale: she fell in love in college, married her sweetheart Eric when they graduated, and two years later stopped taking birth control pills so they could have their first child. But it was not an easy pregnancy, and she didn't feel much like having sex even during the early months. After the baby was born, she went back on birth control pills. But the demands of motherhood and career kept her hopping, and she was often too busy or tired to relax and enjoy sex with Eric.

When their son was three years old, the burden eased. They started to enjoy each other again and decided to have another baby. It was another difficult pregnancy, with frequent indigestion, vaginitis, headaches, fatigue, and irritability. Their daughter was born two months premature, creating a strain on Wendy and Eric's nerves and finances.

With two young children in the house, Eric working long hours to advance his career, and Wendy trying to work part-time, they hardly had a moment to themselves. Wendy had frequent vaginal itching and discharges, rectal itching, headaches, and muscle pains. She was a good mother but didn't take very good care of herself, always eating on the run and never allocating time to an exercise program for herself. She was tired and had`absolutely no interest in sex.

At first Eric was very understanding, but after awhile he started losing patience and wanted to know what happened to that loving, alluring college sweetheart he married. Wendy and Eric started fighting more and more.

Finally, they went to a counselor, who gave them some advice that helped add balance to their marriage. This counselor also happened to know about CRC and the Body Ecology Diet and recommended that both Wendy and Eric try the Diet. They did, and Wendy immediately began to feel better and have more energy. Her vaginitis cleared up and her nerves calmed down. She and Eric were able to spend more quality time together and put joy and sex back into their marriage.

Pregnancy

During pregnancy, a woman's hormonal balance changes dramatically. If her body ecology is weak and she lacks adequate friendly bacteria, this leads to a condition of yeast overgrowth.

More and more babies are being delivered by Caesarean section, and their mothers are given antibiotics to prevent infection. These antibiotics kill any friendly bacteria a mother may have in her system, and they can be passed on to the baby in breast milk, causing trouble for the baby's immature ecosystem. Babies can easily develop infections when they have no internal body ecology and only fragile immune systems to protect them from unfriendly bacteria and viruses.

Throughout pregnancy, and especially if a mother-to-be must take antibiotics, the Body Ecology Diet is critical. Its total exclusion of foods that feed the yeast and its large amounts of cultured vegetables and probiotics (especially bifidus infantis) will help her immensely. Still, she should not be discouraged if her yeast condition does not subside. The high amount of progesterone in her blood increases the amount of sugar, and the yeast will thrive even though she is not feeding them.

The good news is that childbirth is one of the best times to conquer this condition permanently—if you follow the Diet strictly and eliminate all forms of sugars. The act of giving birth is part of the wondrous arrangement of cleansing. The afterbirth and bloody materials that are sloughed off immediately after the baby is born, and the bloody discharge that follows for several weeks, provide a vehicle for yeast and toxins to leave the body.

The sudden hormonal changes that take place and the presence of healing agents that are designed to repair any damage from the birth give the new mother an opportunity to become even stronger than she was before her pregnancy. If she takes large amounts of the right probiotics, eats very, very well for four to six weeks after the baby is born, and rests to the point of doing nothing except caring for the precious new life given to her, a woman can emerge from the demanding process of pregnancy with an almost new body. (Please read the new section on kefir. It contains important information for pregnant and nursing mothers.)

A Word of Caution

It's especially important for a pregnant woman to maintain a healthy vagina so that candida will not transfer to the baby as it passes through the birth canal. Check with your doctor first, but we have found that douching with probiotics, apple cider vinegar, and tea tree oil is fine during pregnancy. Discontinue just before you think your cervix will start to dilate.

About the Colon

Even before a woman becomes pregnant, she should work to create a clean, properly functioning colon. The high levels of progesterone in a pregnant woman drastically slow transit time of food and waste as it passes through the digestive tract; that's why pregnant women so often are constipated. The slower transit allows more time for the mother and the baby to absorb nutrients from the food, but if there is excess waste material built up in the colon, that absorption will be impeded. In fact, toxins will be absorbed, not vitamins and minerals. (See Chapter 17 to learn how to improve the health of your digestive system.)

Monthly Cycle

Remember, menstruation is a cleansing, and women should consider it a wonderful opportunity to eliminate toxins and become even healthier. Let's review the steps that make it easy to appreciate this monthly miracle.

✔ After you ovulate, reduce the amount of salt you take in, so the body will not retain fluids and will easily let go of the uterine lining.
✔ Maintain this through the end of your period. Then, you can slightly increase your salt intake, perhaps by having more contracting foods than you otherwise might (although still balancing them with expanding foods).
✔ Get plenty of rest during your period. Plan quiet activities. Cleansing takes energy.
✔ Eat well. Do not overeat, and do not stray from the Diet or binge on foods with sugar, which could cause havoc in your system.
✔ All-alkaline meals are great when your period begins.

Once a woman knows she has a candida overgrowth and knows what to do about it, she can get well, with her own determination and help from the Body Ecology Diet.

Men and Candida

The damp, moldy, fungus-like nature of yeast dampens the fire nature of man. Candidiasis, while it is not as common as among women, is weakening many men in America today and has become a serious threat to the well-being of the family unit and to society.

Men are traditionally less likely to go to the doctor if they don't feel well and, therefore, are less likely to have taken antibiotics. They also don't have the contributing factors of monthly hormonal changes, birth control pills, and multiple pregnancies. Nevertheless, candidiasis does strike men and is always present in people with AIDS.

For the most part, candida affects different organs in a man than in a woman. In women, the yeast overgrowth often first manifests in the hormonal system, sexual organs, and the digestive tract, surfacing as vaginitis, PMS, constipation, gas, bloating, acne, fatigue. In men, the yeast usually colonize first in the digestive tract and cause digestive disorders. As the condition worsens, they then go systemically to the heart, liver, and kidneys, creating many of the symptoms listed below. (These organs are hearty organs where disorder can fester for years before suddenly manifesting as a heart attack or kidney malfunction, for example.)

While yeast prefer moist, dark environments such as the birth canal, they can live on the skin, and that includes the foreskin of a man's penis and on his scrotum. If a man and woman show signs of having weak immune systems (chronic fatigue, AIDS, cancer), and symptoms of candidiasis persist, they are most likely passing the candida back and forth. It will be essential, then, for both to follow the Body Ecology Diet to improve their health.

Dr. Crook lists several common symptoms men have that suggest candidiasis:

- ✔ Food, chemical, and inhalant allergies.
- ✔ Persistent jock itch, athlete's foot, or other fungal infections.
- ✔ Impaired sex drive.
- ✔ Wife or children with candidiasis.
- ✔ Recurrent digestive complaints, including constipation, bloating, or abdominal pain.
- ✔ Craving for alcohol, sweets, or breads.

The Body Ecology Diet works just as well for men as for women.

Children

Born as contracted, perfect little beings, children need to be nourished so they will develop strong immune systems and establish a healthy lifestyle. Breast milk gives babies their best chance at developing strong immunity, as the mother passes along friendly bacteria (especially Bifidus) to her newborn. However, many mothers, due to their compromised immunity, are deficient in proper intestinal flora, leaving their children prey to yeast overgrowth. This soon sets up a vicious cycle of recurring colds, sore throats, ear infections, and digestive problems like gas, constipation, and diarrhea. For the sore throats and ear infections the baby is given more antibiotics.

Right now, a whole new generation of teens and twenty-year-olds have serious undiagnosed yeast infections from repeated courses of antibiotics since birth. Their immune systems and endocrine glands are so endangered and weak that millions of them suffer from fatigue, depression, irritability, mood swings, allergies, acne, and digestive problems; and they have strong, uncontrollable cravings for sugars.

What Can Be Done to Help?

It is vitally important that our children receive the help they need through diet, education, and emotional support in order to kill off the yeast living within them. They must establish (perhaps for the first time) a new inner ecological world where friendly bacteria thrive. How will they do this?

First, we must stop using antibiotics so carelessly and be extremely mindful of their serious side effects.

Second, when babies are born, they need help establishing a strong body ecology within their digestive tracts. This means help from healthy mothers who have lots of friendly bacteria to pass on to their infants. Pregnant women would do well to be on the Body Ecology Diet, eat lots of cultured vegetables, and take probiotics.

Remember, inside the mother's womb, a baby's digestive tract is sterile. No body ecology has developed. If the baby receives that first bacteria (bifidus infantis) from a mother who has an abundant supply of her own, in a few months the baby will have a mature ecological system too. Nursing mothers of colicky babies have gotten relief from many sleepless nights just by eating raw cultured vegetables and taking large amounts of probiotics. All babies (especially necessary for bottle-fed babies) can be fed tiny spoonfuls of the juice of cultured vegetables. Probiotics, such as Bifidus infantis and, later, Bifidus adolescentis and L. Acidophilus, can be given to babies and toddlers by bottle. (See special new section on kefir, Chapter 24 - in Russia babies are given kefir at the age of four months to insure healthy immune and inner ecosytems.)

Once babies' digestive tracts are flourishing, their teeth have come in, and they can handle foods other than milk, they should be introduced first to vegetables (which are very easy to digest) and later to grains.

Following the food combining rules is very important. Fruit should be eaten on an empty stomach; grains and vegetables can be eaten together. Eggs and meats can be introduced much later and, of course, combined with non-starchy vegetables.

Babies often prefer the sweet vegetables (carrots, squash, sweet potatoes) for their first foods. These help satisfy the sweet craving that all humans have, and encourage growth, since they are expanding foods. We have found that B.E.D. babies even like ocean vegetables (puréed), especially arame cooked with lots of sweet onions and carrots.

Babies love the juice or liquid found in salt-free cultured vegetables. Since breast milk is quite sweet, they will make funny faces when first introduced to these sour new foods. But you'll soon see how quickly they develop a taste for them and eat them eagerly. A child who is fed in this manner never has digestive problems and usually has two to three pleasant-smelling, well-formed, easily-passed stools each day.

Children of all ages can take probiotics; see our recipe for "Acidophilus Milk" using probiotic powder, alcohol-free vanilla, lecithin (for creaminess), and the herb stevia as a sweetener.

> *Because of Donna's concern for children, Body Ecology recently developed Eco-Renew™, a delicious chewable probiotic for children. It has stevia, FOS and billions of DDS-1 bacteria. In our taste test all children loved it (Adults too!). We recommend you give them a few tablets each day instead of a sugary treat. You can find it in your local health food store or call: 1-800-511-2660.*

Teens heal very quickly on the Body Ecology Diet. Most symptoms clear up in a few weeks, and they have rapid improvement in energy, digestion, moodiness, skin, and weight problems.

Although it's difficult, but not impossible, to get teenagers to food combine, they quickly notice an improvement in their digestion. They are also usually thrilled with the loss of weight. Their biggest hurdle to overcome is those first several days without sugar. Beverages made with fresh-squeezed lemon juice, stevia, and sparkling mineral water are a good substitute for colas. Our "Ginger Ale" recipe is a teen favorite.

Today's young adults were born into a world of fast foods; for them it's a way of life. We need to develop fast foods that are healthy foods. Teens also need better choices at school, restaurants, movie theaters, and any other place where they gather to eat out.

Teenagers have always been sensitive about their appearance, and now they're very interested in eating better and looking better. Food education is important; they are ready for it. Perhaps it is time to reactivate those old home economics labs in our high schools.

If we don't teach our children how to take care of their bodies, they won't be needing educating for their minds.

Women: Caveat Emptor

Pharmaceutical companies, aware of the enormous profit in drugs to treat vaginal yeast problems, have begun selling over-the-counter drugs that were previously available only through a gynecologist. Competing with each other for this huge market, the companies expect to reach at least 75 percent of American women.

Yeast infections, these companies would have us believe, are caused by pregnancy, antibiotics, and tight clothing. Television commercials suggest that this problem is unavoidable and "just happens." Nothing could be further from the truth. There is no mystery at all. Pregnancy never *causes* this problem, and tight clothes only make a candida sufferer more uncomfortable. It is the drug companies, the American Medical Association, and the F.D.A. that are largely to blame. By developing stronger and stronger antibiotics without researching their long-term effects, these companies feed upon our fears, our desire to avoid suffering, and our lack of understanding about cleansings.

Even though drug companies promise you a cure, drugs will not correct candidiasis. Using them is dangerous and a waste of time and money. What you are learning in this book is a solution. You must starve the yeast until they die down to a level where they no longer can present a problem, AND you must reestablish a balanced ecology within you. The right foods, the use of probiotics, and cultured foods (apple cider vinegar, kefir, and cultured vegetables) will do it.

Candidiasis in the colon is relatively easy to cure when it first begins. We can use colonics and enemas to flush it out; and we can eat cultured foods and probiotics to reestablish a new inner ecosystem. But once it leaves the colon and becomes systemic, it becomes a serious problem. There is no way to get into the body and scrub away yeast that has begun massing around your heart, lungs, sinuses, brain, liver, sexual organs and nervous system. It is the job of the immune system to conquer the spreading infection. Our immune system knows how to do this but it must have the strength. That's why it's critical to restore and rebuild the immune system with nourishing foods, and eliminate any toxins that may be weakening it. In addition, women must nourish their adrenals and balance their hormones.

CHAPTER 19
How to Strengthen Your Immunity

Since your weakened immune system allowed your candida to overpopulate in the first place, it is essential to strengthen your system in order to restore a healthy balance. There are many ways to do this; *all* are important to regaining your health.

✔ **Welcome the cleansings your body will go through.** As you begin the Body Ecology Diet, the first three weeks (and probably the first few days) will be the most difficult. As the toxins start leaving your body because you are no longer feeding the yeast, they create symptoms that mock candidiasis itself. You may feel fuzzy-headed, weak, and flu-like. It is vital to cleanse your colon and stay with the Diet during this period, and you *will* emerge stronger and healthier.

Our bodies were designed to cleanse *throughout* our lives—each cleansing signifies the underlying health and vitality that we cherish. Some cleansings last a day or two; some require up to three weeks. Just remember to rely on the basic Body Ecology Diet and the techniques and products we recommend, and you will feel better when the cleansing concludes.

✔ **Eat appropriately for your improving condition.** As you start feeling better and better, you'll be very excited, and you'll be tempted to return to some of those "old" ways of eating—sugar, poor food combining, too many contracting foods. Or you may want to reintroduce a food, such as fruit or sweet potatoes, before you're really ready. Resist those temptations! You should be symptom-free for at least three months before you try to reintroduce foods that are not on the basic Body Ecology Diet. (See Chapter 21 on introducing new foods.) Just enjoy the health that the Diet brings, experiment with new recipes, and establish this new foundation of healthy eating that will last a lifetime.

✔ **Control the yeast.** Be sure to avoid feeding the yeast in your system. Follow the Body Ecology Diet. Clean your colon and then recolonize the friendly bacteria in your digestive tract by using probiotics. While many labels on the bottle recommend one to two capsules a day that is never enough for a therapeutic dose. Buy the powered probiotics and take at least 1-2 table-spoons a day. Bulgaricus is excellent and can be taken with your meals. L. acidophilus and any or all of the strains of bifidus can be taken together...but always on an empty stomach first thing in the morning. You may also find L. salivarius or laterosporus strains are good to implant at a later date. (See Chapter 24 on kefir for important new information)

Continue implanting beneficial bacteria for at least three months especially after antibiotic therapy. Many microbiologists recommend cultured foods be eaten throughout your life. Friendly bacteria will enter on **organic** fruits and vegetables and in cultured foods such as cultured veggies, raw apple cider vinegar, kefir and yogurt.

✔ **EXERCISE!** We know—you've heard hundreds of times how important exercise is...maybe you've made a New Year's resolution every year to start an exercise program...and maybe you've even started it, but dropped out days or weeks later. The truth is, exercise is as important to improving your health as the food you eat. You may already be exercising enough—if so, that's great. The information we present below may help you anyway.

Recall from Dr. D'Adamo's blood types theory that Type Os are very physical beings, and they *must* exercise—they won't get well without it. (He says 70% of us have Type O blood.) Only through exercise can Type Os release their stress and tension; movement stimulates their minds. If a Type O student needs to write an exam, an hour of hard physical exercise beforehand will help him/her perform better. When a Type O is upset or angry, exercise will help clear his/her mind. Type Os need stimulating, hard exercise, such as running, squash, cross-country skiing.

Types A and A/B require less vigorous, calmer exercise. Whereas a Type O might swim 100 lengths of a pool, a Type A only needs to swim 10. Other exercises for Type As are yoga, walking, T'ai Chi. This type of exercise sharpens the Type A's mind, whereas too much or too hard exercising would exhaust the Type A and create mental fogginess.

Type Bs, as you know, are in between. They can balance a day of brisk exercise with a day of calming or mild exercise. Type Bs have wide latitude in establishing their exercise program.

✔ **Exercising on a mini-trampoline** (rebounder) is particularly stimulating to the immune system. It is an ideal form of exercise for all blood types because it requires so little energy but quickly rebuilds the immune system. It stimulates the T-cells, which help the body fight foreign invaders. You don't have to do a full aerobic workout on a mini-trampoline. Five minutes once or twice a day will suffice, and it's all right to do a low-impact workout. If you are not able to jump up fully, even raising your heels and keeping your toes on the surface will help. Exercise adds oxygen, a vital partner, to your system. Oxygen helps kill unfriendly bacteria and stimulates you physically and mentally.

There is a big difference in the quality of mini-tramps or rebounders. You'll want the highest quality you can afford…one with a tightly woven mat and strong, durable springs. If you cannot find one in your area, call **FIT FOR YOU** (1-800-521-JUMP).

A final reminder: do not exercise when you're in the middle of a cleansing. It's more important to give your body time to rest. Cleansing takes strength, so save your strength during this period, and resume your exercise program when the cleansing ends.

In conclusion, JUST DO IT. Just decide that exercise is vital to your health, and commit yourself to a new life pattern that incorporates exercise. If you can, find a buddy to exercise with—that makes it more fun and gives you a better chance of sticking with your program. If you are already exercising regularly, congratulations. Keep up the good work.

✔ Manage the stress in your life. There are many ways to do this—many books, courses, people with advice. But the first step is to acknowledge that the stress does need to be managed, to acknowledge that you do need help. If you've been trying to handle it all yourself, try looking outside yourself for the solution. You don't need to carry the world's burdens on your shoulders! Find a way to restructure your life spiritually and mentally that will aid your physical healing.

✔ Teas you can drink that are especially helpful in rebuilding the immune system include mathake, echinacea, dandelion root, and many others (see Shopping List on page 253). All of these add strength to your immunity.

CHAPTER 20

Healing at a Deeper Level: The Liver

Once your colon is clean and functioning well, the yeast have died back to a level where they no longer overwhelm your immune system, and your inner ecology is restored, many of your symptoms will be gone and you will look and feel much better. Now it's time for the next level of healing: restoring and even upgrading the immune system to a point where it's healthier than ever. This means turning your attention to your liver.

We often ignore this important organ, but it plays a vital role in your well-being. You can never achieve true health without a healthy liver. In our chapter on the colon, we said "disease begins in the colon." While this is true, it is also true that wherever disease and disorder exist, you will also find an unhealthy liver.

Know Your Liver

Weighing three to four pounds, the liver is the largest interior organ. It is a humble, hard-working gland. It never "cries out in pain" unless the gallbladder is inflamed. But it does accumulate toxins, often before we are even born.

The liver is not just a large filter, but also a biliary organ and an endocrine gland. It plays a key role in digestion, in the formation of blood, and in defending our bodies against infection. As soon as the body absorbs any substance, the liver intercepts it. The liver then accepts and neutralizes this substance, transforms it, or rejects it. In fact, if the liver did not alter the nutritive substances we eat, they would all be poisonous to us, even the nutrients from "healthy foods."

During digestion, the liver secretes bile to help assimilate fats. The bile lubricates your intestinal walls, regulates the level of your friendly bacteria, destroys unwanted and dangerous organisms as they invade your body, stimulates the peristaltic activity that forces your fecal material to move through and out of your body. Bile, along with digestive fluid from the pancreas, acts upon fats, proteins, and starches, transforming them into useful substances. There is no question that the liver governs digestive functions and must be healed before your digestion, your immune system, and your overall well-being reach an ideal level.

The liver filters and transforms albumin, sugars, and vitamins into useable substances. It transforms carbohydrates into fat (if they are not used immediately) and stores it. Our livers portion out cholesterol according to need and neutralize its excess.

And if all this doesn't make the liver busy enough, it also maintains the fluidity of your blood by regulating its coagulation ability and thus preventing hemophilia and phlebitis. It destroys old red blood cells and helps make new ones, and helps the immune system by providing the proteins necessary to make white blood cells. It regulates body temperature.

Signs of an Impaired Liver

Even though your liver is in distress, you won't be able to say, "Oh, I have a pain in my liver." This silent, hard-working organ never aches. Nevertheless, Chinese medicine says that the liver "cries" when it is in trouble. One outward sign of this is on the face between your eyebrows; you may have one or several deep lines and/or a swollen puffiness. A person with a weak, congested liver barely tolerates the cold in winter and may suffer chills, usually following a meal. If you have an overactive liver,[24] you may often feel feverish and find the summer months very uncomfortable.

If you have begun to clean your colon but still do not have a well-formed and complete evacuation of your stools each day, you must now focus your attention on your liver.

A weak, insufficient, or overactive liver pulls energy away from the spleen, pancreas, and stomach—organs that play a key role in digestion. The intestines, too, are almost totally dependent upon the liver and the bile it produces.

Other symptoms of a weak, congested liver include:
- ✔ Anemia
- ✔ Hemorrhoids
- ✔ Dark, insufficient urine
- ✔ Small red flecks the size of a pinhead that come and go at different places on the body
- ✔ Skin diseases such as eczema, acne, hives, itching, rashes: the skin seems dirty, with dark pigmentation or spots on the face, on the backs of the hands, on the forehead, or around the nose
- ✔ Jaundice (yellow skin)

[24]A congested liver can also at times become overactive, as it works very hard to compensate for the congestion; then it becomes even more exhausted.

✔ Eye problems (loss of elasticity of lens and atrophy of cells within eye lead to sensitivity to light, conjunctivitis, far-sightedness, myopia, cataracts, astigmatism, moving spots, double vision)
✔ The whites of the eye become yellow
✔ Body deficient in minerals
✔ Hormonal imbalances in women due to the liver's influence over estrogen; malfunctioning of ovaries and problems with conception, with the monthly menses, and difficulty at time of menopause; loss of sex drive and femininity, developing more male qualities
✔ Hormonal imbalances in men; may produce feminine qualities, including an increase in breast size, sterility, and impotence
✔ Loss of weight and malnourishment
✔ Obesity and malnourishment
✔ Problems with sinuses, adenoids, and tonsils
✔ Alternating constipation and diarrhea
✔ Headaches, dizziness, shivering
✔ Loss of appetite
✔ Eating disorders
✔ Diabetes
✔ Hepatitis
✔ Cirrhosis

This list goes on and on beyond the scope of this book. We merely want to impress upon you the importance of caring for this precious organ. An impaired liver cannot process toxins, so even the brain and central nervous system are affected. Symptoms may range from depression, spaciness, daydreaming, and an inability to concentrate and remember things, to more serious disorders such as mental aberrations. In its extreme, the influence the liver has upon the brain can be seen during the final stages of cirrhosis when a coma occurs just before death.

You can test the health of your liver right now. Put the fingers of your right hand completely underneath your right rib cage. You will probably notice it is hard, "congested," and quite tender. If all three joints of your fingers don't fit completely under your ribs, your liver needs some tender loving care.

How the Liver Gets In Trouble

Remember that the liver is a large filter, and everything we take into our bodies must pass through it. It stores the remains of all the drugs, vaccines, and medicines we have taken *throughout our lifetime,* and the chemicals, hormones, and preservatives from our food. The hormones in birth control pills leave a dark patch in the liver, which shows up on x-rays. The fats from dairy foods (milk, cheese, and ice cream), from animal foods, and from oily and fried foods are also "fixed" in the liver. Flour products and vitamin and mineral supplements weaken the liver. So does improper food combining. Not only do all these cause a body ecology imbalance, they also cause congestion in the liver.

Filling your stomach beyond the recommended 80% mark causes your liver function to slow down and become insufficient. In fact, people who want to cure themselves of the eating disorder bulimia need to focus on healing the liver and restoring their body ecology, as well as healing the emotions.

Lack of sleep and fatigue (from pushing yourself too much when your body needs to rest) weakens the liver. Ironically, a vicious cycle occurs as the liver weakens, because it becomes more and more difficult to sleep. You'll know you have a congested liver if you feel tired and sleepy soon after eating, yet you have plenty of energy around 1-2 am. You may also tend to worry during this time or have negative thoughts. Digestive problems may bother you late at night, and you may have to urinate more than you do during the day.

A special note to pregnant and nursing women: if you neglect proper eating habits, not only will your own liver suffer, but your baby will be born with a congested liver as well. More and more newborns have damaged livers as a result of their mothers' poor eating habits. The liver of the fetus intercepts everything its mother eats and changes it into either a useful nutrient that aids growth or one that could clog its tiny new organ.

How Can We Help the Liver Heal?

There are several actions that will help heal the liver, and the first is to stop overworking it by changing the way you eat. Continue to clean the colon, then encourage the liver to cleanse with herbs and probiotics. Stimulate it—acupuncture can often be very helpful here. Exercise (walking, rebounding, yoga) is a daily must. You can also rest more, perhaps by taking afternoon naps if you feel tired. Do not, however, lie down right after eating a meal. If you overeat (beyond a stomach that is 80% full) and feel sleepy, don't give in! Keep moving...do the dishes...and expend energy until you burn off that excess food.

In Eastern medicine, the emotion of anger is connected to the liver. Holding in anger can further damage this organ, so try to express not only current anger, but release old anger that may be "stored" in the liver. As the liver cleanses, you may find yourself feeling uncontrollably angry and irritated at just about everyone and everything. Take it easy on yourself, and warn your family and friends not to take your outbursts personally.

Related Problems and Organs

Also in Chinese medicine, the liver is paired with the gall-bladder, so anything that strengthens one strengthens the other. In order to heal the liver, all other organs must be strengthened as well. This includes the kidneys and bladder, which nourish the liver, and the stomach and spleen/pancreas, which are controlled by the liver. (Remember, as the liver weakens, it pulls energy away from the stomach and spleen/pancreas, so often the stomach is not digesting well.) During a liver cleansing, the lower back around the kidneys may ache, reflecting the activity in all these organs.

Chinese medicine recognizes the connection between the liver and the eyes, knees, and skin. As you cleanse, you may have eye symptoms such as tearing, soreness, pinkeye (conjunctivitis), or see tiny moving, floating specs. Your knees may ache and pop, especially when you first wake up in the morning. You may have other aches, as if you have a bad case of the flu; the liver area may be tender to the touch; your urine and stool may change color; you may be constipated, and feel very tired or sleepy, especially after you eat.

Cleansing Equals Healing

Liver cleansing may be one of the most uncomfortable forms of healing. Sometimes you can cause it to happen step by step at a slow pace, but if the body itself organizes a major cleansing, you may feel "ill" for two or three weeks. But this is one of the most important cleansings you will ever go through.

It often happens in the spring, a natural time of cleansing and healing. The greens that aid in liver cleansing are very available during this time, and the weather turns warmer, giving you the chance to bask or walk in the sun—another important way to heal. This is a good time to take herbs and herbal combinations specifically designed to cleanse the liver and colon.

Eating Right

It is vital, of course, to eat right during this time. Rest your digestive tract by eating lightly. Eat small meals so the body will not have to use a lot of energy for digestion, but eat as often as you feel necessary to maintain your energy. Often people lose their appetites when they cleanse, so if this happens to you, drink plenty of lemon juice and water and sip vegetable broths and teas. This is also an excellent time for juicing, especially with green vegetables.

When you do eat, avoid fats from animal foods. Also, limit the quantity of animal foods, or, better yet, eliminate them completely since the weakened liver cannot handle ammonia, a by-product of protein digestion. Stay away from oils, ghee, and butter, because these all slow down liver function. Eat lightly steamed and pureed foods. Eat chlorophyll-rich foods such as lettuce and leafy greens, and eat as much raw food as you can tolerate. Your last meal of the day should be a light one, taken early enough that the stomach is completely empty before you go to sleep. All you may want is soup, vegetable broth, or tea.

Grated radish (daikon) is especially helpful because it takes oil and fats from the body. Leeks have antiseptic properties and aid the bile in keeping the intestines clean. Asparagus and celery are good liver cleansers. Carrots help build the blood and encourage the secretion of bile. Raw cultured vegetables are excellent because they are cleansing and easily digested. Sipping fresh lemon juice (very antiseptic) in water or apple cider vinegar in water (1 Tbsp. in 6 oz. water) also helps. Rosemary and thyme are herbs noted for healing liver congestion, and you may want to cook with them or make a tea by steeping them for ten minutes in hot water. Drink this tea before each meal. Liquid chlorophyll also aids liver cleansing.

Other Tips for Liver Cleansing

The liver cannot cleanse until the colon is open and working well, so make sure your colon is in good shape before you start taking herbs that stimulate liver healing. Liver cleansing herbs include milk thistle, dandelion root, barberry, and artichoke.

It's also very important to avoid becoming constipated. If necessary, have colonics or take home enemas (especially at bedtime) to keep the colon open, since the liver literally dumps its toxins into the colon.

Large amounts of lactic acid bacteria and probiotics (especially L. acidophilus, Bifidus and L. bulgaricus) are critical for keeping the liver clean and healthy. (See more about the liver in the new kefir chapter, Chapter 24)

Patsy went on the Body Ecology Diet and for a two-year period followed the Diet religiously, cleansed her colon, and took plenty of friendly bacteria. Her health improved remarkably, her yeast overgrowth disappeared, and she looked wonderful. Then she reached a plateau and became discouraged. In spite of conquering her yeast imbalance, her digestion was poor. She was still constipated and needed frequent enemas or colonics. She felt sleepy and chilled, especially after eating, and yet was full of energy at night before bedtime. Each morning she woke feeling stiff and tired. She called asking for help.

We were delighted to hear from her and even more pleased with what we were hearing. Patsy had earned a place at the next level of cleansing, and her body was telling her it was time to focus on healing her liver. All her effort and self-discipline had paid off—she was recovering her health and rebuilding her immunity. From a short interview with her we discovered she was eating too much butter and oil. She was not eating cultured vegetables and drinking apple cider vinegar in water, and she did not know about juicing.

The following instructions and menu suggestions were given to Patsy. With the same determination and persistence that had contributed to her conquering her yeast problem, she now turned to healing her liver.

Mornings

Upon rising, drink the juice of one lemon in 6 oz. warm water.

(If the bladder feels weak, as an alternative to the lemon juice and water, take 1 Tbsp. cranberry juice concentrate with 6 oz. water and stevia to taste. You can also take a combination of freshly squeezed cranberry juice and Granny Smith apples at this time. This is a very rich drink and should be slowly sipped and "chewed" with the saliva before swallowing. One 6 oz. glass is sufficient.)

When appetite signals you to do so, follow the above drink with one to two grapefruits.

Or drink raw vegetable juices (preferably a green drink...see recipe in juicing chapter). If carrot juice is used as a base, squeeze lemon juice into the vegetable juice before drinking. Again, be sure to "chew" this juice slowly before swallowing.

Wait at least one hour before eating lunch.

Continue to sip lemon juice and water, if desired, until 10 minutes before eating. Take digestive enzymes ten minutes before eating lunch.

Lunch

About 11 a.m., or when hungry.

(Suggestions given below are designed for someone who brings lunch to work and has a facility for reheating it.)

This should be your largest meal of the day. Eat mostly grains, vegetables, and starchy vegetables. If you do seem to need animal foods for strength, limit them as much as possible. The menus below are only guidelines to stimulate your own creativity.

1. Soup
    Leafy green and raw vegetable salad and small amount of
        B.E.D. Dressing (or a no-oil dressing)
    Tea

2. A leftover grain dish
    Raw vegetables and/or a leafy green salad and a small amount
        of B.E.D. Dressing (or a no-oil dressing)
    Cultured vegetables
    Echinacea tea with stevia (sipped slowly after lunch)

3. Salmon Roll-ups. Use salt-free canned salmon, and roll it up
        inside romaine or leaf lettuce. Cultured vegetables are
        good rolled up with the salmon; so is mustard. If you
        have time, make a delicious pate by blending the
        salmon in your food processor with herbs such as
        parsley, dill, some lecithin granules, and Trocomare.
    Drink warm lemon juice and water to aid digestion at the
        end of your protein meal. (Digestive enzymes should
        also have HCL for protein digestion.)

4. Baked or hard-boiled eggs
    Steamed veggies
    Cultured vegetables or salad with no-oil dressing
    Tea with stevia, or lemon juice and water
        (Digestive enzymes same as above if not eating raw
        cultured veggies)

5. Seasoned, baked new potatoes
    Arame with carrots and onions
        (leftover from last night's dinner)
    Green vegetables or leafy green salad
    Tea

(If you have a microwave in your office, bake a potato and top it with Dr. Bronner's Balanced Mineral Seasoning, apple cider vinegar, and cultured veggies instead of butter or ghee.)

Between meals sip medicinal teas such as Dandelion, Echinacea, Rosemary, and Thyme.

Dinner

At least 4-5 hours before bedtime.

This meal should be one that digests quickly. Be very careful not to overeat. An all-alkaline meal is ideal, avoiding grains and animal proteins, which take much longer to digest. Eat as much raw food as possible. A soup and salad, or a starchy vegetable such as baked acorn squash, baked red skin potato, or corn on the cob can be accompanied by raw vegetables, lightly steamed land vegetables, ocean vegetables, and cultured vegetables. Chew very well.

To aid digestion: if not eating cultured vegetables or taking enzymes, slowly sip the apple cider vinegar and water drink, during and after your meal.

Take digestive enzymes at bedtime for several weeks.

Herbs and herbal blends designed to cleanse and strengthen the liver are available at your local health food stores. Take as directed on the label.

NOTE: Probiotics are not included in this program since Patsy enjoyed making a large batch of cultured vegetables each month and felt the expense of probiotics did not fit her budget at the time. If you are not making and eating cultured vegetables, be sure to include probiotics in your morning routine.* They combine with all morning suggestions, but are best if taken on an empty stomach.

An Important Affirmation

I have now earned the right for my liver to cleanse and become completely healthy.

---

*There is a very strong relationship between friendly bacteria and optimum liver function. A lack of a healthy inner ecosystem rich in the Bifidus strains, *L. acidophilus*, and *bulgaricus* is linked to liver disorders including diabetes and cirrhosis. We strongly recommend that you take large amounts of probiotics to help cleanse and strengthen your liver. Please read *Probiotics* by Leon Chaitow and Natasha Trenev for more information. (Thorsons Publishing Group)

PART FIVE

Creating a Bright, Healthy Future

CHAPTER 21

How to Reintroduce Other Healthy Foods into Your Diet

Let's say you've followed the Body Ecology Diet carefully for three or four months and your symptoms of candidiasis have totally disappeared. You feel terrific, physically and emotionally, and you have a new outlook on life now that the pain and suffering of those symptoms have cleared up. You want to try some foods that are not on the strict version of the Diet.

We're not talking about going back to cake, cookies, alcohol, and other foods that would feed the yeast. We recommend you never go back to these. (You can satisfy that sweet craving with sweet vegetables, and stevia in teas, and Body Ecology Diet desserts.) Although you may be symptom-free, the yeast may have burrowed deep into your organs and tissue, and unless you stop feeding it, it will eventually resurface and you will experience symptoms again. However, you *can* introduce *healthy* foods, and by combining them properly, you can enjoy a greater variety of things to eat.

The very first rule to remember is INTRODUCE ONLY ONE NEW FOOD AT A TIME. Try a small amount with the B.E.D. foods you know you can tolerate, and note if you have any symptoms (such as a headache, intestinal upset, rash) immediately or over the next day or two. If you don't have a reaction, try the food again after a few days (at least four). If you again remain symptom-free, you can start rotating that food through your diet regularly.

The foods you can tolerate often depend on your blood type, so remember this valuable guideline when you add foods to your daily diet (see Chapter 7). Develop your own individual set of foods that you enjoy and can tolerate. People heal at different rates, and the successful introduction of new foods also may depend on factors such as stress, exercise, and the amount of sleep you get. We recommend that you make up your mind to ALWAYS use food combining, the 80/20 rules, and other principles of the Body Ecology Diet to maintain your optimal health.

What to Try First

For all blood types, fruit is one of the easiest, healthiest foods to reintroduce into your diet. Try grapefruit first, then kiwi. These are such sour fruits that the yeast are not interested in them. Remember to eat them alone, particularly in the morning.

Summer is the best time to expand into fruits, because that is when the body needs their cooling, high water content effects. Other sour fruits (see list below) include blueberries, bing cherries, raspberries, strawberries, and blackberries. Oranges are too sweet and are not recommended for a long time. Sour green apples (cooking apples) are a good fruit to try after you know you can safely eat grapefruit, kiwi, and some berries. (Blood Types A and A/B do not do well with apples because they are highly acidic.)

Acidic (Sour) Fruits

Acerola Cherry	Loganberry
Apple, sour	Orange
Cranberry	Peach, sour
Currant	Pineapple
Gooseberry	Plum, sour
Grapefruit	Pomegranate
Grape, sour	Strawberry
Kumquat	Tangelo
Lemon	Tangerine
Lime	Tomato

EAT THESE ALONE or maybe with protein fat. Or, try lemon and tomato with non-starchy green vegetables.

Except for grapefruit, people with Type A blood don't tolerate acidic fruits very well, and they should always avoid or be extra cautious about the sweet fruits, such as bananas and grapes. For other blood types, try fruits in their increasing order of sweetness (see Lee DuBelle's book on food combining), and add melon last.

Tomatoes are considered an acidic fruit, and the best time to introduce them is in the summer, when they're in season and vine-ripened. Eat them raw with fresh green vegetables. Cooked tomatoes tend to be acid-forming in the body, so because we are trying to make our bodies more alkaline, tomatoes are most healthful when they're raw. Type Os seem to tolerate tomatoes much better than Types A and A/B; as always, Type Bs are somewhere in the middle.

Adding Grains

For Types A and A/B, wheat can be very mucous-forming, and wheat and buckwheat are too acid-forming. Types A and A/B do best with the three alkaline-forming grains on the Body Ecology Diet (quinoa, millet, and amaranth), but once their body ecology is well established, they can try other grains. All Type Os do well with quinoa pastas, which usually include some corn, but As should eat quinoa pastas that are wheat-free.

Corn is a tricky food; some people just tolerate it better than others. People with an overgrowth of unhealthy microbes often cannot eat corn. Summer corn (on the cob) is never a problem, but the harder flint corn, which is ground into meal and also made into chips, may take longer to tolerate. There are different types of flint corn—blue, white, yellow—and you may have to experiment to determine which is best for you. Blue is usually tolerated the best by anyone on the B.E.D. Remember, when introducing any new food, it's better to try it with non-starchy green vegetables to get a true test of whether you can add it back into your diet.

Menu Tip:

Try oil-free, baked blue corn chips with vegetable soup or with cultured vegetables to reduce the drying, contracting effect of the chips.

When you try eating rice again, go for the light, long grain rices, like white basmati. Save brown basmati and long grain brown rices for later. Long grain brown rices are less glutinous than the short grain rices. "Texmati" rice is particularly good for Type As.

Cooking Tip:

Before you cook the rice, soak it for several hours to remove the enzyme inhibitors in the outer husk; then drain, rinse, and cook.

Flour products are very "gummy" and create mucus in the colon. You're better off minimizing flour products and getting the benefits of grains through *whole* grains. When you do have that craving for desserts and sweets, occasionally go to our recipes that use stevia and the flours made from the Body Ecology Diet grains.

Dairy

Type As may never want to reintroduce *uncultured* dairy foods because they are too mucous-forming. For Type Os, cultured dairy products are less mucous-forming, so they should first try goat's milk products such as *raw* goat's milk cheese, kefir, and yogurt. These should be eaten alone, or with sour fruits, non-starchy vegetables or cultured vegetables.

Beans

Beans have some protein and some starch in them, so they send mixed signals to the digestive system, and that is why many people have trouble digesting them. Always soak beans overnight to remove the enzyme inhibitors, and cook them with a piece of kombu (ocean veggie) and sea salt (to make them more alkaline). Serve beans with non-starchy green vegetables. The key to introducing them is to try the *larger* beans first, such as garbanzo, kidney, and anasazi. Try a small portion at first, and don't mix types of beans—just one type at a time.

Most beans are too acid-forming for Type As, but As may tolerate soybeans and tofu products.

Other Foods To Try

For all blood types, add **beets, parsnips, sweet potatoes, and yams** once you're *certain* the yeast is under control. These are very sweet vegetables and should be combined with non-starchy green vegetables and especially ocean vegetables. The salt in the ocean veggies balances the sweet taste.

Olive oil can be one of your first additions. Use it in a salad or in cooking; it is very healthy. Olives are considered a protein fat as well as a fruit, and can be added to green salads. Avocados are also a protein fat and can be eaten with a salad that lacks protein or starch. Type As may have trouble digesting avocados because they're very high in oil and fat. If you show signs of a congested liver, avoid avocados.

Soaked and sprouted almonds are the only nut that is not acid-forming. Here is the way to sprout them no matter what your blood type: place a handful in water in a jar and soak them 8 to 12 hours or overnight. They will become plump as they are starting to sprout. Then, drain out the water and sprinkle them in a salad, for instance, or on top of some steamed vegetables, and you will find them easier to digest. **Other nuts** are very high in fat and are acid-forming in the body. Eat them sparingly and combine them with green vegetables. Type Os might tolerate pecans better than other nuts; Type Bs will have to experiment.

Raw mushrooms are not a very healthy food; Type As have particular trouble digesting them. But cooked mushrooms are better for you, and dried shitake mushrooms have special medicinal value, because they help build the immune system.

A Final Reminder

Sugar—even so-called healthy sugars like honey, molasses, and barley malt—doesn't combine well with anything. If you ever try one of these, have it in a tea, perhaps first thing in the morning; it will digest within a half hour or so, and you can then eat other foods. Better yet, use stevia in the tea; it helps regulate the pancreas, and you won't get the rush that honey and other sweets bring.

CHAPTER 22
A Review:
How to Restore Your Body Ecology

At this point, you may feel overwhelmed by the information in this book, and you may not know where to start. Depending on how "sick" you are, you may be able to start with only one change in your diet or lifestyle—or your body and mind may be able to handle several changes. Just do as much as your intuition—some call this your "inner guide"—tells you to do. Start with one change, or a few, or all—but start.

As you begin the Diet, the three most important actions to take are to:

✔ Starve the yeast by using the Diet foods, which feed you, not them.

✔ Begin cleansing the colon.

✔ Implant new colonies of friendly bacteria.

When you eliminate all forms of sugar from your diet, you stop feeding the yeast, and your body will start to discard the dead yeast toxins. You will feel hungry because the yeast are hungry—remember, up until now, they've been using you and your food to stay alive. You can eat as much of the healthy food on the Diet as you want, as long as you follow the principles of the Diet.

Another key step requires your mental and emotional commitment to the Diet and to healing yourself; this will give you the strength to adhere to it when temptation hits. It's also a good idea to tell your friends and family that you're beginning a new way of living and ask for their support. Then, when they see you either doing splendidly on the Diet, or straying from it, they'll be able to act appropriately. Making a public declaration always helps solidify a private resolve.

Here are the rest of the major principles and guidelines of the Body Ecology Diet. They all support one another, so once you declare to yourself that you're on this new path, following the Diet will be simultaneously easy, challenging, and rewarding.

✔ Think of land and ocean vegetables as the basis for all your eating. They are our most nutrient-rich foods, and by following the 80/20 rule you'll always put vegetables on 80% of your plate.

✔ Eat cultured foods (kefir, *see new info in part VI*, cultured vegetables, apple cider vinegar) and take probiotics to help recolonize the friendly bacteria in your digestive tract.

✔ Eat a wide variety of the foods you can tolerate. This way you will be sure to get all the nutrients you need.

✔ Always plan meals around the expansion/contraction and acid/alkaline principles. Use the 80/20 rules to determine how much food you can eat.

✔ Exercise!

✔ Welcome cleansings, knowing they are signs of healing. Rest through them.

✔ Rearrange your emotional attitudes, if necessary, to reduce stress, set priorities, and learn to say no. Fight negative thoughts and attitudes, and start creating more joy in your life. The very energy of joy leads to healing. Take care of yourself.

✔ Live a wholesome life: enjoy the out-of-doors, try to get sunshine on your body, breathe deeply to relax and get more oxygen into your body.

✔ Appreciate the opportunity to heal yourself step by step, knowing that your success will influence others to take a similar path.

CHAPTER 23
Toward a New Science of Healing

Now that you've read all *about* the Body Ecology Diet, you're ready to start *using* it. Try scanning the book quickly again, perhaps highlighting in a new color things you want to remember. We hope this copy will become dog-eared, its pages marked up and grimy from rereading and use—the mark of a worthwhile book.

Before moving on to the recipe section, where you'll find many more cooking tips, menu suggestions, and a shopping list, please consider some ideas about human beings, nature, and healing.

Healing in Ancient and Modern Times

Ancient people were intuitively aware of the inherent order, the natural perfection of the universe. Nature was not an enemy to be conquered, but a friend that supplied food and water for physical needs and beauty to satisfy spiritual and emotional needs. When people got sick, they knew how to use natural remedies to heal themselves, and they trusted the inherent perfection of nature to assist in healing.

But we moderns, as we develop our technological, material world, have moved away from trusting our intuition. We often view nature as a force to be altered and subdued, even for the praiseworthy goal of freeing people from suffering and misfortune. Our drive to create a world free of disease, poverty, and early or unnecessary death often acts at cross-purposes to the natural flow of things.

For example, we use fewer and fewer natural remedies and more and more manmade drugs. We have lost trust in the body's ability to cleanse and heal itself. Young people choosing careers in the healing and helping professions often begin with sincere intentions to return to natural ways, but get waylaid when the demands of big business and overburdened systems pull on them.

It's time to leave this track. We must once again start accepting nature's ways, trusting and nourishing our intuitive selves. We will then be in better balance with our rational, intellectual selves, resulting in exciting opportunities to create the world as we really want it.

What a New Science of Healing Would Look Like

A new approach to healing would promote us as spiritual beings, not just machine-like bodies that break down, wear out, or become vulnerable to attacks from strange viruses and bacteria. The greatest spiritual teachers, such as Jesus, Moses, and Buddha, taught that suffering, pain, and adversity exist to train us in attaining a state of perfection for our ethereal selves. As we overcome hardship, we cultivate the positive nature of our spiritual selves.

Thus, true healing recognizes an inner force that meshes with the laws of nature. Some call this force God, or the Creator, or the Source of all existence. People with candidiasis, cancer, AIDS, and other serious conditions often find they improve and heal only when they pay attention to their spiritual lives and arrive at a new appreciation for the Creator. The writings of Dr. Bernie Siegel and many others prove this. Donna feels that the efforts she has made to grow spiritually and the results that have come out of that effort are an even greater gift than all the answers she has found to overcome candidiasis.

Connecting Emotions to Healing

A new science of healing would also recognize the usefulness of emotions and teach us to rechannel the energy of negative emotions into positive, useful expressions. Dr. John Gray, creator of the HEART seminars,[25] does this by advocating what he calls a "love letter." He encourages his patients to "dump" all their anger in a letter instead of getting mad at someone, fighting and walking away. After all the anger is expressed, people can begin to feel the hurt, sadness, and disappointment that are always underneath. As they continue to express these emotions, they can begin to give up the need to "be right" and ultimately accept responsibility for their actions, including the original, angry blow-up.

Dr. Gray understands that negative emotions are useful; he does not fear them. He guides his patients to view their negative emotions as benchmarks or red flags...signals that they are moving off target from the life of fulfillment they want. Once they look honestly at anger, sadness, and fear, a tremendous capacity opens up for understanding, forgiveness, healing, and love.

An Updated Approach to Healing

We have come to rely too much on medicines and drugs to cure whatever ails us. Even advocates of the "natural foods movement" rely too much on vitamin and mineral supplements and components of plants. There are about 60 nutrients known at this time to be essential to human nutrition. Yet even if you

[25]Gray, 1984

154

swallowed a mega-vitamin/mineral pill consisting of generous quantities of all these nutrients, you could not maintain your health. This is because the whole foods contain elements essential to our health that modern science has not identified. Our arrogance leads us to believe we can duplicate the intricate relationships among these components that nature provides.

Until researchers, doctors, and other health experts come up with new solutions, we may be forced at times to use antibiotics and other medicines. The Body Ecology Diet is essential during these times. We are thrilled by the response to the Diet from the medical community and from holistic health practitioners. We are grateful to all the professionals who are encouraging their patients to use the Diet.

Oriental medicine holds that you can heal yourself by eating properly. In Western medicine, the average new medical school graduate has had only about two weeks' study in nutrition. We challenge medical students to use the super technologies of today and tomorrow to discover more of the natural paths of healing that have been used in the past. Young people who enter the medical profession have declared their desire to help heal; let us keep them from getting discouraged by giving them a true science of healing that is more in tune with the laws of nature.

Why Take Better Care of Our Bodies?

Why should we give up all those foods that taste so good and make us feel full and lazy? After all, they only weaken us, harm our immune systems, and shorten our lifespans.

We've forgotten who we really are. We cannot accept the godliness, the divinity of our true selves. We were created for a purpose: to establish a bright, happy world, one highly evolved on a material level, yet governed by spiritual wisdom. It will be a world rich with music, art, and science, free from the pain of poverty, disease, and hunger.

We are moving toward this paradise, making mistakes along the way, but learning from them. Yet if we continue to eat for pleasure alone, ignoring the purpose of our creation, our minds and bodies will weaken such that we will never find the happiness that is our birthright. Once we discover our inner strength and glory, it becomes easy to turn away from negativity and dissatisfaction. It becomes easy to operate from our positive, altruistic selves and take care of the bodies that house our beautiful souls.

Actions You Can Take to Support Your Body Ecology and Your Planet's Ecology

✔ Create a demand for organic or untreated foods to be sold in your neighborhood grocery store, not just at health food stores. Demand foods free from antibiotics and other harmful additives.

✔ Support the new breed of natural foods supermarkets (such as whole foods markets) that offer healthy foods, organic produce, and extensive in-store soup and salad bars and deli sections that sell wholesome, delicious, ready-to-eat foods. Shop at groceries that are responsive to the changing demands of their public, that patronize local organic farmers, and that are constantly trying to expand their organic produce departments.

✔ Patronize restaurants whose menus offer the healthy, organic foods that are on the Body Ecology Diet. In Atlanta, R. Thomas & Son Deluxe Grill is becoming a well-known showplace for B.E.D. foods. Richard Thomas, former President of Kentucky Fried Chicken, is delighted with the response to the Body Ecology Diet Salad Dressings, Cultured Vegetables, and other dishes his menu lists. You can ask restaurants in your own area to offer B.E.D. recipes, or at least to make available a greater range of simple, healthy dishes that use more vegetables.

✔ Ask for healthy snacks at your local theaters, including popcorn sprinkled with mineral-rich sea salt and popped in coconut oil.

✔ Encourage schools to offer healthier lunches in their cafeterias. Participate in changing curricula so that more nutrition is taught in a more interesting manner. Students can learn how food can be fun and healthy at the same time. Help revive "home economics labs" based on principles of the Body Ecology Diet and ways to cook our recipes.

✔ Buy foods and products that help save the environment, rather than destroy it. Putting a serving of meat on your table requires much more of the world's valuable energy and resources than a serving of fish; grains and vegetables use even less.

✔ Within reason, avoid medicines that suppress your natural healing and cleansing and thus weaken the immune system. Rely on diet, exercise, and good mental attitudes to stay healthy. Emphasize prevention and wellness.

✔ Create or build a community of people committed to this way of life, to these points of view. This will support your goals and forward your purpose.

PART SIX

The Magic
of Kefir

CHAPTER 24 - NEW SINCE FOURTH EDITION!!
The Body Ecology Diet and Kefir

Since the first printing of this book, thousands of people around the world are now eating according to the principles of the Diet. We've received hundreds of letters and are very grateful to know that you are becoming well. Many of you have reported such improvement that you call yourselves "cured." You are symptom-free. Others tell us that they immediately feel better, but that their symptoms return when they stop following the Diet. And for a significant number of you, digestive problems persist or there is unwanted weight loss. This means that the inner ecosystem still is not fully reestablished and needs some additional help. It also means even the healthiest foods may be passing through your body without their nutrients being adequately absorbed.

The solution is to continue your healing process and now focus on restoring the integrity of your digestive tract as quickly as possible so it can begin to assimilate food properly, allowing your body to attain its optimal weight. Remember, you are not completely well until your inner ecosystem is restored.

Without detracting from the importance of The Body Ecology Diet, probiotics, raw cultured vegetables, and **VITALITY** *SuperGreen*™, we have discovered another addition to The Diet that will help you establish a new inner ecosystem. We would now like to introduce you to Kefir...a wonderful ancient food that we believe will help you enter the final phase of getting well, restore the integrity of your digestive tract, and add to the effectiveness of everything else you've done so far.

Donna's Story

Many years ago, I was introduced to kefir, but did not understand or appreciate its value. An excellent colon therapist had mentioned to me that kefir, especially goat milk kefir, has a very beneficial, toning effect on the colon. After a bit of searching, I found a goat farmer and master cheese maker in Pennsylvania who made delicious kefir. I ordered some and tried it, but was highly skeptical since it was made from milk. Milk sent up a red flag for me. Milk is mucous-forming, feeds yeast, and in Chinese medicine, produces a sticky, "damp" quality. Besides, I had always been lactose intolerant and allergic to milk. So, even though I enjoyed it, I quickly dismissed kefir as an unimportant food.

Then, as always happens for me, I began to see signs that I needed to open my mind to new possibilities. For example, I happened to turn on television (I rarely watch) and saw a program about fish in a Canadian lake that produced mucus to protect themselves as the lake's pH level rose due to acid rain. Several weeks later, I lunched with a friend whose daughter had brought home a book describing how a fish had totally covered itself with mucus when it washed up on the beach, protecting itself until the rising tide returned the fish safely back to sea. I realized mucus can be a protection. After a little more reflection, I remembered that all things in this universe have both a positive and a negative side and I had been focusing only on the negative.

I tucked this information away in my mind and, as I began collecting more information about kefir, more parts of the puzzle fell into place. For example, I knew that, at birth, a newborn has no inner ecosystem and must establish it during the first few months of life, ideally from breast milk. Nature decrees that mother's milk be available for all offspring of mammals. This milk lays down a bed of clean mucus, allowing friendly bacteria to establish themselves. Breast milk is an excellent source of protective agents such as lauric acid, a powerful antimicrobial that deactivates pathogenic bacteria, yeast, fungi, and some viruses. This protects the baby until the inner ecosystem is well established with positive bacteria and its immune system matures.

As I began to add up all the facts, I realized that: 1) there is both good, clean-quality mucus and toxic mucus, 2) good mucus coats and protects the interior lining of the digestive tract, and 3) unlike yeast, who burrow into the intestinal walls with their tentacles, good bacteria do not have tentacles. They must be caught by this clean mucus where they nestle into their warm, acidic environment, fed by the sugar (lactose) in mother's milk. Mucus, I finally had to admit, was an essential part of a healthy inner ecosystem.

People with candidiasis have a very unhealthy inner ecosystem. They have an overgrowth of fungus or yeast, and very toxic bowels. In order to heal, they must first cleanse the colon and control the yeast overgrowth. Then they must reestablish an inner ecosystem teeming with beneficial bacteria. At this second stage, a victim of candidiasis could be compared to a newborn babe...both must have this vibrant, living inner world if they are going to assimilate nutrients, create a strong immune system, and live a long, fruitful life.

It was becoming clearer to me that kefir had tremendous healing power. With its laxative effect it helps clean the colon. Its beneficial bacteria and yeast help control the pathogenic yeast and repopulate the colon with a favorable, new life force. And kefir, being cultured, is much healthier than milk.

In ancient times, kefir was given to the people of the Caucasus regions as a gift from the gods. Perhaps these gods were watching over mankind and offering us this miracle food, at a time we desperately needed it. Now, if only I could learn to make kefir and test out my theory. The problem was that no one had grains or a starter culture, there was almost no information available, and the few people who knew about kefir did not want to share their "secrets." Then a miracle happened!

After publication of the first edition of The Body Ecology Diet, I felt drawn to take a spiritual sabbatical to recharge myself and give thanks for the success of the book. I traveled to a sacred area of Japan and attended a ceremony honoring the creation of humanity. A friend from Sendai, Japan, joined me the evening before the ceremony and brought with him Mrs. Kwai, a woman I had never met before. He told me that his friend had felt very strongly compelled to come and bring with her something she thought I needed. Amazingly, it was a little brown pot of kefir grains cultivating in milk. Mrs. Kwai opened the container and, with her strainer and a spoon showed me how to make kefir.

My prayers were being answered. In amazement I brought the kefir back to my room, still not fully appreciating what I had been given. I ate the kefir, loved the taste and felt a surge of strength after my tiring journey.

When I returned home, everything started coming together. I began making kefir every day. At first I was skeptical as I always am about new foods, so I told no one about it. Each morning I had a glass of it and within two weeks couldn't believe how much energy I had. When you are over fifty (as I am), if you eat the wrong foods it shows and you look your age. However, I was amazed that each day I seemed to look younger. Others noticed it, too, and kept telling me how good I looked. Any woman loves that.

One day, I received a call from a woman who was using the Body Ecology principles to heal herself from non-Hodgkins lymphoma. Yes, the lab reports showed no trace of cancer, but I could still hear a weakness in her voice. Intuitively, I knew the kefir would help her.

It did! She called again two weeks later and the change in her voice was remarkable. She said she was feeling much, much better. From that day on I recommended kefir to many more people.

Women with vaginal yeast infections told me that kefir cleared up the infection. Young women with eating disorders, people with Crohn's disease, stomach problems, ulcers, diverticulitis and constipation...by following The Diet and having kefir for their breakfast meal...all reported that they were becoming well.

Thousands of people in my hometown of Atlanta are now on The Body Ecology Diet. They have been spreading the word about it and about kefir too. Many are making kefir at home and love to do so...later, we'll tell you how.

I can't recommend kefir highly enough. It is a nutritious, incredibly delicious food. If your body is ready for it and you find you tolerate it well, kefir can be essential to your achieving maximum health and immunity. As you read this book and begin to drink kefir, you'll realize, too, that it is an ancient remedy for modern maladies: a true gift from heaven. Enjoy!

What is Kefir?

Kefir is a cultured and microbial-rich food that helps restore the inner ecology. It contains strains of beneficial yeast and beneficial bacteria (in a symbiotic relationship) that give kefir antibiotic properties. A natural antibiotic—and it is made from milk! The finished product is not unlike that of a drinking-style yogurt, but kefir has a more tart, refreshing taste.

The Body Ecology Diet recommends avoiding dairy products because they contain a milk sugar called lactose that feeds yeast and creates mucus. But kefir does not feed yeast, and it usually doesn't even bother people who are lactose intolerant. That's because the friendly bacteria and the beneficial yeast growing in the kefir consume most of the lactose and provide very efficient enzymes (lactase) for consuming whatever lactose is still left after the culturing process. Yes, kefir is mucous-forming, but only slightly so if you follow some simple food combining rules (more on the food combining principles later).

And here's the capper: the slightly mucous-forming quality is exactly what makes kefir work for us. The mucus has a "clean" quality to it that coats the lining of the digestive tract, creating a sort of nest where beneficial bacteria can settle and colonize. This makes the other probiotics you may be taking even more potent: They now have a better chance to take hold and proliferate in your intestines, helping you really "get your money's worth." By the way, kefir can be made from any type of milk, including milk made from cow, goat or soy.

Kefir is made from gelatinous white or yellow particles called "grains." The grains contain the bacteria/yeast mixture clumped together with casein (milk proteins) and polysaccharides (complex sugars). They look like pieces of coral or small clumps of cauliflower and range from the size of a grain of wheat to that of a hazelnut. Some grains have been known to grow in large flat sheets that can be big enough to cover your hand. No other milk culture forms grains...making kefir truly unique. Once the grains ferment the milk by incorporating their friendly organisms into the final product, you remove these grains with a strainer before drinking the kefir. The grains are then added to a new batch of milk, and the process continues indefinitely.

Kefir vs. Yogurt

Kefir, experts believe, has more therapeutic value than yogurt. Its very active yeast and bacteria provide more nutritive value than yogurt since they excel in digesting the foods you eat and in keeping the environment of the colon clean and healthy.

Yogurt is made by adding a starter culture to milk and gently heating it to a certain temperature. To make kefir, you must start with the "grains" or a "starter" and no heating is required. This means that if you can obtain a reliable source of fresh, raw milk, you can retain enzymes that would normally be destroyed by the heat of pasteurization. Kefir "cultures" at room temperature in approximately 24 hours, right on your kitchen counter.

Kefir "grains" are a little more difficult to work with since they can be contaminated easily. An even easier way to make kefir is from a "starter." This starter can be purchased from your health food store (or call 1-800-511-2660). We have found that using a new package of starter culture each time ensures that the microbial population of yeast and bacteria is consistent and very viable.

After your inner ecology is restored, you may find that you now digest yogurt well and want to make use of its friendly bacteria. But choose kefir first. The friendly bacteria and yeast in kefir are crucial to the restoration process. We think of them as a SWAT team moving in quickly to begin the therapeutic process, efficiently doing the job they were created to do.

You may see a product in the store that claims to be kefir, but read the label carefully. Unless it has strains of friendly bacteria *and the good yeast*, it is not true kefir. That's why Donna has worked so hard to find a reliable, inexpensive source of real kefir "starter" so you can make it yourself...fresh and delicious.

Helios Nutrition has recently introduced an *organic* kefir made with FOS (food that encourages the growth of microorganisms). Plain flavor is fine. Ask your health food store to carry it. 1-888-3helios.

Benefits as Friendly Bacteria

With more than 400 different species of beneficial microorganisms living inside a healthy gut, why not give them the optimal environment? As we've said, kefir lays down a foundation of clean mucus so these beneficial organisms have a place to thrive. When you add probiotics (friendly organisms purchased from your health food store, see shopping list page 254) they too will find a receptive home much more quickly when a favorable environment has already been created.

The fact that you can easily make kefir fresh every day or so in your own kitchen means that its friendly yeast and bacteria are readily available to do their job in your intestinal tract.

After you restore the balance to your inner ecology using the Body Ecology Diet, cultured vegetables, probiotics, and kefir, your intestinal tract will be teeming with friendly organisms. Then you will be better able to enjoy some foods containing natural sugars (fruits, whole cereal grains, the sweeter vegetables such as yams and parsnips), and you may tolerate that occasional binge on really sugary food such as a piece of cake or candy. The beneficial bacteria gobble up the sugar for themselves first, leaving little to carry into the rest of your body. Of course, we are not endorsing foods with refined sugar, but it certainly doesn't hurt to have yourself prepared and "well-armed."

If you are a parent worried about all the sugary foods your child wants (and often gets), kefir is especially useful for establishing and maintaining a strong immune system in your child. To make a kefir treat that kids love, add the natural, sweet-tasting herb stevia, some non-alcoholic fruit flavorings or vanilla, and/or Omega Nutrition's, butterscotch-flavored Essential Balance Junior™ oil.

Kefir keeps the small and large intestines clean and free of parasites. Once in the large intestine, the beneficial bacteria create lactic acid that balances the pH level there. In this acidic environment parasites and other unfriendly organisms cannot survive. Kefir's beneficial yeast and bacteria are ready to ambush any parasite eggs or larvae before they have a chance to establish themselves and multiply.

With its .02% alcohol content (produced by the yeast), kefir is acidic when you make it; yet it becomes alkaline-forming in the body once you eat it. This means that the overall quality of the blood remains slightly more alkaline and we remain healthy.

The friendly bacteria and yeast in kefir provide a good advance team for other probiotic cultures like acidophilus and bifidus. Kefir "clears the land" and establishes clean, healthy sites for new colonies of friendly bacteria. When the new settlers arrive (the friendly bacteria you buy in your health food store or generate internally by eating cultured foods), they remain and thrive, ensuring you a far better return on your investment.

New research has found that stomach ulcers are often caused by a pathogenic bacteria called Helicobacter pylori. Expensive antibiotic therapy is now being used to kill this bacteria. Kefir may prevent such ulcers. Remember antibiotics kill all bacteria, both the good and the bad, so it is important to remain on the Body Ecology Diet if you must take antibiotics, using it, cultured vegetables, kefir and probiotics to rebuild your inner ecosystem.

We have found kefir to be beneficial in cases of diarrhea, which is common in AIDS or in cancer patients undergoing chemotherapy or radiation.

Benefits Regarding Nutrition

Kefir contains complete protein with all the essential amino acids. By the time you drink kefir, its friendly bacteria have already partially digested the protein, making it much easier for you to digest. High amounts of protein are critical to healing, and your body must have adequate minerals in order to assimilate the protein. Kefir provides these, too. Abundant calcium and magnesium are also found in kefir.

Tryptophan, an essential amino acid found in kefir, combines with the calcium and magnesium to help calm the nervous system. Some people call kefir "Nature's tranquilizer" or "Nature's Prozac." Its calming effect is great for people who are high-strung or nervous, for hyperactive children, or for people with sleep disorders, such as the elderly. The body converts tryptophan into serotonin, an important chemical called a neurotransmitter; increased serotonin levels induce sleep and prohibit waking during the night. This conversion is helped along by Vitamin B6, which is also abundant in kefir.

Kefir also has ample phosphorus, the second most abundant mineral in our bodies. Phosphorus is important in utilizing carbohydrates, fats, and proteins for growth, cell maintenance, and energy. A phosphorous deficiency can result in the loss of appetite.

Kefir and the B Vitamins

People with candidiasis are usually deficient in the B vitamins and in Vitamin K because the body's use of these vitamins depends on adequate levels of friendly bacteria in the intestinal tract. When kefir is included in the diet, your body should soon be able to manufacture sufficient amounts of these needed bacteria. Vitamin K promotes blood clotting, encourages the flow of urine, relieves menstrual cramps, increases vitality and longevity, and enhances liver functioning.

Kefir provides biotin, another B vitamin, which is missing in people with candidiasis. Biotin is a coenzyme that assists in the manufacture of fatty acids and in the oxidation of fatty acids and carbohydrates. Without biotin, the body's production of essential fatty acids is impaired. Biotin also aids in the body's assimilation of protein and other B-vitamins: folic acid, pantothenic acid, and B12. A deficiency of biotin can cause muscular pain, poor appetite, dry skin, lack of energy, or depression and a distressed nervous system.

Kefir is an excellent source of Vitamin B12, which is essential for longevity. It is the only vitamin that contains essential mineral elements. It cannot be made synthetically but must be grown, like penicillin, in bacteria or molds. B12 is necessary for the normal metabolism of nerve tissue and for red blood cell formation. B12 builds immunity and has been used to increase energy and counteract allergens. It is also required for normal growth and is important for fertility and during pregnancy. Plus it works along with folic acid, another member of the B-complex, in facilitating the synthesis of choline. [Choline is a fat and cholesterol dissolver and plays an important role in the transmission of nerve impulses. It helps regulate kidney, liver, and gallbladder functions and aids in the prevention of gallstones.]

B12 helps the placement of Vitamin A into body tissues by aiding carotene absorption or Vitamin A conversion. It also aids in the production of DNA and RNA, the body's genetic material. B12 needs to be combined with calcium during absorption to benefit the body properly; Nature has provided for that in kefir.

Kefir is rich in thiamin (Vitamin B1), also known as the "morale vitamin" because of its beneficial effects on the nervous system and on mental attitude. Thiamin is linked with enhanced learning capacity, growth in children, and improvement in the muscle tone of the stomach, intestines, and heart. It is essential for stabilizing the appetite and improving digestion, particularly of carbohydrates, sugar, and alcohol.

Benefits Regarding Your Overall Health

Kefir helps stop food cravings because the body feels nourished as an inner balance is achieved and nutritional deficiencies are corrected.

Kefir provides a "sour" taste. Chinese medicine teaches us there are five tastes necessary for balance in the body; the sour taste is not commonly found in our American diet.

The skin prospers from kefir. It will become moist and creamy and, over time, you will notice a refinement of the pores. You can use kefir externally to help moisturize your skin; yet, it is beneficial for oily skin too. Fermented milks contain lactic acid which is one of the naturally occurring Alpha hydroxy acid, (AHA) so popular in the cosmetic world today. You'll love experimenting with our skincare recipes in The Magic of Kefir.

Kefir is cooling to the body, so it is ideal to eat when you have a fever or any other condition of body heat.

After taking antibiotics, kefir is very useful for reestablishing friendly bacteria in the intestines. Kefir is "Nature's antibiotic." Using it helps reduce the need for antibiotics in the future.

Kefir's friendly bacteria automatically show up in the vagina, or you can implant them more directly as a douche.

While colonic therapy helps cleanse pathogenic yeast from the large intestine, such yeast colonize in the small intestine as well. Fermented foods like kefir and raw cultured vegetables have a cleansing effect on both intestines. Once these are free of pathogens, the liver is able to function much better, releasing its toxins into a clean colon as it was designed to do.

Kefir helps produce more pleasant breath, healthier bowel movements, and sweeter-smelling stools. And it can eliminate flatulence!

How to Introduce Kefir Into Your Diet

Some people thrive on kefir right from the start and others may need to proceed more slowly. Remember that people with candidiasis lack milk-digesting bacteria, so you may have to build up your "tolerance" of kefir. Start with about four ounces in the morning on an empty stomach. Every second day increase the amount until you are able to drink a full eight ounce glass.

If you are just beginning the therapeutic version of the Body Ecology Diet's health recovery program, it might be best to wait three to six months before introducing kefir. You may first need to clear your body of accumulated toxins and see your symptoms disappear. Moreover, people with candidiasis have what Chinese medicine calls the condition of dampness. Unfermented and improperly combined dairy products can lead to even more dampness and excess mucus. Here are some suggestions for introducing kefir while conquering dampness.

1. Eat Body Ecology Diet foods, which are drying.

2. Use proper food combining techniques to make kefir less mucous-forming. (see below)

3. Drink plenty of water and eat grains that have been soaked and then cooked. These add moisture and fiber to the colon.

4. Clean you colon. If a colon is free of blockages, kefir is tolerated more quickly. We have found that people who report having trouble with kefir, often have not followed the advice on colon cleansing. You probably also need to add acidophilus (Bio-K+) and bifidus bacteria to your small and large intestines. These wonderful bacteria also help to clean and improve the health of your entire digestive tract.

5. Be sure to get adequate exercise. Exercise stimulates the colon and improves elimination.

6. Make your kefir from goat milk if you find cow milk is mucous-forming. The milk from a mother's breast is alkaline-forming. Goat milk is also alkaline, while cow milk is acidic. This could explain why goat milk is often better tolerated by humans. It also has more calcium, magnesium, phosphorus, and potassium than cow milk. Goat milk contains no folic acid, however, so pregnant and nursing mothers should consider a folic acid supplement and eat leafy greens, broccoli, root vegetables and whole grains. Goat milk will also require more starter culture. (Use one and a half packets of starter culture to each quart of goat milk.) If you would like to learn more about the benefits of goat milk, see GOAT MILK MAGIC by Dr. Bernard Jensen.

Food Combining Rules for Kefir

As a dairy product, kefir should be eaten alone, on an empty stomach, or combined with:

1) raw or lightly steamed vegetables (Try a salad with our kefir dressing recipe, or use our recipe to make a kefir dip for raw veggies.);

2) acid (sour) fruits such as strawberries, lemons, limes, grapefruits, pineapples, cranberries, or blueberries;

3) soaked nuts or seeds.

Kefir smoothies are especially delicious and very popular as a morning breakfast for our children. In the beginning the non-alcoholic flavorings work well, but as your child becomes well, you can add acid fruits. Simply blend kefir, your favorite berries or flavorings and stevia. A little unrefined flax seed oil, Essential Balance™, or Essential Balance Jr.™ (all made by Omega Nutrition) is a "must" for children...especially those with eczema and Attention Deficit Hyperactivity Disorder.

To insure that kefir is not overly mucous-forming, do not combine it with proteins (except nuts and seeds) or starches.

Around the world, however, kefir is eaten throughout the day, even as a digestive aid after a meal. Once your inner ecosystem is restored (anywhere from three months to a year), you may experiment and want to try kefir at the end of a meal, even though it is more mucous-forming at this time. See what works for you. Some people think that eating kefir about an hour before bedtime helps them relax and fall asleep. Remember it is rich in tryptophan.

In the chapter on food combining, we recommend you wait three hours after eating dairy foods before dining on protein or starches. However, because kefir's protein is pre-digested and the friendly yeast and bacteria speed up digestion, you need only wait about 45 minutes to an hour before eating something else.

So have kefir as your first food of the day and follow the directions in the next chapter for additions to this morning "cocktail."

Contents of a Spectacular Kefir Drink

Make your kefir with the freshest milk possible, then add as many of the following ingredients as you wish:

- Up to 1 tsp. of unrefined flax seed oil or Essential Balance™ oil, Essential Balance Junior™, (made by Omega Nutrition), a butterscotch-flavored oil that is especially appealing to kids.

- Lecithin to taste. Lecithin assists in the digestion of fat. If you make kefir from skim milk, the only fat will come from the unrefined oil. However, the beneficial microorganisms prefer a little fat; so 2% or whole milk makes a better kefir.

- Fiber, such as Nutri-Flax™.

- Probiotics, if you are taking them currently.

- Natural flavorings or herbs, such as stevia, nutmeg, cinnamon, or non-alcoholic vanilla or fruit flavorings (peach, strawberry, lemon, lime, raspberry, orange, tangerine).

Is Kefir Right For Me?

Some people believe that milk and dairy products should be eaten only by newborns, and that, since no adult animals in the wild drink milk, we adult humans shouldn't either. Others have an ethical objection to dairy products. You need to decide for yourself.

Perhaps you will achieve such great results with kefir that you will want to continue it indefinitely. Or you may want to use it for a short period of time, being mindful of its mucous-forming effects. Or maybe two to three times a week is best for you. Studies show that cultured foods such as our raw cultured vegetables, kefir, or miso and tempeh in the more traditional Oriental diet, are key components in a genuinely healthy diet. It is wise to keep colonizing the intestinal tract with beneficial bacteria. Research shows that beneficial bacteria disappear from the stool once probiotic therapy is discontinued.

We would not recommend anything that we haven't found to be superior in helping people heal, but we also know how important it is to trust the wisdom of what your own body tells you. Learn to listen to its signs and signals.

A Word of Caution

Constipation

Even though kefir traditionally is recommended as a laxative, a small percentage of people find it constipating. This may be because they lack the enzymes necessary to digest the milk protein (casein) or the milk fat. Try making your kefir from non-fat, organic milk. Also combine 2 ounces of water with only 4 ounces of kefir and drink this small amount in the mornings on an empty stomach.

Be sure to add other probiotics that thrive in the small intestine and colon, especially acidophilus and casei (Bio-K+) and various bifidus strains. Expect to take them 2-3 weeks before seeing an improvement. With time, more dairy-loving bacteria and yeast will colonize your digestive tract. Once this happens you can digest dairy better. We also recommend taking a digestive enzyme formulated to digest milk products (see shopping list page 253).

If you become constipated after adding kefir to your diet, ask yourself these questions:

✔ Am I eating enough fiber? Kefir lacks fiber, so be sure to eat plenty of the high fiber foods: vegetables, salads, raw cultured vegetables, and the Body Ecology grains.

✔ Am I following the food combining rules?

✔ Am I eating too much kefir and skipping other meals? Since kefir is so delicious and is the perfect "fast food" it is easy to overeat it, skipping essential high fiber meals.

✔ Am I eating sugary foods and flour products? Both are constipating.

Teeth

A final reminder: brush your teeth after you eat kefir. Its bacteria produce an acid condition in the plaque that can lead to decay without proper care (just as any food left in the mouth without proper rinsing and care can lead to decay).

Vitamin C

Do not take your Vitamin C with a Kefir meal. Kefir is so powerful as a digestive aid that, when it is present in the intestines, it may prevent Vitamin C from reaching the bloodstream. If you have a cold or other condition that creates a lot of mucus, such as an ear infection, stop your Kefir and start taking therapeutic doses of Vitamin C (several thousand milligrams per day, to bowel tolerance).

Where Can I Get Some Kefir?

Kefir made right in your own kitchen, is not only delicious, but it is also more medicinal than store-bought kefir. That's because the bacteria and beneficial yeast are really viable. When you make it yourself, you also have a choice of the quality and kind of milk to use. Choices include non-fat, 1%, 2% or whole cow's milk, goat's milk, soymilk and even raw milk (if available). The great news is that homemade is also unbelievably easy. Just add a simple starter culture (that looks like acidophilus or bifidus powder) to room-temperature milk, shake or stir, then cover it and let it sit for 24 hours on your kitchen countertop. You'll know it is ready when the milk turns thick and you could stand a toothpick up in it. Then, refrigerate your kefir to stop the fermentation process. If you leave it for several hours longer, it will start to turn to kefir cheese.

Of course, there are times when you may want to simply purchase your kefir. Carefully read the label to make sure a product labeled kefir is really true kefir. Kefir produced by **Helios Nutrition** is the only kefir that carries our Body Ecology seal of approval. It's organic, it has FOS (food for the friendly micro-organisms) and it tastes wonderful. The plain flavor (unsweetened) is the one to buy when you have candidiasis. Plain flavor is delicious, but you can change the flavor simply by adding one of the non-alcoholic flavorings found in your health food store.**

An important tip for Goat Milk lovers: If you make your kefir from goat's milk, you will need to increase the amount of starter culture. Instead of using one packet of starter use one and a half packets.

NOTE: Kefir starter culture is available by calling 1-800-511-2660. **Helios Nutrition kefir is available in fine health food stores.

Points To Remember About Kefir

✔ To obtain a microbial-rich, potent kefir, make a new batch every day or two. Use the freshest organic milk you can find to ensure high-quality and good flavor.

✔ Kefir is the healthy equivalent of a "fast food." It provides a filling meal that is nutrient-rich and easy to digest. Its high liquid content makes it an ideal breakfast food, since it's best taken on an empty stomach.

✔ Kefir should be used as one of the first steps in restoring your inner ecology. It will help establish a foundation of beneficial bacteria; then you can add the more expensive probiotics from your health food store.

✔ You can make kefir from cow, goat, or soy milk. You can even culture organic cream and make kefir sour cream.

✔ If you are allergic to lactose, don't worry. The yeast and bacteria in kefir digest the milk sugar lactose. Any remaining is taken care of by the lactase enzymes. After reestablishing your inner ecosystem, you may find that you can more easily digest other dairy foods.

PART SEVEN

Special Foods, Recipes, & Menu Suggestions

by DONNA GATES and HEIDI WOHL

Introduction

By now you've studied the principles of the Body Ecology Diet, thought about how they will apply to *your* life, and are ready to try some recipes. You'll find new recipes in this section, or perhaps variations on some of your favorites. Once you master the principles, the rest falls into place.

We want you to enjoy experimenting with the new foods we introduce on the Diet, such as the grains and sea vegetables. Remember, the information may be overwhelming at first—this is normal—but soon you'll be up to speed and feeling much better.

Heidi's Story

"I grew up on the standard American diet: meat, canned and frozen food, sugar, and lots of junk food when I was a teenager. By the time I was 20, I decided I was addicted to sugar and vowed to do something about it. So I started taking lots of vitamin pills, drank pep up drinks, and I gave up sugar. I did start feeling better, but that was not to last.

"I studied nutrition and tried various diets. I became a vegetarian, gave up cheese and dairy, and tried a raw foods diet. Despite all this, I had lots of viral infections, sore throats, excessive mucus and nasal discharge, and chronic constipation.

"Then I went headlong into studying and practicing macrobiotics for several years. I was sure that would be the answer, but it wasn't. I developed a fungal infection around my mouth, my digestion was poor, and the chronic constipation continued. I always had a bad taste in my mouth.

"I tried acupuncture and received counseling at the highest level of macrobiotics. I was told to cut out virtually all salt, oils, fruit, many vegetables, and strictly limit my fish intake. I was desperate to be healthy, so I took all these steps. At this time I was pregnant. My skin turned yellow, I had no energy, I felt weak and tired all the time, constipation was worse than ever, and I had indigestion after every meal. I continued to believe that brown rice, beans, and greens would save me if only I could eat enough of them.

"Then I met Donna. I began the Body Ecology Diet immediately, and when I did, my digestion improved dramatically, the embarrassing fungal infection on my mouth started to go away, and my spirits lifted. I didn't realize how much my nervous system had been affected by my candidiasis. I began to feel calmer. Things that had caused tremendous stress in the past, even such simple things as preparing a meal and getting it on the table, became pleasant. Taking a car trip to the city, which had been stressful and demanding, suddenly became routine. I began enjoying food once again.

"Now I prepare all the meals for my family based on the Diet guidelines, with reasonable adjustments for individual needs. We've all benefitted from the Diet. I love to cook and create new recipes. All the recipes I've contributed to the Body Ecology Diet will add variety to your meals as well as help you restore your inner balance. They are my gift in gratitude for what the Diet has done for me. Bon Appetit!"

Heidi Wohl

Tying It All Together:
How to Make the Diet Work for You

Yes, there *is* a lot of information to absorb, a lot of things to do to make the Diet an integral part of your life. Remember the principle of step by step. You don't need to do everything the first day. Look back through this book at least one more time before you do anything else. Set aside a time just for planning and organizing. The biggest reason people feel overwhelmed on the Diet is failure to prepare and plan. Take the enthusiasm you have from reading this book and use it to incorporate the Diet into your daily life. Here are some suggestions...step by step.

Step One

Take a look at what you already have.

Standing in your kitchen with paper and pencil in hand, evaluate what's there. What staple foods do you have on hand, and what do you need? Body Ecology Diet staples include: the four grains, onions, garlic, red skin potatoes, cooking oil, spices, apple cider vinegar, teas, and other items from the Shopping List. Get rid of foods that are not on the Diet.

Step Two

Reorganize your kitchen so it works for you.

Arrange the kitchen so the things you use most frequently are closest to your working space. For example, keep the onions, garlic, and your favorite knife near your cutting board. If some members of your family are not on the Diet, put their foods in a separate area of your cupboards or pantry. This will reduce the temptation for you to eat them, and also make it easier for everyone to find what he likes.

You might even want to make sections inside your refrigerator, with one shelf for leftovers, one for fresh foods, etc. Or organize it by meals, breakfast foods here, lunch foods there; or divide it by days or by household members.

Step Three

Start your lists.

Next, start a shopping list. Review Chapter 12 to see what foods are on the Diet, and look at the Body Ecology Diet Shopping List to remind you what to buy. Note the foods you already enjoy and the family recipes you can easily adapt. For example, you may often serve grilled salmon steaks, steamed broccoli tossed with garlic and lemon, and a leafy green salad with grated carrots and Vidalia onion. Make a B.E.D. salad dressing, and you've created your first Body Ecology Diet meal.

Step Four

Plan a few delicious menus of your own or choose some of ours.

Plan at least three days of menus. When you go shopping, you may have to revise your plan, depending on what's available and fresh. If you want to cook Brussels sprouts but when you arrive at the grocery store they look pale and limp, you should be flexible enough to investigate the green beans or broccoli. Try to shop for fresh foods two or three times a week.

Some people find it easier to plan meals for a week or ten days, then rotate this same group of menus and recipes. Repeating the menu you love has certain benefits. You can perfect the seasonings and ultimately save lots of time, as you become quite efficient with repetition. For example, Monday nights might be for curried carrot soup, millet corn casserole, and a parboiled salad; Saturday morning breakfasts might be an arame and onion omelette with steamed asparagus. Put your menu plans on the refrigerator as a support and as a constant reminder so that you do stay on the Diet.

Benefits of Meal Planning

Menu planning makes adherence to the Body Ecology Diet much, much easier. If you have several days' meals, or a week's meals planned on paper, you can shop more quickly and even prepare meals more efficiently. You know what's in your refrigerator, and you know what's needed to put a meal on the table. You can plan ahead by, for example, washing and drying lettuce for the next meal while you're waiting for the breakfast veggies to sauté. Store the lettuce in a clean plastic container, and when you're ready to make a salad for lunch, it will be nice and crispy, and you'll be one step ahead.

Another benefit of meal planning is that you're much less likely to go off the Diet on binges. You've made a plan...now all you have to do is follow it. You can even plan snacks, so that when you suddenly find you're starving, you grab the carrot sticks you've already cut up or the blue corn chips from the cupboard. Try dipping blue corn chips into raw cultured vegetables for a great snack. Make a big pot of vegetable soup, and keep it in the refrigerator where you can dip into it whenever you're hungry. If it's a non-starchy vegetable soup (creamy cauliflower dill or broccoli fennel), you won't have to worry about whether it combines with the grain or animal protein meal you're about to eat in an hour.

You'll also be less likely to run out to a restaurant if you have a meal planned and the food in the house, ready to be cooked. It's difficult (although not impossible) to food combine properly in a restaurant where everyone around you is eating based on desires, not necessarily on health. Most restaurants do not offer the healing food that you can eat at home.

The Art of The Diet

Planning the Body Ecology Diet meals at first will seem strange, just like anything new. It's like standing at the bottom of a mountain and searching for the summit. Don't despair. Soon the various elements of the Diet will become second nature to you, and you will be creating meals as part artist, part cook. At some point, you may not need to sit down and plan every single meal. You might just go to the store, buy lots of fresh vegetables to have on hand, and come home to create a variety of dishes.

Even if you cook a new recipe that doesn't taste quite right, give it another try – it may take a couple of times to get it just the way you like it. Experiment with herbs and spices; develop recipes of your own and send them to us – we will publish them in the Body Ecology Diet newsletter.

Keep in Mind

As you create your menus, remember to use the principles of expansion/contraction, acid/alkaline, food combining, and the 80/20 rules. Your goal is to create balance in your body by balancing the foods you eat. You don't want to eat too much to the extreme expansion or contraction ends of the continuum; you want 80% of your food to be alkaline-forming and 20% to be acid-forming.

As you begin the Diet, you may need more protein foods to enhance the yeast die-off. You may tolerate more cooked foods than raw, but as soon as you can, try to include some raw foods, such as salad or cut-up veggies, at least once a day. You'll get to know your body very well and discover what it needs for you to feel good. If you eat something that's very contracting, such as salty meat, and you start feeling cranky or achy, you can bring your body back into balance by eating foods that are more alkaline and expanding (a salad with apple cider vinegar dressing).

If you're having a snack, ask yourself if it combines with your last meal, which is probably still digesting in your stomach.

There are several additional things to consider in meal planning. Is your body in a cleansing period? If it is, eat lightly and plan foods that are easy to digest. For example, steamed carrots are easier to digest than raw ones. Soups are easier than salads, and blended soups are easiest of all.

Take note of the season, too: if it's hot, plan lighter, cooling foods; in cold weather your body needs heavier, warming foods. Chilled summer soups, raw salads, and fruit are cooling; hot soups and porridge are warming.

If you're constipated, avoid contracting foods, such as meats and eggs. Instead, eat the more expanding foods, such as salad and raw cultured vegetables; drink lemon juice and water. Try grain with vegetable meals, which have lots of fiber. Sprinkle flax seeds on your food, and use the ocean vegetable agar to aid elimination.

If you're a woman, consider where you are in your monthly cycle. From the time you ovulate to the end of your menstrual period, eat foods with as little salt as possible, because you want to encourage a complete cleansing, a complete shedding of the uterine lining, and salt restricts that. After your period, it's okay to increase your salt intake a bit.

Add Fun, Reduce Stress

Getting back to the art and creativity of cooking, remember to vary the color and texture of the foods you make. If you're making millet with cauliflower, brighten the plate with a lightly steamed green vegetable and maybe a few shavings of carrot or bits of red pepper. If you're serving a dark green ocean vegetable, garnish it with lemon or cucumber slices or a red radish cut like a flower. Regarding texture, serve creamy mashed potatoes with a crisp salad, or blended soup with crunchy baked blue corn chips.

Try to serve the food attractively, too. Put your grain serving in a little mold and turn it upside down on the plate, or mound it and surround it with green veggies or top it with a few sprigs of parsley. Sprinkle dill on top of a bowl of soup, or arrange lemon slices and parsley on fish.

You may be a gourmet cook who likes to spend a lot of time in the kitchen, or you may be a working mother who needs to do ten things at once. Wherever you fit, you can adapt all the things you've ever learned about cooking and food to the Body Ecology Diet. The only thing you need to change is the food itself, and after practicing with the Diet a bit, it won't seem like much of a change at all. You can use healthy cooking and eating to express your inner self, to express the newfound vitality you will feel as you use the Diet to rebuild your immunity.

Cooking to Heal

The Body Ecology Diet foods build the immune system and nourish the body and the spirit. They should be cooked with the intention to heal. A cook's vibrations are always in the food he or she cooks. Many spiritual leaders choose a spiritually elevated follower to cook for them. They know that only a well-balanced, centered person has the power to create meals with a harmonious and positive energy. Creating a meal can be an expression of love for those who will eat it. Whether you cook for yourself or for those you love, it's important to cook with the intention to heal, with calmness and appreciation for the benefits the food can bring.

Hopefully, you'll continue to learn about the energetics of foods and of the impact foods have on your body. For example, the sweet vegetables (onions, carrots, winter squash) nourish the spleen, which is often weak in people with candidiasis. You never want to cook with *refined* fats and oils, because your organs—already weakened by yeast and toxins—cannot process them. Excessive gas and bloating could indicate that the liver isn't handling any fats. You can alleviate this by temporarily using no-oil salad dressings until you tolerate the *unrefined*, essential fatty acid oils we recommend. Taking digestive enzymes high in lipase, not overeating, not eating late at night, and using herbs such as milk thistle, fennel, and dandelion also helps heal the liver. Blood sugar problems, including hypoglycemia, and diabetes also indicate inappropriate absorption of refined fats and protein.

As we've indicated, the amount of salt you use is critical. Signs of too much salt include dark circles under the eyes, irritability, craving for sweets; and in children, whining.

What About Breakfast?

When you wake up in the morning, your body is in an acid condition after being asleep all night. Ideally, you want to use alkaline foods to bring back the balance as your body recovers from the overnight detoxifying and cleansing stages. **VITALITY SuperGreen**™ is an ideal alkaline, nutrient-rich, morning breakfast drink and is convenient if you're in a hurry.

Many people are used to a grain breakfast, but remember to balance your grain such as millet or amaranth with lots of water and some leftover or freshly chopped vegetables. This has the additional benefit of adding water to your system, which has been without it all night.

If you have a pressure cooker, cook 1 cup millet with seven cups of water. Include sea salt and any veggies, such as carrots, onions, or leftover ocean veggies from the night before, or add a strip of the ocean vegetable kombu to the pot before cooking. Cook it under pressure for about 30 minutes. This "gruel" or "porridge" is excellent for correcting constipation.

Vegetable soup is excellent for breakfast: it adds water to the body and gives you valuable nutrients to start the day.

For a sweeter start to your day, try cooking Quinoa Flakes (Ancient Harvest) with vanilla flavoring, cinnamon, and stevia. Add flax seed oil or Essential Balance™ after it cools a bit. You can also have puffed millet with the Body Ecology Diet "Milk" (see recipe).

Once you can tolerate flint corn, try boiling onion and fresh corn together with white corn grits. With this or any cooked grain/veggie combination, you can cook it up the night before, pour it into a baking dish and let it cool overnight. In the morning slice it into squares and sauté it in a little coconut oil or ghee, making a "grain fritter." Serve with a favorite steamed vegetable and tea.

Eggs are fine for breakfast, too—just remember they need to be balanced with foods that are more expansive and alkaline. That means vegetables, ocean vegetables, and raw cultured vegetables. A cup of hot water and lemon will aid digestion. Make an omelette with vegetables, or fold in greens from last night's dinner to make a balanced breakfast.

Many people eat fish or meat for breakfast. If you combine these with lightly steamed vegetables, you'll have a fine meal. A glass of unsweetened cranberry juice sweetened with stevia and taken one half hour before you eat your meat or fish meal will keep you from feeling too contracted. Of course, this type of heavy breakfast would sound most appealing in the cold winter months and totally unattractive in the heat of the summer.

Include *at least* 1/4 cup of cultured vegetables with your morning meals. Animal protein foods and grain dishes always digest better when eaten with these enzyme-rich vegetables. No medicine can replace the benefit of the friendly bacteria they create.

Only after your body ecology is well restored can you introduce fruit. If you've been symptom-free for three months, try grapefruit or kiwi. Remember to have it in the morning when your stomach is empty. You can eat grapefruit or kiwi for breakfast, then wait at least 30 minutes and eat another type of food if you wish. If you do heavy physical work during the day, a breakfast of fruit alone probably doesn't have enough sustaining power to keep you going until lunch. That fish or meat with vegetables breakfast we mentioned above will. But if you work at a desk, you might be able to eat fruit for breakfast and mid-morning snacks and not have other foods until lunch.

Authors Note: In this latest edition we have included a new section on kefir. It makes a perfect breakfast food. If you tolerate it well, you'll find a wonderful new way to enjoy a high-protein breakfast and help reestablish a healthy inner eco-system. It is quick, convenient, and provides an ideal delivery system for the Omega-3, Omega-6, and GLA (Borage Seed) oils.

Lunch and Dinner

There are endless combinations of lunch and dinner possibilities. The following menu suggestions are only guidelines to start you on your way. As you become more adept at developing your own delicious recipes and menus, please send in your ideas and suggestions; we would love to publish them in the Body Ecology Diet Newsletter. We are always amazed at how creative our readers are and how clever they are at applying the principles of the Body Ecology Diet.

The Body Ecology Diet Menu Suggestions

For the week of: _____ Name: _____

	Breakfast	Lunch	Dinner	Snack
Monday	Baked Eggs Arame with Onions and Carrots Leftover Green Vegetable Raw Cultured Vegetables Chamomile Tea with Stevia	Watercress Soup Curried Summertime Corn Salad Tea	Broccoli Fennel Soup Millet Amaranth Corn Casserole Salad with B.E.D. Dressing Tea with Stevia	Tea with Stevia B.E.D. Cookies Popcorn and Carrot Sticks
Tuesday	Stevia-Sweetened Cream of Buckwheat OR Savory Cream of Buckwheat with Sautéed Vegetables Digest Ease Tea	Cauliflower Dill Soup Salmon Steaks Green Beans and Garlic Raw Cultured Vegetables Tea	Baked Potatoes Topped with Carrot Cauliflower Tarragon Mustard Sauce and Raw Cultured Vegetables Parboiled Salad Tea with Stevia	Celery Sticks with Soaked Almonds
Wednesday	Cranberry Juice (wait 30 minutes) Puffed Millet Cereal with B.E.D. "Acidophilus Milk"	Scrambled Eggs with Onion, Shitake and Red Pepper Asparagus Spears Raw Cultured Vegetables Tea with Stevia	Waffles Topped with Italian-Style Carrot Sauce Salad with Italian Dressing Raw Cultured Vegetables Tea	B.E.D. Vanilla Pudding
Thursday	Soft Cooked Millet Porridge with Onions and Carrots Raw Cultured Vegetables Echinacea Plus Tea with Stevia	Carrot Cauliflower Tarragon Soup Quinoa Salad on Bed of Leaf Lettuce Raw Cultured Vegetables Tea with Stevia	Baked Eggs Carrot Salad Steamed Kale and Daikon Raw Cultured Vegetables Tea	Celery Sticks with Soaked Almonds
Friday	Puréed Non-Starchy Vegetable Soup Baked Chicken or Fish (leftover from day before) Warm Water with Wedge of Lemon	Potato Corn Chowder with Savory Crackers or Blue Corn Chips Salad with B.E.D. Dressing Tea	Vegetarian Kasha Meatloaf with Gingery Carrot Sauce Mixed Vegetable Sauté Salad with B.E.D. Dressing Tea	Almondine Dip with Crudités
Saturday	Vegetable Omelette Steamed Broccoli Raw Cultured Vegetables Ginger Root Tea with Stevia	Salad Plate Special: Corn Salad, Cole Slaw, Raw Cultured Vegetables, New Potato Salad on Bed of Leafy Lettuce Tea	Millet "Mashed Potatoes" with B.E.D. Gravy Broccoli Spears Sweet Carrot Gelatin Salad Tea	Raw Cultured Vegetables with Blue Corn Chips
Sunday	Grain Fritters with Onion and Fresh Corn Steamed Green Vegetable Pau D'Arco Tea with Stevia	Grilled Swordfish Steak Sweet Carrot Gelatin Salad Brussels Sprouts Raw Cultured Vegetables Tea	Rosemary Roasted Potatoes Collard Greens Corn on the Cob Arame with Onions and Carrots Raw Cultured Vegetables	Celery Sticks with Soaked Almonds

Shopping List

These menu plans are given only as examples of balanced B.E.D. meals. You'd have to be in the kitchen all day or hire a cook to prepare them *all* as shown. With more experience and careful planning, you can develop time-saving menus of your own.

FIGURE 9

Menu Blank

For the week of: _____   Name: _____

	Breakfast	Lunch	Dinner	Snack	Shopping List
Monday					
Tuesday					
Wednesday					
Thursday					
Friday					
Saturday					
Sunday					

The Body Ecology Diet Soups

Mention the word soup, and most people can picture a steaming bowl of delicious, nutritious food...or they can remember the great aromas that drew them to their mothers' kitchens...or they recall how a bowl of cold soup calmed them down on a hot summer day. The Diet has soups just as good as these. They're simple to make, easy to digest, and very healing.

Traditionally, soup is served at lunch or dinner, but we recommend you eat it for breakfast, too. Because it has a high water content and is alkaline-forming, it is ideal in the morning, when your body is dehydrated and acid from several hours' sleep. You can make your breakfast soup as light or heavy as you want, eating anything from a vegetable broth to a vegetable soup with cut-up vegetables and even grains in it.

Soups are a godsend for busy people. Pull out that crockpot you never use, and cook soup in it while you're out working or running errands. You can make a large amount and keep it in the refrigerator for several days, so you always have a complete, healthy meal at your fingertips. When you have something like this so available, it's easier to stay on the Diet without binging or deviating from the guidelines.

If you don't like to cook, or feel you're not particularly good at it, soups are pretty foolproof. You can season them to your individual taste preferences, add leftovers to fill them out, and change the taste each time you make them. It's a chance to be creative and daring—it's almost impossible to make a mistake! Children—who are often picky eaters—seem to love soup.

Try what Heidi calls a "Clean Out the Refrigerator" soup. Look for vegetables or leftovers that will spoil unless they're used soon, and invent a soup from them. Or make a soup using scraps of onion skins, carrot peels, celery leaves, broccoli stems, cabbage cores, and fresh herbs. The skins and peels of vegetables contain extraordinary amounts of nutrients, but use them only if they're organic, because pesticides and toxins accumulate on the skin or in the area between the root and leaves, as on carrots.

Aren't sure how to use those good-for-you sea vegetables? Put several three-inch strips of kombu in the pot when you start your soup. Remove and chop them up when the soup is cooked.

If you have an especially weak intestinal tract, we highly recommend that you blend soups, which makes them even easier to digest. You can use a hand-held blender such as the Cuisinart® Quick-Prep™ to purée the soup right in the pot and save yourself some cleanup time.

Most of our soups taste terrific either hot or cold, so adjust them to the seasons. Our "cream" soups, such as Creamy Dilled Cauliflower, don't really use cream or any dairy ingredient; they are blended and only taste rich and creamy.

In vegetable soups (starchy or non-starchy), you can use a bit of oil, butter, or preferably ghee. The best way to start is to melt the ghee, then add seasonings, then sauté the onions and other vegetables for a few minutes each in this mixture before adding your water or broth. The sautéing, especially of the onions, yields a more flavorful soup, but if you're short on time, just put everything in the pot and start it cooking.

Usually you should add salt during the final 10 - 20 minutes of cooking, or after pureeing, but if you want the vegetables to stay firm, add salt in the beginning. Add just enough to bring out flavor in the ingredients, but not enough for the soup to taste "salty."

Many traditional soup recipes, especially those containing animal protein, can be adapted to Body Ecology Diet principles. So go to it, and have some fun!

Special Note

For especially delicious soups—and a real time saver—replace the garlic and oil in our recipes with a combined "garlic oil."

We make garlic oil from whole bulbs of organic garlic and unrefined safflower oil. It keeps well in a glass jar in the refrigerator, and you can use it to sauté onions for soups. It seems to replace the "body" found in meat stocks that chefs strive for in vegetarian soups. Often, however, these chefs resort to stocks that contain yeast or hydrolyzed vegetable protein, a naturally occurring MSG which is found in all fermented soy products.

To make garlic oil, peel two entire bulbs (not cloves) of garlic and place the cloves in a blender; pulse until coarsely chopped. Slowly add two cups of unrefined safflower oil while blending. Pour into a glass jar and refrigerate until needed.

If you own a Cuisinarte® Quick-Prep™ or similar hand-held blender, it's even easier. Simply chop the garlic right in a wide-mouth glass jar. Then slowly add the oil while blending.

Garlic is a powerful antifungal, excellent for warding off parasites, yeast, and pathogenic bacteria. This great recipe idea isn't just for soups. Use garlic oil to replace garlic and the oil or butter in any of our Body Ecology Diet recipes.

Non-Starchy Vegetable Soups--
They go with everything!

Carrot-Cauliflower with Tarragon

This is one of our most popular soups and is great to serve to even your most difficult-to-please guests. It combines with animal protein and grain entrees. Make enough to have for several meals. It disappears quickly in our families.

Ingredients:
1 Tbsp. organic, unrefined coconut oil, ghee or butter
1 head of cauliflower, chopped
Approximately 4 cups carrots, chopped
1 large onion, chopped
3 Tbsp. fresh tarragon, chopped, or 1 Tbsp. dried
    (or to taste)
Water to cover
Sea salt or Herbamare (just enough to bring out
    a delicious taste)

1. In a soup pot, melt oil and then add tarragon
    if using it dried.
2. Add onion, sautéing until translucent.
3. Add carrots, cauliflower and water (also add
    tarragon if using fresh).
4. Simmer until tender (approximately 25 minutes)
5. In blender, purée.
6. Return to soup pot, adding sea salt or Herbamare.
7. Simmer for 10 minutes and serve.

Creamy Dilled Cauliflower Soup

This is a very elegant soup and is excellent with animal protein meals such as grilled salmon steak. Everyone loves it!

Ingredients:
1 Tbsp. organic, unrefined coconut oil, ghee or butter
1 large onion, chopped
4 - 6 cloves garlic, chopped (or to taste)
1 large head (or two small heads) cauliflower,
    cut into chunks
Handful of florets separated from the head of
        cauliflower
6 Tbsp. fresh dill or 2 Tbsp. dried
4 - 6 cups water
Sea salt or Herbamare to taste

1. In a stockpot, melt oil, then add dill if using dried.
2. Add onion, sautéing until translucent.
3. Add garlic and sauté a few minutes, being careful not to overcook garlic.
4. Add cauliflower chunks (and fresh dill if using) and enough water to cover.
5. Simmer until tender.
6. Purée in blender and then return to stockpot.
7. Add approximately 4 cups water depending on desired thickness of soup (thicker and creamier is usually preferred)
8. Add sea salt or Herbamare to taste, and florets.
9. Simmer until florets are tender. Adjust seasonings and serve.

Variation:
1. Add 1 tsp. Desert Spice from Nile Spice Foods, Inc.
2. After blending, add sliced shitake mushroom and cook about ten minutes more.

Watercress Soup

Another very elegant soup, watercress is especially healing for the liver. Also excellent for dinner guests; it goes very well with animal protein meals. Delicious with starchy vegetables and grains, too.

Ingredients:
1 large onion, chopped
1 Tbsp. organic, unrefined coconut oil, ghee or butter
5 very large cloves (or more) garlic, chopped
1 cup celery leaves
6 cups water
Sea salt and Herbamare to taste
1/2 tsp. (or to taste) Dr. Bronner's Balanced Mineral
      Seasoning (optional)
1 bunch watercress, washed well, large stems
      removed, and chopped

1. In stockpot, sauté onion in oil over very low heat until translucent.
2. Add garlic and celery tops and sauté slowly (approx. 5 minutes more).
3. Add water, sea salt, and Herbamare, and continue simmering for 10 minutes.
4. Purée soup in blender for several minutes until very smooth.
5. Return to stockpot, adjust seasonings.
6. Drop watercress into soup.
7. Bring to boil, turn off, and cover a few minutes before serving.

Broccoli with Fresh Fennel Soup

Very popular as a breakfast soup. Fennel aids digestion. Be sure to buy a bulb of fennel that has a generous amount of the feathery fennel tops. They look a lot like fresh dill. Use the bulb later in a vegetable soup like the Harvest Soup on page 176.

Ingredients:
1 large head broccoli (separate florets and stems)
1 large onion, chopped
4 - 6 cloves garlic, chopped
1 Tbsp. organic, unrefined coconut oil, ghee or butter
Feathery fennel tops from one bulb fresh fennel
6 cups water
Ground fennel seed, 1 tsp. or more to taste
Sea salt to taste or Herbamare
Scallions and parsley, finely chopped, for garnish

1. Remove tough outside layer of broccoli peel from stems, and chop (discard any woody pieces)
2. Sauté onion, garlic and ground fennel seed in oil until onion is translucent.
3. Add broccoli stems and most of florets, reserving a handful of the smallest ones to use later. Add fennel, and water.
4. Simmer until tender, about 20 minutes.
5. Purée mixture in blender (or use Cuisinart™ Quick Prep) for several minutes until very smooth.
6. Return to stockpot, adding sea salt or Herbamare to taste.
7. Simmer 10 more minutes, adjust seasonings before serving. Garnish with parsley, scallions or chopped red bell pepper strips.

Starchy Vegetable Soups

Teresa's Authentic Peruvian Quinoa Soup

Extremely healing and easy to digest, this soup is a meal in itself. Accompany it with a raw leafy green salad or some cultured vegetables for even better balance.

Ingredients:
1 - 2 Tbsp. organic, unrefined coconut oil,
　　ghee or butter
2 large onions, chopped
2 large leeks, washed well and chopped
2 stalks celery, chopped
3 carrots, cut into $1^{1}/2$ inch matchsticks
5 cloves garlic, chopped
1 large red bell pepper, chopped (optional)
1 cup peas
2 large red skin potatoes, diced
$1/2$ medium butternut squash, remove skin and seeds,
　　dice same as potatoes
$1/2$ head small cabbage, coarsely chopped
Leaves from 1 large bunch cilantro, chopped
1 cup fresh parsley, chopped
1 tsp. cumin (optional)
1 cup quinoa
8 cups water
Sea salt or Herbamare to taste

Sauté in oil the garlic, onions, leeks, and celery for several minutes. Add other ingredients and simmer till tender. Add sea salt the last ten minutes of cooking.

Potato/Corn Chowder

Ingredients:
1 - 2 Tbsp. organic, unrefined coconut oil, ghee or butter
1 onion, diced
1 tsp. thyme
2 bay leaves
4 - 6 cloves garlic
4 medium red potatoes, diced
4 cups corn
6 cups water
1 Tbsp. sea salt
1 leek, washed, halved lengthwise and sliced
3 stalks celery, diced
1/4 tsp. pepper

1. In coconut oil, ghee or butter, sauté onion with thyme, bay leaves, and garlic until onion is translucent.
2. Add potatoes, 2 cups corn, water, and sea salt.
3. Simmer until potatoes are tender (approx. 20 minutes).
4. Remove bay leaves and 1/4 of the soup. Purée and return to pot.
5. Add remaining corn, leeks, celery, and pepper.
6. Adjust seasonings.
7. Simmer until veggies are just tender (10-15 minutes).

Harvest Soup

Ingredients:
1 - 2 Tbsp. organic, unrefined coconut oil, ghee or butter
1 large onion, chopped
3 cloves garlic, chopped
4 - 5 medium carrots, chopped
3 medium red potatoes, chopped
1 medium fennel bulb with stalk and leaves (optional)
Broccoli stems from one bunch of broccoli, chopped
Sea salt or Herbamare to taste
Ginger Curry flavoring to taste (Nile Spice Foods)

1. In stockpot, sauté onion in oil, ghee or butter.
2. Add other vegetables and enough water to cover.
3. When vegetables are tender, purée ingredients and return to the stockpot.
4. Add more water to achieve desired consistency, sea salt, or Herbamare and other seasonings.
5. Simmer 10 more minutes and serve.

Squash and Ginger Soup

Ingredients:
1 - 2 Tbsp. organic, unrefined coconut oil, ghee or butter
1 acorn squash, skinned and chopped
2 medium carrots, chopped
2 medium onions, chopped
2 celery sticks, chopped
3 cloves garlic, minced
Large piece of ginger root (3 - 4 inches long), grated
Water to cover
Sea salt or Herbamare to taste
Minced parsley as garnish

1. Sauté carrots, onions, celery, and garlic in oil.
2. Add squash and ginger.
3. Cover with water.
4. Simmer for 30 minutes or pressure cook for 12 minutes.
5. Purée and adjust water to desired creaminess.
6. Add sea salt or Herbamare, and simmer at least 10 minutes more.
7. Serve garnished with parsley.

Lima Bean Cilantro Soup

Ingredients:
1 - 2 Tbsp. organic, unrefined coconut oil, ghee or butter
2 - 10 oz. packages frozen lima beans
2 large onions, minced
6 - 8 cloves garlic, minced
4 carrots, peeled and cut in half
8 cups water
2 tsp. sea salt or to taste
Pinch red pepper flakes (optional)
1 bunch cilantro, coarsely chopped

1. Sauté onion and garlic in oil for several minutes.
2. Add water, carrots, lima beans, and sea salt.
3. Simmer until vegetables are tender.
4. Remove carrots, cool, and slice into 1/4 " or thin rounds.
5. Purée approx. 3/4 of soup and return to pot with carrots.
6. Adjust seasonings.
7. Add cilantro and simmer for two minutes. If cilantro is unavailable try parsley, spinach, watercress, kale. Cook accordingly.

Animal Protein Soups

Fish Chowder   Remember: animal protein soups combine only with non-starchy vegetables, ocean vegetables and raw salads.

Ingredients: (Makes 2 servings)
1 Tbsp. organic, unrefined coconut oil, ghee or butter
$1/2$ cup leek or onion, minced
1 clove garlic, minced
$1/2$ cup carrots, thinly sliced
$1/2$ cup celery, thinly sliced
2 cups vegetable broth
$1/4$ cup parsley, chopped
$1/2$ bay leaf
1 whole clove
A few yellow celery tops, chopped
$3/4$ cups white fish (sole, bass, etc.) cut into cubes
$1/8$ tsp. kelp
$1/8$ tsp. sea salt or to taste
2 Tbsp. parsley or chives, minced

1. Sauté leek or onion and garlic in oil over low heat.
2. Add carrots and celery and continue to sauté for several minutes.
3. Add broth, cover, and simmer until vegetables are partially tender, about 5 minutes.
4. Add parsley, bay leaf, clove, celery tops, and fish.
5. Simmer 3 minutes more.
6. Add kelp and sea salt and remove bay leaf.
7. Serve with snipped parsley or chives.

Creamy Salmon Soup with Greens

A high calcium soup.

Ingredients:
1 - 2 Tbsp. organic, unrefined coconut oil,
    ghee or butter
1 large onion, cubed
3 carrots, chopped
1 large daikon, chopped
1 bunch kale, chopped
2 heaping tsp. dried dill
2 - 7 oz. cans salmon (including bones)
3 Tbsp. lemon juice (or to taste)
Sea salt to taste

1. In a saucepan, sauté onion in oil.
2. Add daikon and carrots and continue to sauté for several minutes.
3. Add dill and a small amount of water.
4. Place lid on saucepan and simmer on low heat for 15 minutes.
5. Add kale and cook until kale is tender.
6. Place in a blender, add salmon and blend. Add spring water as necessary to make blending go smoothly.
7. Return to stockpot.
8. Add sea salt.
9. Cook 10 more minutes.
10. Squeeze in lemon juice before serving.

Asparagus Soup

This soup is delicious hot or cold. Because of the chicken broth it only combines with non-starchy vegetables.

Ingredients:
1 - 2 Tbsp. organic, unrefined coconut oil,
    ghee or butter
3 - 4 large yellow onions, chopped
5 cans chicken broth
3 ½ lbs. fresh asparagus, cut tops off and set aside,
    cut stalks into 1" pieces (cut and discard
    tough ends)
Sea salt to taste
Pepper to taste

1. Sauté onions in oil until soft and golden.
2. Heat broth, and add cooked onions and 1" asparagus stalk pieces.
3. Cook on low heat until asparagus is soft.
4. While cooking, add sea salt and pepper.
5. Purée, then return to heat and add asparagus tops.
6. Cook for 10 more minutes (take off heat before tops become too soft).
7. For a cool soup, refrigerate.

The Body Ecology Diet Grains

A whole new world of grain dishes and recipes can open up for you as you explore the four grains on the Diet: millet, quinoa (keen-wah), buckwheat, and amaranth. You may be used to eating a lot of wheat and rice, breads and cereals, but if you try our recipes with an open mind, your cravings for these "common" breads and grains will diminish.

As you begin the Diet, you may be eating more protein meals than grain meals, but as you feel better, try to eat a grain meal (with vegetables, of course!) at least once a day. When the grains are soaked and then cooked with vegetables, they are more flavorful and even more healing.

Store grains in the refrigerator to keep any insects at bay. Soaking the grains in water for 8 to 24 hours before cooking them is a must. This makes them easier to digest. Be sure to wash them well; quinoa has a bitter outer coating and millet tends to carry a lot of "dirt" and scum. Buy a strainer with very fine mesh (particularly for amaranth and quinoa) and rinse the grains under running water for a couple minutes before starting to cook them.

The basic water-to-grain ratio is 2-1 for quinoa and buckwheat, although it can vary according to taste, recipe, and method of cooking (e.g. pressure cooker). A 3-1 ratio of water-to-grain is better for amaranth and millet. You can add salt to the pot as you start cooking; this is particularly important for buckwheat, which is acid-forming and needs the salt to make it more alkaline. Roasting millet before cooking brings out a nutty sort of taste that is particularly good. To roast the millet, just dump it in a dry pan after you soak and wash it, turn the heat on very low, and stir slowly until the millet dries and you smell a nutty flavor. The millet won't brown.

In addition to the recipes in this section, here are some suggestions for simple ways to use the Body Ecology Diet grains:

For breakfast, make Cream of Buckwheat or Quinoa Flakes with stevia, cinnamon, vanilla, and ghee—or throw in small squares of nori as it's cooking for a more savory flavor. Linda cooks amaranth with dulse, then adds ghee and a pinch of pepper. For breakfast, Heidi serves quinoa or amaranth with carrots, peas, and onions. All the grains are very compatible with red potatoes, and you can combine them with onions, peas, parsley, and dill. Buckwheat also goes well with corn, cabbage, onions, and some Dr. Bronner's seasoning.

For summer lunches, you can toss (soaked then cooked) millet or quinoa into a fresh green salad or into a cooked vegetable dish served at room temperature. You can make any number of sauces, such as cauliflower curry, or gingery carrot sauce, and spoon them over the grains. Enjoy!

Grain Dishes

Basic Amaranth Recipe – Pressure Cooked

Ingredients: (makes 2 cups)
1 cup amaranth
2 cups water
1/4 tsp. sea salt or to taste
1 Tbsp. organic, unrefined coconut oil,
    ghee or butter (optional)

1. Combine the amaranth, water, and salt in
    pressure cooker.
2. Adjust heat to maintain high pressure and cook for
    6 minutes.
3. Reduce pressure with a quick-release method.
4. Remove the lid, tilting it away from you to allow any
    excess steam to escape.
5. Stir well, adding oil, ghee or butter if desired.
    If the mixture is too thin, boil gently while stirring
    constantly until thickened, about 30 seconds.

Heidi's Onion Pie

Crust:
2 cups amaranth flour
1 tsp. sea salt
5 Tbsp. butter or
    4 Tbsp. organic, unrefined coconut oil
Approximately 1/2 cup water

1. In a bowl or food processor, place flour, sea salt, and
    butter or oil.
2. Cut or pulse butter into dough until crumbly, gradually
    adding water until dough begins to form a ball.
3. Remove from bowl or processor and form into flat ball.
4. Place on wax paper, sprinkle flour around the ball, roll
    the ball out using wax paper both under and on top of
    the dough to facilitate rolling.
5. Transfer the crust to a round pizza pan.
6. Crimp edges.

Sauce:

4 - 6 large onions, thinly sliced in $1/2$ rounds

4 cloves garlic, minced

1 Tbsp. Italian Blend or oregano, parsley,
   rosemary, basil, and celery seed

$1/2$ tsp. basil

1 Tbsp. organic, unrefined coconut oil, butter, or ghee

1 cup water

$1^{1}/2$ - 2 tsp. sea salt

$1/2$ cup amaranth

Pinch of red pepper flakes

$1/2$ red bell pepper, minced

2 - 3 green onions, thinly sliced rounds

1 Tbsp. fresh herbs such as basil or cilantro, minced
   (optional)

1. Sauté onion, garlic, herbs, and pepper flakes in oil,
   butter, or ghee.
2. Reduce heat, cover and cook until onions are tender,
   approximately 15 minutes.
3. Add water, sea salt, and amaranth.
4. Bring to a boil, reduce heat and simmer, covered, for
   approximately 20 minutes.
5. Remove lid and boil off excess liquid.
6. Add red pepper, scallions, and optional fresh herb for
   the last 2 - 3 minutes of cooking.

General Directions: (Makes 4 servings)

1. Preheat oven to 400 degrees.
2. Bake crust for 10 minutes.
3. Add toppings.
4. Sprinkle with Herbamare, garlic powder, and/or
   pepper flakes if desired.
5. Bake for approximately 20 minutes.

Basic Quinoa Recipe

Ingredients:
1 cup quinoa
2 cups water
1 pinch sea salt

1. Rinse quinoa several minutes in a strainer.
2. Place water and salt in a saucepan and bring to a rapid boil.
3. Add quinoa, reduce heat, cover, and simmer until all the water is absorbed and the grains become translucent and pop open (15 - 25 minutes).

Variation: For a rich, nutty flavor, toast quinoa (with or without organic, unrefined oil) in a skillet, stirring constantly, before adding to the water.

Curried Quinoa

Ingredients:
1 - 2 Tbsp. organic, unrefined coconut oil or ghee
1 Tbsp. curry powder
1 tsp. sea salt or Herbamare
2 cups cooked quinoa
2 medium onions, diced
2 cups cooked vegetables (peas, corn, potatoes, red bell pepper, cabbage, yellow squash, etc.)

1. Melt ghee or heat oil in wok or skillet.
2. Add curry powder and sea salt.
3. Sauté onion for several minutes until translucent.
4. Add other cooked vegetables. Sauté several minutes.
5. Add quinoa and adjust seasonings.

Heavenly Quinoa Hash

This protein rich meal is a perfect way to use leftovers.
From *Delicious* Magazine (Makes 6 servings)

Ingredients:
1 cup quinoa
2 cups water
1/4 tsp. sea salt
1 large onion, sliced
4 - 6 garlic cloves, minced
1 red pepper, diced
1/2 tsp. ginger, minced
2 red skin potatoes, cooked and diced
1/4 cup minced parsley
2 Tbsp. organic, unrefined coconut oil, ghee or butter
Herbamare and/or sea salt to taste

1. Rinse quinoa several minutes in a strainer.
2. Place water and salt in a saucepan and bring to a rapid boil.
3. Add quinoa, reduce heat, cover, and simmer until all the water is absorbed and the grains become translucent and pop open (15 - 25 minutes).
4. Sauté onion in oil, ghee or butter until translucent.
5. Add garlic and red pepper and sauté until tender.
6. Add potatoes, ginger, and parsley and sauté for few minutes more.
7. Fold in cooked quinoa, and sauté until heated.
8. Taste and adjust seasonings before serving.

Quinoa (or Buckwheat) Stuffed Peppers

Ingredients: (Makes 6 servings)
2 cups cooked quinoa, other B.E.D. grains or
    combination
1 - 2 Tbsp. organic, unrefined coconut oil,
    ghee or butter
1 medium onion, chopped fine
1 tsp. sea salt or to taste
3/4 tsp. pepper
2 Tbsp. dried sweet basil
2 Tbsp. paprika
4-6 cloves garlic, chopped fine
2 stalks celery, chopped fine
1 lb. greens such as kale, parboiled 5 minutes,
    chopped
6 red peppers, seeded and parboiled 5 minutes

1. Sauté onion in oil or ghee with seasonings until
   translucent.
2. Add garlic, celery, and kale, cook until tender.
3. Blend with cooked grains.
4. Taste mixture and adjust seasonings.
5. Stuff red peppers with quinoa mixture.
6. Bake at 350 degrees in oiled casserole for 45 minutes.

Basic Buckwheat Recipe

Ingredients:
1 cup buckwheat
2 cups water
1 tsp. sea salt or to taste

1. Soak and rinse buckwheat in strainer.
2. Place water and salt in a saucepan and bring to a
   rapid boil.
3. Add buckwheat, reduce heat, cover, and simmer until
   all the water is absorbed (approx. 15 minutes).

Variation: For a rich, nutty flavor, toast buckwheat
    (with or without organic, unrefined coconut oil,
    ghee or butter) in a skillet, stirring constantly,
    before adding to the water.

Buckwheat Croquettes

Ingredients:
2 - 3 Tbsp. organic, unrefined coconut oil, ghee or butter
1 large onion, minced
2 stalks celery, finely minced
2 cloves garlic, finely minced
1/2 cup parsley, finely minced
1 carrot, finely grated
2 cups cracked, roasted buckwheat
3 cups vegetable broth or water
1 tsp. Herbamare
1/2 tsp. sea salt
1 Tbsp. Dr. Bronner's Balanced Mineral Seasoning
1/2 cup arrowroot
1 cup millet, quinoa or amaranth flour

1. Sauté onion in 1 Tbsp. of oil, ghee or butter until slightly browned.
2. Add celery, garlic, parsley, carrot, and broth or water.
3. Cover and cook for 5 minutes.
4. Add buckwheat.
5. Cover and cook on low for 10 minutes.
6. Turn off heat and allow to steam, covered, for 10 more minutes.
7. Add flour, mix well, and set aside to cool.
8. When cool, form into patties.
9. Fry burgers in just enough oil, ghee or butter to prevent sticking to pan.
10. Drain on paper towels and serve.

Buckwheat with Corn and Cabbage

This is a nice meal served with garlic green beans and a grated carrot salad.

Ingredients:
1 - 2 Tbsp. organic, unrefined coconut oil,
    ghee or butter
2 cups corn kernels
3 cups chopped cabbage (preferably savoy)
1 large onion, chopped
1/2 red pepper, minced
4 cups vegetable stock or water
1 1/4 tsp. sea salt
1/4 tsp. pepper
1 Tbsp. Dr. Bronner's Balanced Mineral Seasoning
2 cups roasted buckwheat
1/4 - 1/2 cup parsley, minced

1. Sauté vegetables except parsley in oil for about
    5 minutes
2. Add stock or water, salt, pepper, and Dr. Bronner's.
3. Bring to boil.
4. Add buckwheat.
5. Simmer for 20 minutes.
6. Turn off heat, fold in parsley and allow to sit covered
    for 10 minutes.

Vegetarian Kasha "Meatloaf"

Good with Squash and Ginger Soup and green vegetables.

Ingredients:

1 cup buckwheat cooked in 3 cups water with
    ³/4 tsp. sea salt for 45 minutes.
1 - 2 Tbsp. organic, unrefined coconut oil,
    ghee or butter
1 medium onion, chopped fine
4 garlic cloves, chopped fine
4 stalks of celery, chopped
1 red pepper, seeds removed, and diced (optional)
1 Tbsp. (or to taste) Dr. Bronner's Balanced
    Mineral Seasoning
Sea salt and black pepper to taste
2 ears fresh corn, cut off the cob
2 cups fresh spinach or cabbage or kale, chopped
1 can water chestnuts, drained and chopped (opt.)
1 bunch scallions, chopped fine

1. Melt oil or ghee in large skillet.
2. Sauté onions, garlic, celery, and red pepper until soft.
3. Add Dr. Bronner's, sea salt, black pepper.
4. Add corn, greens, and water chestnuts, sauté until soft.
5. Add cooked buckwheat and sauté all together well.
6. Taste and adjust seasonings.
7. Fold in scallions.
8. Pour mixture in oiled loaf or casserole pan.
9. Bake at 400 degrees for 45 - 60 minutes.
10. Serve with a sauce such as Gingery Carrot Sauce, Italian Carrot Sauce, or The Body Ecology Diet Gravy.

Variations:

1. Instead of pouring the mixture into a pan: scoop out the seeds and membranes of 4 red pepper shells or carve out the center of 4 onions. Then, fold the mixture into the pepper shells or onion bowls and bake the stuffed peppers/onions at 350 degrees for 30 minutes.

2. Instead of pouring the mixture into a pan: fold the mixture into steamed cabbage leaves, wrap the leaves in a roll, and bake at 350 degrees for 30 minutes.

Basic Millet Recipe

Ingredients:
1 cup millet
3 cups water
1 tsp. sea salt or to taste

1. Wash millet well and drain.
2. Boil water and sea salt. (To get fluffy millet, boil water and salt before adding millet. If you start grains in cold water, they become creamier and sticky.)
3. Add millet, cover, reduce heat, and simmer for 25 to 30 minutes.
4. Let stand covered for 5 to 10 minutes to increase fluffiness if desired.

Variation: For an even more delicious flavor, roast millet in heavy skillet until millet has a nutty smell.

Millet "Mashed Potatoes"

Ingredients:
1 Tbsp. organic, unrefined coconut oil, butter, or ghee
1 small onion, chopped
1 cup millet (washed)
$1/2$ head cauliflower, chopped
$2 3/4$ cup water
$1/4$ tsp. salt

1. Sauté onion in oil in pressure cooker.
2. Add millet and lightly sauté.
3. Add cauliflower, sauté.
4. Add water and salt.
5. Bring to pressure, reduce heat and cook 25 minutes.

Variation: Add 1 medium chopped carrot when sautéing cauliflower.

Millet and Sweet Vegetables

With the sweet vegetables (onions, carrots, butternut squash) this dish strengthens the spleen/pancreas and stomach. For the first two to three months you may find that this dish prepared with the butternut squash is too sweet and feeds the Candida. Leave the butternut squash out of the recipe. The onions and carrots should cause no problems.

Ingredients:
2 cups millet, rinsed and dry roasted in skillet
2 medium onions, finely chopped
3 carrots, diced
1 small butternut squash, with skin cut off and cubed
1 tsp. sea salt
5 1/2 cups water
1 Tbsp. organic, unrefined coconut oil,
      ghee or butter
Several pinches of herbs may be added such as
      thyme, rosemary, sage, and celery seed

1. Into pressure cooker place millet, vegetables, sea salt, and water. (This dish can also be prepared in a saucepan. Increase the amount of water to 6 cups and follow the same directions.)
2. Dissolve sea salt into water and gently pour water around sides of millet and vegetables.
3. Close cover and bring up to pressure and cook on low flame for 30 minutes.
4. Reduce pressure and open lid.
5. Fold in oil, ghee or butter.
6. Stir well and serve.

Variations:
1. To create a creamier consistency, purée the millet/ vegetable mixture with oil, ghee or butter in a blender.

2. Add 3 inch strips of kombu ocean vegetable in the pressure cooker with the millet and vegetables. The dish will not be as sweet but it will have extra minerals.

Tex-Mex Millet and Amaranth Corn Casserole

Ingredients:
1 Tbsp. organic, unrefined coconut oil, ghee or butter
1½ cups millet, washed and drained
½ cup amaranth, rinsed in fine strainer and drained
1 Tbsp. sea salt
6 cups water
Kernels from 8 ears of corn, or 16 oz. frozen corn
1 large onion, minced
1 large red bell pepper, diced
1 mild green chili pepper, diced (optional)
1 tsp. Herbamare
1¾ tsp. Frontier Herbs Mexican Seasoning (salt free)
½ tsp. ground cumin

1. In bottom of large stockpot sauté onion, green chili pepper, Mexican Seasoning, and cumin in oil, ghee or butter with sea salt until onion is translucent.
2. Add millet, amaranth, corn and water.
3. Bring water to a boil, cover, turn heat on low and let cook 30 minutes.
4. Fold in red pepper and Herbamare, adjust seasonings to taste.
5. Pour into a 9" by 13" buttered casserole dish, dotting with butter or ghee if desired.
6. Bake 30 minutes at 350 degrees.

Variation: Use 2 tsp. Frontier Herbs Italian Seasoning (salt-free)
    instead of Mexican Blend

To bring out a more delicious corn flavor, make a "stock" by cutting the fresh corn off the cob and simmering the cut corn and the corn cobs in 7 cups of water for 20 minutes. Puree and drain. Use 6 cups of this corn stock in recipe.

Heidi's Savory Crackers–Mexican Variation

Ingredients:

1/2 cup amaranth flour
1/2 cup blue corn flour
1/4 cup arrowroot powder
1/4 tsp. sea salt
1/2 tsp. baking soda
3 Tbsp. softened butter
1/2 tsp. chili powder
1/2 tsp. cumin seed
5 Tbsp. water (approximately)

1. Heat oven to 350 degrees.
2. Sift or blend dry ingredients together with a wire whisk.
3. Using a whisk, pastry cutter, or fork, work butter into flour mixture.
4. Add just enough water to make dough stick together to form a ball.
5. On a floured surface, or between wax paper, roll dough flat (approximately 1/4 inch thick).
6. Sprinkle surface lightly with Herbamare and Dr. Bronner's salt.
7. Transfer to greased cookie sheet.
8. Cut into rectangles, squares, triangles and diamond shapes.
9. Bake for 15 minutes or until edges just begin to brown.
10. Remove from oven and place on wire rack.
11. Place rack of crackers on cookie sheet and put back in oven to become crisp.
12. Turn off oven and serve.

Bill and Mike's Waffles

Waffles, like any flour food, should be an occasional meal. They go nicely with vegetable soup at any time of the day. We have even used them to make sandwiches. We make ours with B.E.D. mayonnaise and a variety of roasted or grilled veggies. These waffles can be frozen or kept for several days in the refrigerator.

(Makes 4 nine-inch square waffles, which break into smaller squares that fit into a toaster for reheating.)

Ingredients:
2 cups flour (amaranth, half amaranth and half
    millet, or other grain flour combinations)
$1/2$ tsp. sea salt
$1/4$ cup melted butter ($1/2$ stick)
2 tsp. baking powder (aluminum-free)
2 eggs (whites and yolks in two separate bowls)
1 - $1^{1/3}$ cups water (depends on flour used)

1. Pre-heat waffle iron to medium or dark setting (a little experimentation will determine which is best).
2. Combine flour, sea salt, and baking powder in mixing bowl.
3. Use whisk to thoroughly mix dry ingredients.
4. In separate bowl, combine egg yolks, water, and melted butter, whisk together until barely blended.
5. Add liquid ingredients to dry and whisk together until a smooth batter is formed. (You may need to add more water to batter to correct the consistency. Batter should pour easily into a waffle iron and spread into all corners–not too thick.)
6. In separate bowl, beat egg whites until they form soft peaks–firm but not dry.
7. Carefully fold egg whites into batter. (Try to fold in completely without stirring too much.)
8. Using a glass or plastic measuring cup (aluminum causes batter to break down), pour about 1 cup of batter evenly into all areas of waffle iron (1 cup for a nine inch square iron). Do not use too much; the batter should not overflow.
9. Waffles should cook in 10 - 14 minutes. If in doubt wait until steam stops rising from waffle iron before looking. Cook until crisp and brown.
10. Always cool extra waffles on wire rack.

The Body Ecology Diet Sauces

The soups, especially the creamy soups, such as Broccoli with Fennel and Creamy Dilled Cauliflower, make wonderful sauces. You can jazz up the Dilled Cauliflower by adding shitake mushrooms and create a dish that is very similar to Campbell's cream of mushroom soup. This can be used as a base in many recipes…even some adaptations of old-time family favorites.

When you make the Carrot Cauliflower with Tarragon Soup, pull out a few cups of soup just after you have blended it, and add a tablespoon (or even more) of whole grain mustard (made with apple cider vinegar). You now have a delicious new sauce. Heidi steams large chunks of vegetables (onions, celery, carrots, potatoes, broccoli) and pours them into a baking dish with this tarragon/mustard carrot sauce over the top. She bakes her vegetable casserole for about 30 minutes. It is absolutely delicious.

The Body Ecology Diet Gravy

This delicious recipe is greatly enhanced by the addition of sauted onions and shitake mushrooms. Its great for special occasions, such as Thanksgiving and holidays, when a traditional gravy is needed.

Ingredients:
2 Tbsp. organic, unrefined coconut oil, butter or ghee
$2^{1}/_{2}$ - 3 Tbsp. amaranth flour
2 cups vegetable broth or water
$^{1}/_{4}$ tsp. fresh minced garlic
Dr. Bronner's Balanced Mineral Seasoning to taste
Sea salt, Trocomare or Herbamare, to taste

1. In a small skillet, make a roux by melting ghee, butter or oil and quickly stirring in flour.
2. Very slowly add vegetable broth or water, stirring constantly.
3. Add garlic and seasoning, adjust to taste.

Variation: Sauté sliced onions and shitake mushrooms in the same skillet you will be using to make the gravy. Remove them and make gravy. Fold onions and shitakes back in and reheat before serving.

Curried Cauliflower Sauce

Great on millet.

Ingredients:
1 - 2 Tbsp. organic, unrefined coconut oil,
    ghee or butter
1 large onion, chopped
2 cloves garlic, minced
$1^1/_2$ tsp. ginger root, grated
1 Tbsp. curry powder or to taste
$^1/_4$ tsp. cayenne
1 head of cauliflower, chopped
1 cup water
Sea salt, Herbamare or Trocomare to taste
Lemon juice to taste

1. Sauté onion, garlic, ginger root, curry powder, and cayenne in oil or ghee.
2. Add cauliflower and water.
3. Simmer or pressure cook until tender.
4. Add sea salt and lemon juice.

Easy Bernaise Sauce

Ingredients:
1 egg
1 tsp. raw, organic apple cider vinegar
1 tsp. mustard
1 Tbsp. lemon juice
$^1/_2$ cup melted butter (1 stick)
Sea salt to taste ($^1/_2$ - 1 tsp.)

1. In a blender, combine all ingredients except butter.
2. In a small pot, melt butter.
3. Add melted butter very gradually to blended mixture and serve.

Gingery Carrot Sauce

Great over grains, serves 4 people.

Ingredients:
1 Tbsp. organic, unrefined coconut oil, ghee or butter
20 - 25 small carrots, chopped (or 15 large)
2 large onions, diced
3 cloves garlic, minced
2$\frac{1}{2}$ stalks celery, chopped
1 small red pepper, chopped
Water or stock to cover
3 Tbsp. Dr. Bronner's Balanced Mineral Seasoning
2$\frac{1}{2}$ tsp. sea salt or Herbamare
1 Tbsp. Italian seasoning
2 tsp. garlic powder
Ginger juice to taste*

1. Sauté carrots and onions in oil, ghee or butter.
2. Add celery and red pepper and continue to sauté until tender.
3. Add water and sea salt.
4. Pressure cook 15 minutes or boil until very soft.
5. Purée.
6. Add seasonings and enough water to make sauce.
7. Stir and simmer 10 - 15 minutes.
8. Adjust seasonings.

Variation: Add pinch of cumin, coriander, or cardamom to carrots as they sauté.

*To make ginger juice: grate ginger, pick up by handful, and squeeze the juice into small measuring cup.

Mock Tomato Sauce

The beet in this recipe is added merely for color and will not cause a problem. This recipe is included for those who love tomato sauces. Adding apple cider vinegar at the end of cooking will more closely duplicate the acidic quality in a tomato sauce. Great over millet or buckwheat croquettes.

Ingredients:
3 tablespoon coconut butter
4 cups diced red onion
3 tablespoons garlic, finely chopped
3 tablespoons pizza seasonings (Spice Hunter)
1 medium zucchini, diced
7 cups butternut squash, baked
3 cups of beet stock*
2 tablespoons of sea salt
6 cups water
1 cup apple cider vinegar

1. Sauté onions and garlic in coconut butter until golden.
2. Add pizza seasoning and zucchini and continue to sauté.
3. Take off heat.
4. Bake butternut squash in oven (you will need two squash).
5. Poke holes in squash to prevent it from exploding.
6. Bake squash until very soft, approximately 1½-2 hours.
7. When done, slice in half and let cool enough to handle.
8. Scoop seeds and measure 7 cups of squash meat.
9. Add to mixture of onions and zucchini.
10. Add water and bring up to temperature.
11. Add beet stock.
12. Continue to simmer and puree until smooth.
13. Add water and salt level for desired thickness and flavor.
14. When room temperature add apple cider vinegar.

* Beet stock is made by simmering 1-2 sliced beets in 2 cups of water for 30 minutes.

Luscious Lemon Butter Sauce

Good poured on an all-vegetable platter.

Ingredients: (Makes approximately 2 cups)
1/2 cup butter (1 stick) or ghee
1 Tbsp. organic, unrefined oil
2 medium onions, finely chopped, or 2 small
    scallions, thinly sliced
1/3 cup fresh lemon juice
1/2 heaping tsp. dried tarragon or 1 heaping Tbsp.
    finely torn fresh tarragon
1/2 heaping tsp. dried basil or 1 heaping Tbsp.
    finely chopped fresh basil

1. Heat butter or ghee and oil in small skillet.
2. Add onions, and sauté until soft.
3. Add remaining ingredients, and simmer 10 minutes.
4. Remove from heat and serve.

Variation: Use 1/2 heaping tsp. of dried dill or 1 Tbsp.
    fresh dill instead of tarragon and basil.

Pesto

Ingredients:
3 - 4 cups fresh basil
3/4 cup organic, unrefined flax or pumpkin seed oil*
1 tsp. sea salt
Rind of 1 lemon
3 Tbsp. lemon juice (approximately 1 juicy lemon)
3 - 4 cloves garlic
1/2 cup flat leaf parsley
1 Tbsp. lecithin

1. In a blender, combine ingredients.
2. Blend until thoroughly puréed.
3. Serve over noodles, grains, red potatoes, a salad
    or a platter of vegetables.

*At the time when you are able to introduce olive oil into your
diet, it can be used in this recipe in place of the unrefined oil.

The Body Ecology Diet Salads and Salad Dressings

Salads are special foods and the Body Ecology Diet salads are even more so. Salads can be a meal in themselves...they can be made with raw or with cooked and chilled ingredients...they're simple to prepare...they take easily to food combining...and they are an important part of a health-building diet.

Although raw foods may be difficult for you to digest, especially when you first start the Diet, they are so rich in enzymes, vitamins, and minerals that it's important for you to include a properly prepared salad in your meals at least once a day as soon as you are able. For easier digestion, try salads with parboiled vegetables and a no-oil dressing (more about this below).

On hot summer days, crisp, cool salads are ideal meals or even snacks. Around the year, you can easily carry them to work and even carry the dressing separately to add at the last moment. When your body becomes contracted from too much salt or a stressful day, balance it with an expansive salad. If your body is too acidic, an alkaline salad can come to the rescue.

Need some salad ideas? See our recipes—and consider the great variety of available lettuces, land, ocean, and cultured vegetables. The more color, the better: green broccoli; asparagus; English peas; yellow squash; red pepper or onion; cool white cucumber or jicama. You can make grain salads with the four Diet grains and potatoes, or protein salads with chopped salmon, tuna, chicken or turkey. Or mix some soaked almonds, sunflower, or pumpkin seeds in with those veggie salads for extra crunch.

Please don't forget those very special ocean vegetables. Left-over hijiki with onions and carrots (see ocean vegetable recipes) is delicious when tossed with leafy lettuce and radicchio and topped with The Body Ecology Diet Salad Dressing. Or soak some arame in water for 10 minutes, drain and chop, and add it to your green leafy salad. Wakame is delicious in a cucumber salad with diced red pepper and red onion. Cut sheets of nori into small strips or squares to sprinkle on any salad for a color and taste bonus.

Raw cultured vegetables add color and zest to any salad. We even add them to our dressing recipes and to mayonnaise.

Importance of Organic, Unrefined Oils

We used to think the carefully processed oils found in health food stores were ideal for our salad dressing, but many people still have trouble digesting them. Donna was working with an enzyme therapist who tested urine samples to determine whether her students were digesting proteins, fats, starches, etc. Over and over the urine tests showed no one was digesting fats. This problem sent Donna on an intensive search for an answer. In the process, Donna, with the help of her creative staff and top Atlanta chef Greg Gammage, discovered the technique for creating delicious oil-free salad dressings (more below). She also discovered that the *quality* of oils is crucial to digestion. The liver, a key digestive organ, cannot handle **refined** oils. It must have totally **unrefined** oils and simply isn't programmed for refined, processed, or denatured oils.

Only two companies supply truly unrefined *culinary* oils: Omega Nutrition and Flora Oils. They are processed with an amazing amount of care. Omega Nutrition was the first in the industry to develop the process whereby organic seeds such as flax, pumpkin, rapeseed, sunflower, or safflower are squeezed to release their oil. They call this special process "omegaflo™." The oil is never exposed to light or oxygen. No preservatives are used. The oils are packaged in black opaque containers, which are stamped with an expiration date.

Unrefined oils have a different flavor than oils you may have used before, so they may take some getting used to. They come in an array of tasty flavors: Brazil nut, pistachio, sesame, hazel nut, and olive. None of these is on the Diet initially, but you can see how you will tolerate them once your body ecology is restored. The *cooking* oils tolerated best are: sunflower (especially popular with children), and safflower (the lightest in flavor).

Flax seed oil, pumpkin seed oil, and canola oil (made from rapeseed, not used at B.E.D. because of its strong, bitter flavor) are never used for cooking. Heat destroys the precious Omega-3 essential fatty acids that we are all so deficient in today. Add flax seed and pumpkin seed oils to any salad dressing recipe, or you can sprinkle them and some raw apple cider vinegar on a baked red skin potato or on grains. Flax seed oil can be taken directly by mouth (1 to 2 tablespoons per day).

Olive oil is enjoying high praise among nutritionists these days and many people report they tolerate it well. Why? It's unrefined. Since olives are fruits, this is *not* recommended for initial use when you first start the B.E.D., but it is one of the easiest to add to your diet when your health improves. Many stores sell high-quality, extra virgin, unrefined olive oil. Olive oil has no essential fatty acids.

All these unrefined oils should be easy to obtain, but aren't. Few people, even health food store owners, understand the importance of these oils. Either order the oils by calling the toll-free number listed below, or give this number to your health food store. These oils cost a little more than the poisonous refined oils but are extremely concentrated, so you only need a little, and your liver will appreciate it.

Canadians, Australians, and Europeans use unrefined oils and prefer to taste the stronger flavor of the seeds. The European way to make a salad is one you may want to adopt. Put 2/3 parts oil to 1/3 part apple cider vinegar or lemon juice, a little salt, pepper, garlic, herbs, and mustard into the bottom of a wooden salad bowl and mix this together. Then add a delicious variety of lettuces and toss together.

High-quality unrefined oils will not spoil in shipping; they have excellent heat integrity. When you receive them, refrigerate a bottle for immediate use, and freeze the rest. The shelf life is eight months to a year when refrigerated, and much longer if the oil is frozen.

To order these unrefined oils call: 1-800-511-2660.

Organic, Raw, Unfiltered Apple Cider Vinegar

People are often surprised to learn they can eat vinegar on the Body Ecology Diet. It's true you can, but only if it is raw, unfiltered apple cider vinegar that has been aged in wood barrels. Several companies make apple cider vinegar, and you will find a nice selection in your health food store, but in our search to find the very best, we chose vinegar from Omega Nutrition. Omega uses *organic*, table grade (not ground-fall), tree-picked apples. In the manufacturing process they do not use heat, clarifiers, enzymes, or preservatives.

Other apple cider vinegars are treated during fermentation with meta-bisulfite, a preservative that is not required by law to be listed on the label. Omega's process ensures that the vinegar contains natural sediment with pectin, trace minerals, beneficial bacteria, and enzymes. Omega stores the vinegar in black drums until it can be bottled in black containers, which protect the vinegar from light. Light causes free radical activity and a breakdown of vital nutrients. Vinegar packaged in clear glass bottles is vulnerable to oxidation, causing it to turn a brown color. (Body Ecology's apple cider vinegar, made by Omega, is available from the above 800 number.)

Thanks to vinegar's mineral content (especially potassium), it has the ability to normalize the body's acid/alkaline balance. Its antiseptic qualities cleanse the digestive tract. The acidity aids in the removal of calcium deposits from joints and blood vessels but has no effect on normal calcium levels of the bones or teeth. Pectin in unfiltered apple cider vinegar promotes elimination and healthy bowels. The potassium in the vinegar regulates growth, hydrates cells, balances sodium, and enables proper performance of the nervous system.

No-Oil Dressings For Better Digestion

Many people have trouble digesting fats and oils...or need to reduce the fat in their diets. When you start the Body Ecology Diet, you may want to give your liver a rest and maximize your healing by using our no-oil dressings, developed using a readily available gel fiber called xanthan gum.[26] They are a real taste treat and a solution to one of our most frustrating menu-planning problems.

We often found ourselves wanting to serve a salad with an animal protein meal, because raw vegetables found in salads are ideal for balancing the contracting nature of animal foods. You'll remember from the chapter on food combining that oil inhibits the secretion of hydrochloric acid needed to digest these proteins. Fats and oils must be avoided when eating these foods, but who wants to eat a salad without a delicious dressing on it?

Xanthan gum was a terrific discovery. We simply took out the oil in the dressing recipe, substituted an equal amount of water and a little xanthan gum to thicken, and added a variety of herbs and seasonings. Our problem was solved. Now you can create salad masterpieces with sliced egg, salmon, swordfish, tuna, soaked almonds, pumpkin and sunflower seeds and one of our no-oil recipes. Once you become familiar with xanthan gum, you'll soon be creating dressings of your own.

We think no-oil dressings and dressings made with only the finest *unrefined oils* is the direction the American diet will be taking as we try to reduce fat and cholesterol from our diets. We are proud that the Body Ecology Diet is able to introduce them to you.

[26]Xanthan gum is produced by the pure culture fermentation of the microorganism, Xanthomonas campestris. It is 100% pure and contains no sugar, salt, starch, yeast, wheat, corn, soy, or milk; it seems to be tolerated by even the most sensitive people. Available from NOW Natural Foods (1-800-999-8069) and Bob's Red Mill Natural Foods, Milwaukie, Oregon 97222 (503) 654-3215. Please tell your health food store to order it for you.

Salad and Salad Dressing Recipes

Raw foods are usually difficult to digest since most people with a body ecology imbalance have weak digestive tracts. Raw foods also weaken the spleen. They are, however, rich in necessary enzymes and we have found that, properly prepared, a salad once a day is an important part of the Body Ecology Diet. Preparation suggestions in parentheses make these vegetables easier to digest.

The Body Ecology Diet Salad

Choose among these vegetable greens to create an infinite number of delectable salad combinations:

Beet Tops	Endive	Parsley
Cabbage	Escarole	Radish Tops
Chard	Kale	Spinach
Comfrey	Lamb's quarters	Turnip Tops
Dandelion	Lettuce	Watercress

Sprouts that can be added include:
Alfalfa
Radish
Sunflower

Stems and Roots:

Broccoli (steamed)	Jerusalem artichokes
Carrots (shredded)	(shredded)
Cauliflower (steamed)	Jicama (shredded)
Celery	Summer squash
Corn (blanched)	Zucchini

Especially nutritious additions:

Arame (soaked or cooked)	Nori (shredded)
	Red onions
Chives	Scallions
Hijiki (cooked)	Wakame (soaked)

Seed and herb seasoning suggestions:

Basil	Dill	Paprika
Cardamom	Garlic Powder	Parsley
Caraway	Horseradish	Poppy Seed
Cayenne	Marjoram	Pumpkin Seed
Celery	Nutmeg	Sage
Cinnamon	Onion Powder	Thyme

The Body Ecology Diet Salad Dressing with Apple Cider Vinegar

Ingredients:
$1/4$ cup organic, unrefined oil
$3/4$ cup water
$1/3$ cup raw, organic apple cider vinegar
2 Tbsp. Dr. Bronner's Balanced Mineral Seasoning
2 Tbsp. Sea Seasonings Dulse with Garlic
1 Tbsp. mustard
$1/2$ tsp. xanthan gum (thickener)

To make this dressing quickly, place all the ingredients in a container with a lid and shake vigorously.

To prepare an even creamier version, place the apple cider vinegar and the seasonings in a blender. Blend at medium speed, slowly adding the oil. This "emulsifies" or thickens the salad dressing, and it will not separate. Add xanthan gum after oil, and blend.

The Cuisinart® Quick-Prep™ or any other brand hand-held style blender works very well, too.

The Body Ecology Diet Salad Dressing with Fresh Lemon Juice

Ingredients:
$1/4$ cup organic, unrefined oil
$3/4$ cup water
$1/3$ cup fresh lemon juice
2 Tbsp. Sea Seasonings Dulse with Garlic*
2 Tbsp. Dr. Bronner's Balanced Mineral Seasoning*
1 Tbsp. mustard
$1/2$ tsp. xanthan gum (thickener)

Place all the ingredients in a jar, shake very well. If time permits, refrigerate before serving over chilled salad.

*In place of these ingredients, sea salt, Herbamare, Trocomare, or other seeds and herbs may be added to taste.

Variations: Add any of the following if desired: chopped parsley, diced cucumber (peeled), $1/4$ small red or Vidalia onion (minced), 1 minced scallion, minced garlic to taste, 1 minced celery stalk.

Parboiled Salad

Ingredients:
Variety of lettuce, torn into bite-size pieces
Vegetables to chop for parboiling:

Broccoli	Daikon	String beans
Cabbage	Kale	Yellow squash
Carrots	Peas	Zucchini
Corn (cut off cob)	Radishes	Celery
Scallions	Cucumbers	Red onions

1. Cut various vegetables into pretty shapes (shredded, matchsticks, half moons, diced, flowers, stars), using vegetable cutters if you wish.
2. Quickly parboil in rapidly boiling water. Make sure you don't overcook. They are best when taken out of the water right after they have turned their brightest color (e.g., broccoli turns a beautiful bright green).
3. Remove from heat and chill well.
4. In a bowl, place lettuce and chilled vegetables.
5. Toss with a salad dressing of your choice.

Fresh herbs are great, too (chop and add raw): parsley, dill, mint, basil, watercress, arugula.

Ocean vegetables are wonderful: dulse, wakame, arame—just soak till soft, drain, squeeze out extra liquid and chop. (You don't have to cook wakame or arame, but you can cook them for 15 minutes if desired.)

Soaked and sprouted almonds and raw sunflower seeds add a nice festive touch, but do not add if your salad has a starchy vegetable like parboiled red potatoes.

Grain Salads

On the Body Ecology Diet remember only four grains can be eaten initially. With time you will want to introduce other grains back into your diet. This recipe works well for millet, quinoa, buckwheat or a combination of the three grains. Later it works well with rice, bulgur, barley, etc. Amaranth is too sticky for a grain salad.

Cooked, leftover grains can be converted easily into a grain salad since they are usually drier than freshly cooked grain.

When cooking fresh grain to use in your grain salads, bring the water to a boil before you add the grain. Once the grain is cooked, remove it from the heat and let it sit for 15 minutes or longer to dry out and become more fluffy.

Toss together 2 - 4 cups of any cooked grain (including combinations) with raw or slightly blanched vegetables, add a dressing of your choice, sprinkle in some seasonings or sea salt, and your grain salad is complete.

Vegetables should be diced or finely chopped, and ocean vegetables (which make an excellent addition to a creative grain salad) should be soaked or cooked (see Chapter 12).

Vegetable suggestions:

Carrots	Scallions	Yellow squash
Cucumbers	Radishes	Green beans
Celery	Peas	Broccoli
Red onions	Corn	Ocean vegetables

Quinoa Salad

Ingredients:
2 cups uncooked quinoa (or millet)
2/3 cup frozen peas
2/3 cup frozen or fresh corn
2/3 cup red bell peppers, finely diced
1 bunch scallions or 1 red onion, finely chopped
    (optional)
1 cup or more Rosemary Vinaigrette (see recipe)

1. Cook grain until cooked but slightly resilient.
2. Steam carrots, peas, and corn 4 - 6 minutes
    (should be cooked but still slightly firm).
3. In a large bowl, combine all ingredients.

Quinoa Tabouli

Ingredients: (serves 4)
1 cup quinoa
2 cups water
1/2 tsp. sea salt
1 cup cucumber, diced small
1/2 cup parsley, finely chopped
1/2 cup scallions, finely sliced
Lettuce leaves as a garnish

1. Cook quinoa and sea salt in 2 cups of water, until translucent; remove from heat and let sit 10 - 15 minutes to become fluffy.
2. When cool add cucumber, parsley, and scallions.
3. Add Mint-Garlic Dressing (see recipe).
3. Chill in refrigerator before serving.
4. Serve on lettuce leaves.

Celery Root Salad

Ingredients:
Celery root, grated in food processor
Homemade mayonnaise
Pinch of sea salt
Herbs to taste

Combine all ingredients in a salad bowl and serve.

New Red Potato Salad in Red Onion Dressing

Ingredients: (makes 6 servings)
2 lbs. small red potatoes, washed and scrubbed well
Sea salt or Herbamare to taste
Freshly ground black pepper
3/4 cup homemade mayonnaise
1/2 cup sweet red onion, finely chopped
1/2 cup dill, fennel, or parsley, preferably flat-leaf type, minced
Fresh dill or parsley sprigs for garnish

1. Cut potatoes into bite-size cubes and cook until tender.
2. When cool, add other ingredients.
3. Chill before serving.

Variations:
1. Add watercress, mustard, 1 - 2 Tbsp. raw, organic apple cider vinegar or herbs such as curry powder, garlic, Italian seasonings, etc.
2. These same ingredients can be used with the Body Ecology Diet Salad Dressing, and it's even healthier.

Marinated Corn Salad

Ingredients: (makes 4-6 servings)
1 3/4 cups yellow corn cut from cob (about 4 ears)
1/4 cup water
1/2 small red pepper, cut into 1/2 inch strips
1/2 cup celery, chopped
2 Tbsp. green onions, thinly sliced
1 Tbsp. pimiento, chopped
1 Tbsp. fresh parsley, chopped
3 Tbsp. organic, unrefined flax or pumpkin seed oil
1 Tbsp. raw, organic apple cider vinegar
Sea salt and pepper to taste

1. Combine corn and water in a medium saucepan.
2. Bring to a boil; cover, reduce heat, and simmer 7 - 8 minutes or until corn is tender.
3. Drain corn and combine with red pepper and next 4 ingredients and set aside.
4. Combine oil and remaining ingredients in a jar; cover tightly and shake vigorously.
5. Combine marinade and corn mixture; cover and chill at least 4 hours before serving.

Summertime Curried Corn Salad

For special occasions.

Ingredients:
6 to 8 ears fresh corn or 3 cups frozen
1 small zucchini, diced
1 large red bell pepper, diced
1 bunch scallions, white and tender part of green,
       cut into 1/4 inch pieces
1/2 cup Italian parsley, chopped

Dressing:
1/4 cup organic, unrefined flax or pumpkin seed oil
4 Tbsp. raw, organic apple cider vinegar or
       lemon juice
1 tsp. curry powder
1/2 tsp. sea salt
1 - 2 cloves garlic, minced

1. You can use the corn raw or, if you prefer, blanch it
       quickly and cool.
2. Combine the raw or cooled corn, zucchini, pepper,
       scallions, and parsley.
3. Combine the oil, vinegar or lemon juice, curry powder,
       sea salt and garlic.
4. Combine the vegetables and dressing and marinate
       2 - 4 hours.

Variation: Add 1 - 2 Tbsp. homemade mayonnaise for a
       creamier dressing.

Carrot Salad

This salad is excellent for helping eliminate toxins in the colon.

Ingredients: (serves 1-2)
2 Tbsp. organic, unrefined coconut oil
1 Tbsp. organic, unrefined olive oil
4 - 6 large carrots, peeled and trimmed

1. Finely grate the carrots in food processor and
       toss with both oils.

Cole Slaw

Basic Ingredients: (serves 4)
1 small head white cabbage
2 cups boiling water
3 grated carrots
Sea salt to taste
Seasoned mayonnaise or B.E.D. dressing

1. Cut the cabbage in chunks and grate in food processor or by hand.
2. Place cabbage and carrots into a large mixing bowl and wilt by pouring the boiling water with sea salt over them (this makes for easier digestion). Stir several times and drain.
3. Toss with seasoned mayonnaise or the Body Ecology Diet Salad Dressing.

Variations: Other ingredients can be added such as scallions, red pepper, celery, sliced red radishes or daikon, dill, caraway or celery seed, sunflower seeds, chopped parsley, chives, dill, fennel, or other fresh herbs.

For a sweet cole slaw add a few drops of stevia concentrate.

Asparagus, Green Beans, and Artichoke Salad

This elegantly arranged salad can stand alone or as an entree at an alkaline-forming, all-vegetable meal. It is also delightful with a grain meal. Artichokes are a starchy vegetable, so remember not to serve this salad with animal protein. (Serves 6)

Ingredients:

1 lb. cooked asparagus spears, fresh
1/2 lb. green beans, fresh
Small cooked artichokes, 1 per person, fresh or frozen
      artichoke hearts (see cooking directions below)
1/2 cucumber, peeled and thinly sliced
1 red bell pepper, cut into thin strips
1/2 head cauliflower, broken into small florets and
      steamed lightly or quickly blanched and held
      under cold water to stop the cooking
1/2 cup organic, unrefined oil
1/4 cup raw, organic apple cider vinegar
Salt and pepper to taste
1 level Tbsp. or to taste dried basil
1 fresh lemon (if cooking artichoke)

1. Toss all the vegetables together in a salad bowl.
2. In a screw top jar put oil, vinegar, salt, pepper, and
      basil. Shake well to combine.
3. Pour the mixture over the salad and toss gently but well;
      chill.
4. Toss again lightly, and serve from the bowl or transfer
      to a platter lined with thinly sliced cucumbers, and
      arrange tossed salad ingredients in center of platter
      with artichokes on top.

To cook the artichoke:

1. Cut off base so it is flush flat. Snap off the small bottom
      leaves. Cut about 1 inch off the top of the artichoke.
2. Trim off the outer leaves with scissors to form a nice
      round shape.
3. With both thumbs open the artichoke from the middle
      to expose the choke inside. Use a teaspoon to scrape
      out all of the hairy choke, and push the artichoke
      back into shape. Brush with lemon juice to prevent it
      from discoloring and boil in salted water for 15
      minutes. Drain and leave to cool before using.

Green Bean Salad

Ingredients:
1 lb. green string beans
2 Tbsp. organic, unrefined oil
1 tsp. raw, organic apple cider vinegar
Salt and pepper to taste
1 small onion, shallot, or 3-4 scallions, finely chopped
1 tsp. dried tarragon, oregano, dill, or garlic
    (optional)
1 sprig of parsley

1. Cut the washed beans into 1-inch lengths and blanch
    or lightly steam. Drain and rinse with cold water and
    let cool.
2. Combine oil, vinegar, salt and pepper in a salad bowl,
    whisking together well, and add the chopped onion
    and herbs.
3. Add the cooled beans and toss it all together gently.
    Leave to marinate in refrigerator for an hour.
4. Toss again before serving and garnish with parsley.

No-Oil Salad Dressings

Jeannine's Italian Dressing

Ingredients:
1/2 cup raw, organic apple cider vinegar
1/2 cup freshly squeezed lemon juice
1 1/2 cup water
2 Tbsp. minced garlic
3 Tbsp. Tree of Life whole grain mustard
2 Tbsp. finely chopped fresh parsley
2 tsp. sea salt
1/8 tsp. pepper
2 Tbsp. red pepper, finely chopped
1/4 tsp. each: dried oregano, basil, and thyme*
1 tsp. xanthan gum (thickener)

Blend first 10 ingredients, then add the xanthan gum, blend or shake well. Refrigerate overnight.

*1 Tbsp. of Spice Hunter Seasoning packet can be added instead (see Shopping List).

Lemon Rosemary Garlic Dressing

Ingredients:
1 cup raw, organic apple cider vinegar
1 1/2 cup water
1/2 cup freshly squeezed lemon juice
2 Tbsp. minced garlic
1/2 tsp. pepper
1/2 tsp. celery seed
6 Tbsp. red onion, diced
2 Tbsp. red pepper, diced
1 tsp. dill weed
2 Tbsp. fresh parsley, minced
3 tsp. sea salt
2 Tbsp. dried rosemary, crushed, or 4 Tbsp. fresh
    rosemary, crushed
1 tsp. xanthan gum (thickener)

Blend first 12 ingredients, then xanthan gum; blend or shake well. Refrigerate overnight.

Rosemary Vinaigrette Dressing

Ingredients:
$1/2$ cup raw, organic apple cider vinegar
$1/2$ cup freshly squeezed lemon juice
1 cup water
4 Tbsp. mustard
1 tsp. freshly ground pepper
1 tsp. rosemary
$1/2$ tsp. sea salt
1 tsp. xanthan gum (thickener)

Blend first 7 ingredients, then xanthan gum; blend or shake well. Refrigerate overnight. This dressing is great on potato salad.

•

Salad Dressings with Organic, Unrefined Oil

Rosemary Vinaigrette Dressing

Ingredients:
1 tsp. rosemary
1/4 cup organic, unrefined oil
3/4 cup water
1/2 cup raw, organic apple cider vinegar
1/2 cup freshly squeezed lemon juice
4 Tbsp. mustard
1 tsp. freshly ground pepper
Sea salt to taste
1/2 tsp. xanthan gum (thickener)

1. In a jar with a tight-fitting lid, combine first 8 ingredients and shake well. Add xanthan gum and shake well.
2. Chill before serving. (Dressing keeps up to a week.)

Watercress Dressing

Ingredients:
2 Tbsp. fresh lemon juice
1 Tbsp. raw, organic apple cider vinegar
1/2 tsp. dried tarragon
1/4 cup organic, unrefined oil
Salt and pepper to taste
1 bunch watercress, finely chopped

1. Mix together the lemon juice, vinegar, tarragon, oil, salt and pepper until well blended.
2. Then stir in the finely chopped watercress.

Mint-Garlic Dressing

Good with Quinoa Tabouli.

Ingredients:
1/4 - 1/3 cup fresh lemon juice, to taste (start with less)
1/2 cup organic, unrefined oil
1 - 2 cloves garlic, minced (or to taste)
1 Tbsp. fresh mint leaves, minced

1. Add lemon juice, mint, and garlic in a blender.
2. Slowly add oil to emulsify.

Italian Dressing

Ingredients: (yields 1 1/4 cups)
1 cup organic, unrefined oil
1/2 cup raw, organic apple cider vinegar
1 tsp. sea salt or to taste
1/8 tsp. white pepper
1/2 tsp. dry mustard
2 tsp. Italian-blend seasonings
1 clove garlic, minced

1. Combine all ingredients in a jar; cover tightly and shake vigorously.
2. Adjust to taste.
3. Chill thoroughly.

Variation: Fresh lemon juice in place of apple cider vinegar.

Mayonnaise

Ingredients:
2 egg yolks (free range)
2 Tbsp. raw, organic apple cider vinegar
1 Tbsp. fresh lemon juice
$1/2$ tsp. mustard
$1/8$ tsp. cayenne pepper
1 tsp. sea salt or to taste
1 cup B.E.D. Essential Balance Oil

1. In blender combine egg yolks, vinegar, lemon juice, mustard, cayenne pepper, salt, and $1/4$ cup oil.
2. Blend for 30 seconds.
3. Very slowly, through opening in blender lid, add remaining oil while blender is turning. Continue to blend until smooth.
4. Scrape into a glass jar with a screw top and it will keep safely in your refrigerator 7 - 14 days.

Variations:
1. Add garlic powder, a dash of white pepper, $1/4$ tsp. mustard powder, and herbs (chervil, tarragon, dill, oregano, basil, cumin, coriander, curry, paprika).
2. Cayenne and/or lime juice gives the mayonnaise a nice flavor for topping aspics or for mixing into any salads made of lightly steamed and chilled vegetables such as carrots, broccoli, cauliflower, daikon, kohlrabi, celery root, etc.
3. Mayonnaise can be sweetened with stevia if desired.
4. In place of the vinegar, add 2 tsp. lemon peel, finely grated and 2 tsp. fresh lemon juice and add 1 tsp. fresh mustard.

Note: Olive oil can also be used in this recipe in place of the Essential Balance Oil. A combination of olive oil and Essential Balance is delicious too!

Almond Mayonnaise

This recipe is adapted from *The American Vegetarian Cookbook*, a masterpiece by Marilyn Diamond, co-founder of the Fit For Life movement. While Marilyn has included it in her book as an alternative to mayonnaise made with eggs, we think it makes an excellent party dip or snack food when served with raw vegetables.

Ingredients: (yields 1 1/2 - 2 cups)
1/2 cup raw almonds
1/2 to 3/4 cup water
1/4 tsp. garlic powder
3/4 tsp. sea salt
1 cup organic, unrefined oil (flax or pumpkin seed)
3 Tbsp. lemon juice
1/2 tsp. raw, organic apple cider vinegar

1. Cover almonds with boiling water, allow to cool slightly. Slip off skins and have all other ingredients ready.
2. Place almonds in blender or food processor and grind to a fine powder. Add half the water along with garlic powder and seasonings. Blend well, then add the remaining water to form a smooth cream.
3. With blender running low, remove insert top and drizzle in the oil in a thin stream until mixture is thick.
4. Keep blender running and add lemon juice and vinegar. Blend on low 1 minute longer to allow mixture to thicken to desired consistency.
5. Scrape into a jar with a screw top and refrigerate. This will keep 10 days - 2 weeks.

Note: If you have trouble digesting oil, eliminate the oil completely and increase the water.

Introduction to Ocean Vegetables

We say ocean vegetables, and you may think, ugh–seaweed. Or you might think, I can follow everything on the Body Ecology Diet except this. Well, we now want to do whatever we can to encourage you to incorporate these great nutritional gifts into your diet at least once or twice a day. Your current state of health, your desire to restore your body ecology, and the necessity to survive in an increasingly more hazardous environment make ocean vegetables one of the most important new foods you will encounter in your lifetime.

Ocean vegetables are important to restoring your body ecology because they naturally control the growth of pathogenic bacteria, fungi, and viruses. A body ecology imbalance or immune disorder causes a severe mineral deficiency, plus we have been eating foods grown in mineral-deficient soil for most of our lives. Ocean vegetables are rich in minerals and trace elements lacking in our diets today, and these are organized in such a way that the body can utilize them easily. So we digest and assimilate them well, and they are key to restoring and maintaining proper acid/alkaline balance in the body.

With a body ecology imbalance, the stomach lacks hydrochloric acid and the enzymes needed for digesting *protein*. Proper assimilation of protein is necessary in order to absorb minerals, so a mineral deficiency develops, even if sufficient minerals are contained in our food. Our mineral needs are as great as our need for oxygen, and an imbalance of minerals can cause problems such as mood swings and muscle paralysis.

Ocean vegetables strengthen the nervous and immune systems, and they actually have the ability to remove radioactive elements, carcinogens, and even environmental pollutants from those of us who are environmentally sensitive or allergic. They can also provide the calcium that we miss by not having dairy products, and they offer large amounts of chlorophyll.

Ocean vegetables (you may also find them called sea vegetables) are really algae colonies or single-cell organisms. They're red, blue, green, and black. They thrive only in clean water and are harvested just like land vegetables, at certain times of the year; then they are sun dried, packaged and stored. They grow on rocks or other ocean surfaces.

More Benefits

Oriental and island people have used ocean vegetables for thousands of years. They call them "beauty foods" because they help prevent aging and enhance and prolong the color of hair and lips. The long, lustrous hair of Orientals is often attributed to a diet rich in ocean vegetables such as black hijiki and arame. In areas of Japan where ocean vegetables are harvested, the sixty-year-old women who gather them from the sea often look as if they are in their thirties.

Native Americans reportedly traveled to the coasts to collect these special edibles, then returned home with a lightweight addition to their food supply. Dulse is so well accepted in Canada's maritime provinces that you will find it alongside the fresh fruits and vegetables in grocery stores. Ocean vegetables such as agar often are used as stabilizers in processed foods, though we're not aware of that because the law does not require them to be listed as ingredients.

People who eat a macrobiotic diet are familiar with ocean vegetables and their amazing regenerative powers. Thanks to the many years of effort by macrobiotic leaders, ocean vegetables are now widely available in this country and so are many delicious, creative recipes. We've included only three recipes in this section, but we encourage you to take macrobiotic cooking classes or refer to the many macrobiotic cookbooks for recipes. Most of these recipes call for shoyu or tamari, but you can just substitute salt. Mirin, a sweet wine, is often used to counter the salty taste, so don't use that either. Long, slow cooking, at a very low temperature, using lots of onions and carrots to sweeten, is the more delicious and medicinal way to cook the stronger flavored ocean vegetables like hijiki and arame.

Ocean vegetables are a rich source of organic compost material for farmers. According to one fascinating report, the Irish transformed a barren, rocky seaside cliff into fertile soil by fertilizing it with ocean vegetables. If you want to see what they do to your body, try working some into a house plant and watch it grow.

Ocean Vegetables and The Thyroid

With a body ecology imbalance, the thyroid never functions properly. Thyroid problems can lead to obesity, excessive thinness, hypertension, flatulence, stubborn cases of constipation, fatigue, nervousness, depression, headaches, and neck and shoulder pain. Ocean vegetables have a medicinal and regulating effect upon the thyroid.

A weak thyroid causes weak digestion because of its influence on the liver, gallbladder, pancreas, bile ducts, and colon. As you will remember from the chapter on colon care, cleansing of the colon is vital to restoring your health. Ocean vegetables, high in natural mineral salts, have a *toning* effect on the colon. Constipation is usually a combined problem of the colon, the liver, and the adrenals. Ocean vegetables supply all these organs with the minerals needed to function properly.

The thyroid affects your sensory nerves. Within two to three weeks of eating ocean vegetables every day, you will notice a calmness in both mind and body. Ocean vegetables reduce tension, help us cope with stress, and enable our bodies to store vitality and energy.

The thyroid influences the health of the ovaries, the prostate gland, and the pyloric valve. If you suffer from indigestion, it's especially important to eat ocean vegetables. It's common to have problems with the pylorus, the valve at the end of the stomach that must open and close at the correct time to allow food to pass into the small intestine. Ocean vegetables are an excellent remedy.

Easy Ways to Use Ocean Vegetables

To ensure that you assimilate the precious minerals in your ocean vegetable dishes, be sure to eat protein-rich foods. B.E.D. grains are high in protein, and the ocean vegetables themselves contain more protein and amino acids (the building blocks of protein) than beans. Ocean vegetables combine well with grains, starches, and with protein flesh foods.

DULSE can be eaten right from the package as a snack. In the early 1900s, taverns served dulse as a snack, since its saltiness increased patrons' thirst and therefore tavern revenues. Little did they know it also helped balance the effect of the liquor and beer, which leach minerals from the body. Dulse is high in iron. Carry it with you and eat some when you need energy or brain food. It's an important ingredient in our Body Ecology Diet Salad Dressing. Donna sautés thinly sliced onion, then adds dulse, a little water, and some sea salt, covers this with a lid and lets it simmer for about 20 minutes for a delicious quick vegetable to top a leftover grain. Children love dulse.

NORI is also popular with children and can be carried as a snack food. When a sheet of nori is filled with a hot B.E.D. grain or animal food, then rolled up, it makes a convenient "sandwich." Nori is used in Japanese restaurants for making sushi. Try toasting it by passing it quickly over a burner until it changes color from black to green, then crumble it or cut it into thin strips, and use these to garnish soups, grain dishes, or salads.

KOMBU can be soaked overnight in spring water to create a mineral-rich broth. Use this medicinal stock when making soups or for cooking your grains. If you dry strips of kombu at a low temperature in your oven, they become crispy like bacon and make a great snack.

AGAR is used to create delicious aspics, puddings, and jellos. You'll find it in several recipes in this book: Vanilla Pudding, Sweet Carrot Gelatin Salad (see stevia recipes), and Jelled Butternut Squash. It is superior to animal gelatin, lubricates the digestive tract, and has mild laxative properties. The flakes are easy to work with. As a rule of thumb, for every cup of liquid in your recipe add a *heaping* tablespoon of agar flakes. For a savory aspic, simmer fish stock with seasonings and diced non-starchy vegetables, chill and serve.

Agar is fun to work with. If your mold or aspic needs more seasoning or failed to gel properly, you can melt it down in a saucepan, work with it a little more, then gel it again. Always add the agar to cold water, never hot, and cook it about 20 to 30 minutes on a low simmer. It starts to gel at room temperature but firms up faster with refrigeration.

ARAME'S fine shredded strands have a crisp texture and sweet, nutty flavor. It should be soaked about 15 minutes, chopped and tossed into a salad without cooking. If you want to cook it, we've included a simple basic recipe using lots of carrots and onions to sweeten it. We often mix arame with onions and carrots into leftover grain, form it into patties, and sauté it in unrefined oil or ghee. Delicious!

HIJIKI has a mild and slightly salty or "fishy" flavor. It quadruples in volume when you soak it. It requires more thorough rinsing, longer soaking, and a longer cooking time than the other ocean vegetables. Simmer at least 45 minutes to an hour until it's really tender. Cooked with onions and carrots shown in our recipe, it practically melts in your mouth.

WAKAME adds a pretty green color and a delicate flavor to soups and salads. Soak it until soft, cut off the tough spine, chop it and add to any soup or salad of your choice. Our Cucumber, Wakame, and Red Pepper Salad is very popular.

Tips On Preparing and Storing Ocean Vegetables

These foods can be stored for years. Buy them in bulk to save money, and store them in a cool, dry place. Don't seal them tightly in plastic because if any moisture gets into the container, mold will grow. Before you cook them, check ocean vegetables for tiny shells or stones caught in the folds; rinse them briefly before soaking or putting them in the cooking pot.

Even though they come from a salty environment, ocean vegetables are not salty. Like ocean fish, they absorb very little of the ocean's salt, so be sure to use a high-quality sea salt and season lightly, just to taste.

When you soak ocean vegetables, please don't use the soaking water for cooking. However, your plants will love it.

Ocean Vegetable Recipes

Cucumber, Wakame, Red Pepper Salad

Ingredients:
1/4 of 2 oz. bag of wakame
4 large cucumbers, peeled and very thinly sliced
2 tsp. Herbamare or sea salt
1 large red pepper, diced
1 small red onion, finely chopped
1/3 cup raw, organic apple cider vinegar
2 Tbsp. organic, unrefined oil
Pinch of pepper

1. Soak wakame for 15 minutes, in enough water to cover.
2. Sprinkle Herbamare or sea salt on cucumbers and let set for several minutes to release the juices.
3. Remove "stem" and discard the soaking water from wakame.
4. Chop wakame and add to cucumbers.
5. Add diced red pepper and red onion to cucumbers and wakame.
6. Toss in vinegar, oil, and pepper.

Jelled Butternut Squash

Ingredients:
3 cups water
5 - 6 Tbsp. agar-agar flakes
1 small onion, diced into small chunks
4 cups butternut squash, diced into 1/2" chunks
1 tsp. Herbamare or sea salt
1/2 tsp. dill weed

1. Place the water and agar-agar flakes in a pot.
2. Bring to a boil, stirring frequently to dissolve the flakes.
3. Add the squash, onion, and Herbamare, reduce heat to medium-low and simmer until tender.
4. Purée until smooth.
5. Add dill.
6. Pour the hot purée into oiled gelatin mold
7. Refrigerate until jelled.
8. Slice and serve garnished with parsley, thinly sliced red pepper strips, and a dollop of B.E.D. Mayonnaise. A pinch of curry or Nile Spice's Ginger Curry can be added to the mayonnaise. Rosemary Vinaigrette Dressing (see recipe) also makes a nice topping. Toast slivered, sprouted almonds and sprinkle on top.

Variation:
1. For a spicier version, add 1 tsp. Nile Spice Foods Ginger Curry Spice.
2. Try using carrots, broccoli, or cauliflower in place of squash. Top with your favorite salad dressing.
3. To make a sweet version, use 1 tsp. Frontier Herbs butterscotch alcohol-free extract and stevia liquid concentrate to taste.

Hijiki (or Arame) with Onions and Carrots

Ingredients:
2 oz. bag dry hijiki
1 large onion, diced
2 large carrots, diced
1 tsp. organic, unrefined coconut oil
Sea salt to taste
Water to cover

1. Soak hijiki for 15 minutes.
2. Sauté onion in oil, add carrots.
3. Drain hijiki, dice, and add to onion and carrots.
4. Cover with water and simmer for 45 minutes to an hour, checking occasionally to make sure water has not evaporated.
5. Add sea salt to taste during the last 10 minutes of cooking.

Variation: Add diced red skin potatoes and/or peas.

Note: To create one of our most popular salads, we chill this basic recipe and toss with leafy lettuce and top with B.E.D. Salad Dressing.

Introduction to Stevia

Stevia is an extraordinarily sweet herb...200 - 300 times sweeter than sugar. It has a slight licorice-like flavor that most of us with a sweet tooth, and all the children we have ever met, love. For some people who only like the taste of real sugar it may take a little getting used to, but it has such important medicinal value that it is well worth learning to eat.

Stevia is almost calorie-free, so weight watchers love it. It is ideal for children since it prevents cavities. Unlike sugar, it does not trigger a rise in blood sugar. You won't get a sudden burst of energy followed by fatigue and a need for another "fix." Most importantly for our purposes, it does not feed yeast or other microorganisms, and it increases energy and aids digestion by stimulating the pancreas.

The Japanese are the greatest consumers of stevia today and have been using it for 30 years. A member of the chrysanthemum family (closely related to tarragon and chamomile and distantly related to lettuce, artichokes, safflower oil, and sunflower seeds and oil), it is totally safe and has been used for centuries by the Indians of South America. It grows wild there.

Stevia is available in a number of forms, including crushed green leaves, and a crude greenish-brown syrup. These two forms have a strong, licorice-like aftertaste, but are the most medicinal way to use stevia. To satisfy our perfectly natural desire for sweet-tasting foods, we prefer using white stevia powder or **Sweet N Better** (Body Ecology's stevia liquid concentrate, made from our white powder). You can find stevia in many health food stores today, but be aware that there are two strengths available and you may be disappointed in some brands. In our test kitchens we only use our own stevia products since they are a blend of 55% stevioside and 45% rebaudioside crystals. Since there is only a very tiny amount of rebaudioside in each leaf of the stevia plant, rebaudioside is very expensive to extract, but it yields the most delicious taste. If you have trouble obtaining the same high quality stevia used in our recipes, call us at (800) 511-2660. Your local health food store can order it from us too.

If you purchase white powder, we'd like to share an important tip. Since the powder is so potent, at times you may find it difficult to work with and will over-sweeten your foods. A tiny pinch of the *powder* is so potent, people often put in too much and find that it is just too sweet for them. That's why we recommend using the liquid and experimenting with a few drops at a time to find your own personal level of desired sweetness.

Create a liquid concentrate (or "working solution") by diluting 1 tsp. of the powder in 3 Tbsp. of filtered water. The powder may stick to the spoon, but will soon dissolve. Pour this liquid concentrate into a small bottle with a dropper top and refrigerate to increase its shelf life. One teaspoon of this "working solution" will approximately equal one cup of sugar. We found ourselves using this working solution so often, we created **Sweet N Better** which you do not need to be refrigerate.

Baked goods sweetened only with stevia do not rise as high as cakes and muffins baked with sugar, honey, fruit juice and other popular sweeteners. They also do not brown as much. Check for doneness by touching and not by color. Stevia tastes strong in bland foods, so use much less. It disappears in stronger flavors like carob or chocolate, so use more. Stevia recipe books published by authors unaware of candidiasis combine stevia with various other sweeteners.**

**NOTE: You will find lots more stevia tips in Donna's latest book, "The Stevia Cookbook: Cooking with Nature's No-Calorie Sweetener." But please be advised that Donna wrote this book for main-stream America hoping to teach them about this wonderful alternative to sugar. Her book contains over 100 recipes using only stevia as a sweetener, but many of those recipes (like cheesecake) are not appropriate for anyone fighting a serious immune disorder like candidiasis or cancer.

VISIT OUR STEVIA WEBSITE AT STEVIA.NET.

Stevia Recipes

Body Ecology Diet "Acidophilus Milk"

Good over Arrowhead Mills Puffed Millet Cereal if you use a dairy-free brand of friendly bacteria.

(Many of our mothers have found their very young children have enjoyed this "milk" in a bottle. It's a good way to make sure your baby is getting plenty of the friendly flora, and it satisfies their desire for sugar.)

Ingredients:
1 cup water
1/2 tsp. B.E.D. stevia liquid or tiny pinch stevia
    powder to taste
1 Tbsp. probiotics such as "Life Start," "Mega-
    dophilus," "Maxi Dophilus," "Maxi Bifidus,"
    "Dr. Dophilus," etc.*
1 tsp. vanilla (non-alcoholic)
1 tsp. lecithin granules (opt.)

Purée all ingredients in a blender or shake in a jar.

*If using over cereal, be sure to make your "Acidophilus Milk" with a dairy-free probiotic. If you make this milk with a probiotic grown on dairy, drink it alone on an empty stomach at least one-half hour before eating a starch or protein. Since dairy does combine with acidic fruits, there is no problem drinking this "milk" and then eating a grapefruit or drinking lemon and water.

Ginger Ale

The ale tastes best when the syrup concentrate is allowed to sit in the refrigerator overnight before using.

Syrup concentrate for the ale:
3$^{1}/_{2}$ cups water
4-inch-long piece of ginger, peeled and chopped
2 Tbsp. vanilla flavoring (non-alcoholic)
3 tsp. lemon flavoring (non-alcoholic)
$^{1}/_{2}$ tsp. stevia powder (or to taste)

Serving the ale:
1 cup Quibell Sparkling Mineral Water per serving

1. Boil down ginger in water for 10 minutes.
2. Strain out ginger pieces and pour ginger juice into jar.
3. Add vanilla and lemon flavorings and stevia.
4. Let cool and store in refrigerator as a syrup concentrate.
5. Add $^{1}/_{8}$ - $^{1}/_{4}$ cup of syrup to 6 - 8 oz. of Quibell Sparkling Mineral Water and serve.

Vanilla Pudding

Ingredients:
4 cups water
1 Tbsp. agar powder or 4 heaping Tbsp. agar flakes
2 Tbsp. arrowroot
$^{1}/_{2}$ tsp. sea salt
1 Tbsp. lecithin granules
2 Tbsp. ghee
1 Tbsp. Stevia Working Solution (1 tsp. white stevia powder dissolved in 3 Tbsp. water)
4 Tbsp. vanilla
3 small yellow squash, chopped, cooked, drained and puréed

1. Dissolve agar in 2 cups water.
2. Dissolve arrowroot in 2 Tbsp. water.
3. Combine and cook on low heat until thickened.
4. Add sea salt, lecithin, ghee, stevia, and remaining water.
5. Simmer 10 - 15 minutes, pour into baking dish to cool and gel (several hours or faster with refrigeration).
6. When firm, place in blender and blend until smooth.
7. Add puréed yellow squash and vanilla and continue blending until very creamy.

The recipe on this page is not a strict Body Ecology recipe. We offer it as an answer to the many requests for a party recipe that children will eat. With no sugar, wheat and refined oils, it is a better choice than cookies found in grocery or even in health food stores. You'll be able to enjoy an occasional treat of this quality once you have reestablished your inner ecology and find your digestion is working well. Look for more sugar-free recipes in *Stevia: **Cooking with Nature's No-Calorie Sweetener*** by Ray Sahelian, M.D. and Donna Gates (available Spring 1998).

Norma's Almond Butter Cookies

This recipe is wheat-free and gluten-free.
Ingredients:
1 stick of unsalted butter, softened
3/4 tsp. Body Ecology's white stevia powder
1 large egg
1 cup almond butter
2 tsp. non-aloholic vanilla flavoring
1/2 tsp. sea salt
1/2 tsp. baking soda
1 1/2 cup (Fern's) Rice Baking Mix

To Make Cinnamon Sprinkle:
1 tsp. ground cinnamon
1/8 tsp. Body Ecology's white stevia powder
Dash of Madagascar Bourbon Pure Vanilla Powder
(optional - Nielsen Massey Vanillas Inc.)

1. Preheat oven 350°. Grease a cookie sheet and set aside.
2. In a medium bowl, beat butter with a wire wisk until light and fluffy.
3. Add stevia and cinnamon. Beat until smooth.
4. Beat in egg, almond butter, vanilla flavoring, sea salt, baking soda and Rice Baking Mix until blended.
5. The dough should be thick enough to hold its shape on a tablespoon. Drop cookie dough onto cookie sheet.
6. Score cookies by lightly pressing the back of a fork across the cookie twice in a cross-cross pattern.
7. Sprinkle each cookie lightly with cinammon sprinkle mixture.
8. Bake 15 minutes or until lightly browned.

Cinnamon/ Stevia Sprinkles

Tasty over breakfast cereal, cookies, and squash dishes.

Ingredients:
1 tsp. ground cinnamon
$1/8$ tsp. white stevia powder
Dash of Madagascar Vanilla Powder (optional)

1. Place ingredients in a small jar or shaker and shake until mixed well.
2. Store with other spices and serve as a garnish.

Sweet Carrot "Gelatin" Salad

This recipe is great for potlucks. If you increase the amount of ingredients, do not increase the amount of stevia. Always be sure to test for taste.

Ingredients:
$3^{1}/2$ cups water
3 medium carrots, shredded
2 stalks celery, finely shredded
1 Tbsp. agar powder (or 4 Tbsp. agar flakes)
$1/4$ tsp. salt
$1/8$ tsp. stevia powder
$1/2$ cup total of lemon and/or lime juice
Grated rind of 1 lemon

1. In saucepan, dissolve agar powder in 2 cups cold water.
2. Add lemon rind and salt.
3. Bring to a boil, boil five minutes.
4. Add celery and boil one minute more.
5. Add carrots, stevia, $1^{1}/2$ cups water, and continue boiling 3 minutes more so that carrots are desired chunkiness.
6. Mix well.
7. Pour in lemon juice.
8. Pour mixture into mold, bowl, or square baking dish.
9. Serve on bed of lettuce with a dollop of mayonnaise.

Corn Chutney

Ingredients:

1 - 2 onions, chopped
6 ears corn, kernels removed
3 Tbsp. organic, unrefined oil
1/2 red pepper, diced
1/2 green pepper, diced
9 Tbsp. raw, organic apple cider vinegar
3 Tbsp. stevia concentrate
      (1 tsp. stevia in 3 Tbsp. water)
2 - 3 cloves garlic, minced
2 Tbsp. grated ginger
3 tsp. chili powder
1/8 tsp. cinnamon
1/8 tsp. ground cloves
1/8 tsp. nutmeg
1/4 - 1/2 tsp. curry powder
1 Tbsp. arrowroot powder dissolved in 2 Tbsp. water

1. In a frying pan, sauté onions.
2. Add all additional ingredients except arrowroot.
3. Cook for 5 - 10 minutes.
4. Add arrowroot dissolved in water.
5. Stir well, simmer for another 3 - 5 minutes, and serve.

Appendix A

The Body Ecology Diet℠ Shopping List

Buy organic foods whenever possible.

A sensitivity to any one of these foods, while uncommon, is a sign of the first stages of immune deficiency. As you strengthen your immune system, you should soon be able to enjoy all of these foods. Suggested brand names are listed in parentheses.

While these are not endorsements, we have carefully examined the ingredients in the brand names mentioned below and have given them the B.E.D. stamp of approval. As we learn about new products that help reestablish your immune system without feeding the yeast, we will expand and update this shopping list.

ANIMAL PROTEIN
- natural without antibiotics or hormones
Eggs, fertile, from free-roaming chickens
Fish, cold-water
Red meats
    (Belle Brook Farms 1-800-830-2354),
Free-range poultry (Wellington, Shelton's,
    Bell and Evans, and Murray's)
Natural turkey hot dogs (Applegate Farms),

BAKING PRODUCTS
Alcohol-free flavoring extracts
    (Frontier Herbs, Spicery Shoppe, and
    St. John's Herb Garden)
Baking powder (Featherweight)
Pure Vanilla Powder (Neilsen-Massey Vanillas, Inc.)

BUTTER, GHEE
Butter, raw when available, lightly salted or
    unsalted (Kate's, Alta Dena, Cabots, other
    brands)
Ghee, also called clarified butter
    (Purity Farms is organic)

CANNED AND DRIED GOODS
Bamboo shoots (Ka-me)
Dried daikon
Salmon, **salt-free**
    (Featherweight, Season Brand)
Tuna, **salt-free** (Deep Sea, Ocean King,
    Miramonte, Featherweight, Season Brand)
Water chestnuts (Ka-me)

ENZYMES
Complete Milk Digestant (Malabar)
    for kefir meals.
Plant enzymes (Omega Nutrition) for grain and
    vegetable meals
Di-Acid Stim (Atrium) for protein meals

FERMENTED FOODS
Omega Nutrition's (Body Ecology approved)Apple
Cider Vinegar—in light-proof bottles
(raw–organic–aged in wood)

Raw Cultured Vegetables [Cabbage Dill
    Flavor #1, Vegi-delite live zing salad
    (Rejuvenative Foods 1-800-805-7957)]

FRUIT
Cranberries, fresh or frozen
Cranberry juice concentrate (Hain), pure,
    unsweetened
Lemons, fresh
Limes, fresh

GRAINS (*Remember to soak 8-24 hours*)
Amaranth
Buckwheat, also called kasha
Cream of Buckwheat cereal (Pocono)
Millet
Puffed Millet Cereal, dry (Arrowhead Mills)
Quinoa
Quinoa Flakes (Ancient Harvest)

HERBS AND SPICES
Sweet 'N Better
    Body Ecology's own great tasting liquid herbal
    concentrate with no aftertaste.

White stevia extract*

Dr. Bronner's Balanced Mineral Seasoning,
    (two-tone green label only)

Herbamare and Trocomare

Garden herbs (fresh or dried)
    All traditional land herbs and spices are
    on the B.E.D. Herbs such as cinnamon,
    coriander, curry, garlic, ginger, and turmeric
    are beneficial because they are antifungal.

Sea salt (In our Body Ecology test kitchen we use
    Celtic Sea Salt. A wonderful grinder is available
    for table use 1-800-511-2660)

Seasonings from the ocean (Sea Seasonings
    Brand): Dulse, Dulse with Garlic, Nori with
    Ginger, Kelp with Cayenne (good substitute
    for salt & pepper)

Seasoning Packets from The Spice Hunter
    (can be used for seasoning or in salad

Many, but not all of these products listed in our shopping list are available by calling 1-800-511-2660. Please share this number with your local health food store so they can stock up on the products you need.

dressings with unrefined oil and apple cider vinegar): Cajun Fire, Mediterranean Dressing, Garlic & Herb Dressing, Five Onion & Herb

LAND VEGETABLES
All land vegetables *other than* beets, mung bean sprouts, mushrooms (except cooked shitake), parsnips, green peppers, yams and all potatoes (except red potatoes)

NUTS AND SEEDS
Raw or roasted (always soaked first)
Almonds, Caraway, Flax, Pumpkin, Sunflower

OCEAN VEGETABLES
(Sea Seasonings, Eden, other brands)
Agar, Arame, Dulse, Hijiki, Kelp, Kombu, Nori, Sea palm, Wakame

ORGANIC, UNREFINED OILS
Body Ecology approved Omegaflo® (Omega Nutrition)
Body Ecology's Coconut (for cooking and baking)
Flax seed (also available in capsules)
Garlic Chili Flax Seed Oil
Pumpkin seed, Safflower, Sunflower
Essential Balance™
Essential Balance Jr.™ (butterscotch flavor)

SALAD DRESSINGS & CONDIMENTS
Dressings:
   No-oil Italian Garlic Gusto and
   No-oil Dill by Cook's Classic
Horseradish (made with apple cider vinegar)
Mustards:
   Tree of Life's Whole Grain, Eden's "Hot" Mustard, Anne's Original Mountain Herb, or Zake's Fire Country are all made with raw, unpasteurized apple cider vinegar and without sweeteners.

SNACKS
Guiltless Gourmet Baked Blue Corn Chips*
Santa Cruz Baked organic blue corn tortilla chips*
Popcorn* (air popped or with coconut oil)

TEAS
Traditional Medicinals is our favorite tea company, however, there are many excellent herbal teas available. Read labels carefully, and avoid teas with citric acid and from fruits. (For example, raspberry fruit is not okay, but raspberry leaf, stem, or root is fine.)
Pau D'Arco, Ginger Aid, Echinacea Plus, Chamomile, Weightless Cinnamon, Mint, Green Tea, Mother's Milk, Raspberry Leaf

PERSONAL CARE PRODUCTS
Thursday Plantation Tea Tree Oil Suppositories
Tea Tree Oil castile soap, dental floss, shampoo, mouthwash, lip balm
Toothpaste (NutriBiotic DentalGel, Desert Essence Tea Tree Oil & Neem Toothpaste)
ProSeed Feminine Rinse (douche concentrate)
ProSeed Healthy Gums
ProSeed Nail Rescue (antifungal nail formula)

ANTI-FUNGAL, ANTI-VIRAL, ANTI-BACTERIAL, IMMUNE BOOSTERS
Olive Leaf Extract
Osage Orange or Yeast Ease (Jernigan Nutriceuticals)
MSM Organic Sulfur with Ester C
Proseed Triple Yeast Defense
Proseed Soothing Ear Drops

OTHER VALUABLE PRODUCTS
VITALITY SuperGreen™ (Body Ecology's)
EcoRenew (Body Ecology's delicious, tangy, raspberry flavored chewable probiotic)
Bio-K+ (Acidophilus/Casei (for the small intestine) (800-593-2465) Natren's Lifestart and other bifidus strains for the large intestine) Continental Acidophilus Culture
Nutri-Flax (Omega Nutrition)
Ester-C (Natrol)
NuPlus Simply Herbs, plain flavor (Sunrider)
Lecithin granules
Xanthan Gum (see page 204)
Trace-Lyte Liquid Minerals (crystalloid)
Cal-Lyte (calcium and magnesium w/ crystalloid minerals)
Atri-Aloe V (gentle colon stimulant)
ParaGONE (Renew Life Formulas)

KEFIR PRODUCTS
Body Ecology's Kefir Starter (for homemade)
Helios Nutrition plain flavor (available at fine health food stores)

OTHER BOOKS YOU'LL WANT TO READ
The Magic of Kefir
   by Donna Gates with Linda Schatz
The Stevia Story
   by Donna Gates with Linda and Bill Bonvie
The Stevia Cookbook: Cooking with Nature's Calorie-Free Sweetener
   by Ray Sahalien M.D. and Donna Gates

---

*These foods are not tolerated by everyone. Avoid them the first six weeks, then introduce them by rotating them into your diet once every four days and eat them with alkaline, non-starchy vegetables; avoid eating them alone.

Appendix B

How to Lobby for Approval of Stevia

Background

The food and drug administration (FDA) requires extensive documentation of the safety of any substance approved for sale as a food or drug. Typically, this involves years of testing and millions of dollars. However, there is a category of substances, called Generally Regarded as Safe (GRAS), that can be approved without going through the full extent of this process.

The FDA has approved use of stevia as a dietary supplement, but not as a food additive. The FDA says it needs more scientific testing and proof that stevia has not harmed anyone. Yet the FDA *could* approve stevia in the GRAS category if it wanted to. Currently, at least two petitions are pending to have the FDA approve stevia as GRAS.

What You Can Do

Write directly to the FDA or to your Congressional representatives. Introduce yourself as a concerned citizen who wants stevia to be sold without restriction. (You can include some of the background information on stevia from Chapter 12.) If you write to your Senators or Congresspersons, you can ask them to lobby the FDA on your behalf. Be sure to include your address and ask for a reply.

Sample Letter

Dr. Jane Henney
Commissioner
5600 Fishers Lane
Rockville, MD 20852

Dear Dr. Henney:

Please approve stevia as a food additive in the category GRAS. Stevia, an herbal sweetener, has been used for hundreds of years without harm to anyone. The benefits this substance could have for millions of Americans far outweigh the cost of additional testing and documentation.

Please let me know what action you will take in this matter of vital importance to America's health.

Thank you.

(your name and address)

Or write to your Congressional representatives and have <u>them</u> apply pressure to the FDA to grant the GRAS petitions:

The Honorable (Representative's name)
U.S. House of Representatives
Washington, DC 20515

The Honorable (Senator's name)
U.S. Senate
Washington, DC 20510

Bibliography

PART I

Introduction: A Silent Spring Within

(Chapters 1,2,3, and 4)

Annechild, Annette, and Laura Johnson. *Yeast-Free Living*. New York, NY, The Putnam Publishing Group, 1986.

Carson, Rachel. *Silent Spring*. Boston, MA, Houghton Mifflin Company, 1987.

Chaitow, Leon, D.O., M.D. *Could Yeast Be Your Problem? Candida Albicans*. Rochester, VT, Healing Arts Press, 1988.

Crook, William G., M.D. *The Yeast Connection: A Medical Breakthrough*. Jackson, TN, Professional Books, 1985.

De Schepper, Luc, M.D., Ph.D., C.A. *Candida*. Santa Monica, CA, 1986. (213) 828-4480

Finnegan, John. *Yeast Disorders: An Understanding and Nutritional Therapy*. Mill Valley, CA, Elysian Arts, 1989.

Glasser, Ronald J. *The Body Is The Hero*. New York, NY, Bantam Books, 1979.

Lappe, Marc. *When Antibiotics FAIL: Restoring The Ecology Of The Body*. Berkeley, CA, North Atlantic Books, 1986.

Lorenzani, Shirley S., Ph.D. *Candida: A Twentieth Century Disease*. New Canaan, CT, Keats Publishing, Inc., 1986.

Miller, Jonathon D., M.A., M. Div. *Candida Yeast: The Battle In Your Body*. Akron, OH, Lifecircle Publications, 1986.

Remington, Dennis W., M.D., and Barbara W. Higa, R.D. *Back To Health: A Comprehensive Medical And Nutritional Yeast Control Program*. Provo, UT, Vitality House International, Inc., 1987.

Robbins, John. *Diet for a New America*. Walpole, NH, Stillpoint Publishing, 1987. (1-800-847-4014)

Rochlitz, Steven. *Allergies And Candida: With The Physicist's Rapid Solution*. Setauket, NY, Human Ecology Balancing Sciences, Inc., 1989.

Schmidt, Michael A., Lendon H. Smith, and Keith W. Sehnert. *Beyond Antibiotics: Healthier Options for Families*. Berkeley, CA, North Atlantic Books, 1993.

Sehnert, Keith W., M.D. *The Garden Within: Acidophilus-Candida Connection*. Burlingame, CA, Health World, Inc., 1989.

Tenney, Louise. *Candida Albicans: A Nutritional Approach*. Provo, UT, Woodland Books, 1986.

Trowbridge, John P., M.D., and Morton Walker, D.P.M. *The Yeast Syndrome*. New York, NY, Bantam Books, 1986.

PART II

Principles of the Body Ecology Diet

Chapter 5 - The Principle of Expansion and Contraction

Aihara, Herman. *Basic Macrobiotics*.
New York, NY, Japan Publications, Inc., 1985.

Garvy, John W., Jr., N.D., D.Ac. *Yin and Yang: Two Hands Clapping*.
Newtonville, MA, Wellbeing Books, 1985.

Heidenry, Carolyn. *Making The Transition To A Macrobiotic Diet: A Beginner's Guide To The Natural Way Of Health*.
Wayne, NJ, Avery Publishing Group Inc., 1987.

Kushi, Michio, with Alex Jack. *The Book of Macrobiotics: The Universal Way of Health, Happiness, and Peace*.
New York, NY, Japan Publications, Inc., 1989.

Kushi, Michio, edited by Marc Van Cauwenberghe, M.D. *Macrobiotic Home Remedies*. New York, NY, Japan Publications, Inc., 1985.

Lu, Henry C. *Chinese System Of Food Cures: Prevention And Remedies*.
New York, NY, Sterling Publishing Co., 1986.

Rogers, Sherry A., M.D. *You Are What You Ate: A Macrobiotic Way, An Rx For The Resistant Diseases Of The 21st Century*.
Syracuse, NY, Prestige Publishers, 1988.

Tara, William. *Macrobiotics and Human Behavior*.
New York, NY, Japan Publications, Inc., 1984.

Chapter 6 - The Principle of Acid and Alkaline

Aihara, Herman. *Acid and Alkaline*.
Oroville, CA, George Ohsawa Macrobiotic Foundation, 1986.

Chapter 7 - The Principle of Blood Types

D'Adamo, Dr. James. *The D'Adamo Diet*.
Toronto, Canada, McGraw-Hill Ryerson, 1989.

D'Adamo, Dr. James, with Allan Richards. *One Man's Food...Is Someone Else's Poison*. Toronto, Canada, Health Thru Herbs, Inc., 1980.

Nomi, Toshitaka, and Alexander Besher. *You Are Your Blood Type: The Biochemical Key To Unlocking The Secrets Of Your Personality*.
New York, NY, Pocket Books, 1988.

Chapter 9 - The Principle of Food Combining

Diamond, Harvey, and Marilyn Diamond. *Fit For Life*.
New York, NY, Warner Books, 1985.

Diamond, Harvey, and Marilyn Diamond. *Fit For Life II: Living Health*.
New York, NY, Warner Books, 1987.

Diamond, Marilyn. *A New Way of Eating*.
New York, NY, Warner Books, 1987.

DuBelle, Lee. *Proper Food Combining Cookbook*.
Phoenix, AZ, Lee DuBelle, P.O. Box 35860, 1984.

DuBelle, Lee. *Proper Food Combining Works: Living Testimony*.
Phoenix, AZ, Lee DuBelle, P.O. Box 35860, 1986.

Fogel, Elaine. *The Food Combining Handbook And Cookbook*.
Ontario, Canada, Mystery Laine Publishing, 1983.

Grant, Doris, and Jean Joice. *Food Combining For Health: A New Look At The Hay System*. Rochester, VT, Thorsons Publishing Group, 1984.

Grant, Doris, and Jean Joice. *Food Combining For Health: Get Fit With Foods That Don't Fight*.
Rochester, VT, Thorsons Publishing Group, 1984.

Kahn, Pam, with Dennis Nelson. *Food Combining Recipe Book*.
Santa Cruz, CA, The Plan, P.O. Box 872, 1986.

Mannix, Jeffrey. *Food Combining: The High-Energy Weight Loss Plan*.
New York, NY, Contemporary Books, Inc., 1983.

Nelson, Dennis. *Food Combining Simplified: How To Get The Most From Your Food*.
Santa Cruz, CA, The Plan, D. Nelson, P.O. Box 2302, 1985.

Null, Gary, and Staff. *Food Combining Handbook*.
New York, NY, Jove Publications, Inc., 1973.

Shelton, Herbert M. *Food Combining Made Easy*.
San Antonio, TX, Willow Publishing, Inc., 1982.

Smith, Esther L. *Good Foods That Go Together: The Official Cookbook Of The Hay System*.
New Canaan, CT, Keats Publishing, Inc., 1975.

PART III

Description of the Body Ecology Diet

Chapter 12 - What Is the Body Ecology Diet?

Finnegan, John. *The Facts About Fats: A Consumer's Guide To Good Oil*.
Berkeley, CA, Celestial Arts Publishing, 1993.

Howard, Dr. Edward. *Enzyme Nutrition: The Food Enzyme Concept*.
Wayne, NJ, Avery Publishing Group, Inc., 1985.

Jennings-Sauer, Cheryl. "The Egg's Return," *American Health*,
April, 1988.

Roberts, H.J. *Aspartame (NutraSweet®) Is It Safe?*
Philadelphia, The Charles Press, Publishers, Inc., 1990.

Santillo, Humbart. *Food Enzymes: The Missing Link to Radiant Health*.
Prescott Valley, AZ, Hohm Press, 1987.

PART IV

Rebuilding the Immune System

Chapter 17 - How to Care for Your Colon

Chaitow, Leon, N.D., D.O., and Natasha Trenev. *Probiotics: The Revolutionary, 'Friendly bacteria' Way to Vital Health and Well-Being*.
Hammersmith, London, Thorsons, 1990.

Gray, Robert. *The Colon Health Handbook - New Health Through Colon Rejuvenation*. Reno, NV, Emerald Publishing, 1986.

De Schepper, Luc, M.D., Ph.D., C.A. *Peak Immunity*.
Santa Monica, CA, 1989. (213) 828-4480

Weinberger, Stanley. *Healing Within: The Complete Colon Health Guide*.
Larkspur, CA, Colon Health Center, 1988.

Chapter 19 - How to Strengthen Your Immunity

Muramoto, Noboru B. *Natural Immunity: Insights On Diet And AIDS.* Oroville, CA, George Ohsawa Macrobiotic Foundation, 1988.

Tenney, Louise. *AIDS, A Nutritional Approach.* Provo, UT, Woodland Books, 1986.

PART V

Creating a Bright, Healthy Future

Chapter 23 - Toward a New Science of Healing

Gray, John, Ph.D. *Feelings First! An Illustrated Guide to Enriching Your Relationships.* Santa Monica, CA, Heart Publishing Co., 1984.

Index

The Body Ecology Mission

Our mission at BODY ECOLOGY is to change the way the world eats, thus ending disease. We want every home in America to be using the healthy products we recommend in this book.

Please help us spread the word about these foods.

✔ Organic, unrefined seed oils, coconut oil, extra virgin olive oil, raw butter and raw cream are the best fats to eat. Avoid bleached, refined and deodorized vegetable oils commonly found in most foods. Also avoid margarine.

✔ Stevia is an excellent choice to satisfy your sweet tooth.

✔ Taking an alkaline, mineral-rich superfoods formula is even better than man-made supplements for building up protein, mineral and essential fatty acid deficiencies.

✔ Raw apple cider vinegar is the only really healthy vinegar.

✔ Ocean vegetables and organic land vegetables should make up a significant portion of each meal.

✔ Cold water fish, free-range poultry, and eggs from free-running, fertile chickens, are your best sources of animal protein.

✔ Eating a variety of cultured foods found all around the world helps create a healthy inner ecosystem and contributes to a long, healthy lifespan. Kefir and cultured vegetables are the first ones to introduce if you have Candidiasis.

Other Books by Donna Gates

You can find Donna Gates' other fine books at your local health food store and in major chain book stores.

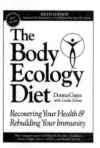

The Body Ecology Diet
Recovering Your Health & Rebuilding Your Immunity
by Donna Gates with Linda Schatz

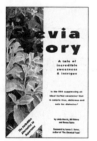

The Stevia Story
A tale of incredible sweetness & intrigue
by Donna Gates, Linda Bonvie, and Bill Bonvie

The Magic of Kefir
An ancient food for modern maladies
by Donna Gates with Linda Schatz

The Stevia Cookbook
Cooking with Nature's Calorie-Free Sweetener
by Donna Gates and Ray Sahelian, MD

Other Body Ecology Approved Products

Look for the Body Ecology logo on other Body Ecology approved products including:

Omega Nutrition's complete line of organic unrefined oils, coconut oil, apple cider vinegar and Nutri-Flax, and Helios Nutrition's organic kefir with FOS.

THE BODY ECOLOGY DIET STARTER KIT

INCLUDES:
- ✔ Vitality Supergreen, 10 oz.
- ✔ Essential Balance, 12 oz.
- ✔ Coconut Oil, 12.75 oz.
- ✔ Sweet 'N Better, 1 oz.
- ✔ Apple Cider Vinegar, 32 oz.
- ✔ Plant Enzymes/Kamizym-D, 90 caps (for vegetarian meals)
- ✔ Di-Acid Stim (for protein meal)
- ✔ Celtic Sea Salt 1/2 lb.

SPECIAL PRICE
With The Body Ecology Diet Book $108.48
Without The Body Ecology Diet Book $91.84

We Would Love To Hear From You!

Try our new website BodyEcologyDiet.com

You'll find information about our products, new recipes each month, and a calendar listing cities where Donna will be lecturing.

Your comments are important.

Everyone is excited about our new "bulletin board" on our BodyEcologyDiet.com website where you can post your questions, comments, and contribute recipes and experiences on The Diet. Many people feel they are all alone in conquering this condition. Communicating with other BEDers really helps.

Our other websites you might want to visit are: Kefir.net and Stevia.net

Our Email address is BodyEco@aol.com

Visit your local health food store for all the products recommended by Donna in this book. If they do not carry the products you need, ask them to order them for you.

Another source for many of the products in this book is Omega Nutrition located at 6515 Aldrich Road in Bellingham, Washington 98226 or on our website at www.omeganutrition.com (800 511-2660, 800 661-3529 or 800 4-STEVIA). Please tell Omega that you heard about their products from *The Body Ecology Diet.*

Notes

Notes